Grassroots Initiatives

A Selection from New Society

Another title in this new series:

Joan Davidson
How Green is Your City?
Pioneering Approaches to Environmental Action

Grassroots Initiatives

A Selection from New Society

With an Introduction by David Lipsey

Bedford Square Press

Published by
BEDFORD SQUARE PRESS of the
National Council for Voluntary Organisations
26 Bedford Square, London WC1B 3HU

First published 1988

ISBN 0 7199 1220 2

Typeset by Cylinder Typesetting, London

Printed and bound in England

British Library Cataloguing in Publication Data

Grassroots initiatives: a selection from
New Society. — (Community action).
1. Great Britain. Community action group — case studies
I. New society. II. Series.
361. 8'0941
ISBN 0 7199 1220 2

Contents

EDUCATION

HOUSING

CRIME AND COMMUNITY

FAMILIES AND YOUNG PEOPLE

EMPLOYMENT

ARTS

Introduction

Britain is arguably now the most centralised of all the major Western democracies. Both the main political parties have paid lip-service to local issues. But actions speak louder than words.

Local government was first rendered less local by Peter Walker's notorious efficiency reorganisation in 1972; then rendered less efficient by constant spending cuts and increasing Whitehall control over its operations. The British welfare tradition, from Beveridge on, has been a centralised one, with centrally determined social security benefits, often administered by centrally controlled officials, and relying overwhelmingly on the taxpayer for its funds.

We lack a countervailing tradition of corporate involvement in community affairs. Prince Charles's gallant effort to establish the 'one per cent club', of businesses prepared to donate one per cent of their profits to non-commercial causes, has struggled to persuade companies to sign up. The growing North-South divide, and the magnetic attraction of people of talent to the capital, have reinforced these centripetal forces. The gloomy picture of Britain as a nation where all power lies at the centre, crushing energies which lie outside it, has a dismal ring of truth.

It may look like that to a London-based government; to the media which still look to it for most of their inspiration; and to the pressure groups which attach themselves to it. Yet it is not the whole truth. There is a different perspective. Those who adopt it say simply this: that there is more going on, out there, than immediately catches the Londoner's eye. It is some of the things going on 'out there', unknown to the metropolitan insider, and hence unsung, that this book is designed to tell us about.

Grassroots Action consists of a selection from a series in *New Society* called 'Initiatives'. The philosophy behind the series is simply stated. We sought to discover, from all over Britain, projects where local groups or local people have found innovative solutions to particular social problems. Some have been fostered by the much-derided local authorities. Others are the product of voluntary groups, sometimes with local-authority financial support, sometimes paying their own way. Sometimes projects have been initiated or facilitated by professional community workers. At other times, they have involved education, primarily – encouraging black people to run their own businesses, for example. Yet others, perhaps the most exciting of all, are examples of pure self-help. A group of elderly people on Tyneside gets together to provide entertainment, support and companionship for one another. The Sikh community in Derby gets together to provide practical help to its members with translation and communication. They did it for themselves.

Each initiative, of course, has faced its own problems: fundraising, constitution-making, defining objectives, and organising to achieve them. Some of the perils and pitfalls that can arise from pioneering action come out of their stories. But individual problems do not detract from the overall impression that these collected experiences convey: of the degree of compassion that people have for one another, and of the willingness of so many people everywhere to give freely of their energy and commitment to do something to alleviate individual misery.

It's necessary to retain a sense of proportion. These local activities cannot be taken as representing predominant trends in society. They do not prove that there is not, still, selfishness; nor do they refute the thesis of some writers – for example, Jeremy Seabrook – that the general drift is still away from regard to the collective interest and towards the individual interest.

There is room for misrepresentation of their scope too, as when the government justifies cutting back central financial provision on the grounds that the 'community' can take over its tasks. Unaided, it cannot; and the state cannot evade its moral responsibilities by claiming otherwise. Individual initiatives and governmental initiatives work best when they are seen as complements to each other, not as alternatives.

But – vitally – there is also here a counter to despair. When we are bemused by our apparent helplessness in the face of huge centralised forces, we can turn to something more hopeful. These local initiatives do not solve the problems of the universe. But they do, frequently, solve the question of one or more individuals. From the metropolitan perspective they may seem to amount to little or nothing. As the grassroots, they may amount to everything, to the difference between happiness and misery, between meaningless and meaningful existence.

There are signs that, at last, all this is coming to be recognised. From the political right, once itself the motive force behind much local charitable activity (even if sometimes in the less-than-perfect forms of the Squire and his Lady Bountiful), one catches a hint of an understanding that society is more than a collection of atomised individuals, brought together only by the market-place. The government's interest in the organisation of a concerted inner-city policy is an example. On the left, there is questioning of both the central and the local state. Labour-controlled local authorities, such as Islington and Stirling, experiment with radical forms of decentralisation. The politics of, for example, the Militant Tendency in Liverpool, opposed to all local activity unless it is controlled by the council, are condemned by Labour leaders and party members alike.

And so, in some respects, the philosophical tide is turning in favour of the ways of caring in society represented by the Initiatives in this book. Taken together, they are intended to inspire, so that the tide runs yet more strongly.

David Lipsey
November 1987

Trespassers will be enrolled

SALLY DEALLER

A centre in the Black Country introduces women to new technology.

"It is more enjoyable than housework. It impresses the children. Mine are always playing on computers at school and I have shown them things."

Jane Babb, 33 year old divorced mother of three, is one of four mums huddled around a table covered in graph paper in a room full of computers, *Tomorrow's World*-style.

They are designing chess pieces by computer to be turned out of a tube of solid metal by a computer-operated lathe. In the background, two younger women are programming a robotic arm to pick up a wooden maquette by jiggling with a screen full of figures. "That's easy," says Chris Downes, a solid woman dressed in black who looks much older than her 29 years. "There's nothing much to it. It looks difficult but it's not."

Jane and Chris are among the first students to take part in the Women into New Technology course, at Bilston Community College in the Black Country, aimed specially at mums going back to work. We are in the Computer Aided Design and Computer Aided Manufacture Centre (the CADCAM centre) with 13 BBC microcomputers and the latest in computer-operated lathes. At the back of the room are two machines, featured on *Tomorrow's World* four years ago as the latest in high-tech engineering. Bought by the college a year later they are not out of date.

The course is for women only and the college had to apply for exemption from the Sex Discrimination Act, 1986, to be allowed to run it. But the women are taught by a man — lecturer Roger Saunders — who teaches what is known as "computer numerical control of machine tools." Teaching the women — he calls them "ladies" — is the same as teaching anyone else, Roger says. "You forget who they are and just get on with the job."

Debs, petite with blonde-tipped curls, has two children aged seven and eight and a husband who was "a bit funny at first" when she started the course. "I think he's a bit worried that I'm meeting all these men. I wouldn't say he's encouraging me but he's not put a downer on me either." Ask them what they are getting out of the course and they come up with intangibles like "confidence", and it "makes you feel more independent". Alan Birks, the college vice-principal, says the course is a source of dignity, increased self-respect and confidence. The college must offer them the opportunity to carry on being students, he says.

But Debs is upset by one lecturer who accuses them all of "smug self-satisfaction" at being students. "I nearly told her she's pretty self-satisfied herself at being a lecturer," she says. But it still stings. The machines they are learning to use are taking over Black Country workshops — but will they get jobs in them?

The centre opened in September last year in the industrial training block at Bilston, where more than 100 boys used to learn engineering. "That's now a dirty word around here, I'm afraid," says equal opportunities organiser Monica Hartill. The engineering and the boys have gone. Since 1979, 100,000 jobs have disappeared in the Black Country, one in four from manufacturing. Traditional metal-bashing industries have fared even worse. These are now fewer than ten engineering apprentices at the college.

Alan Birks says that in 1979: "People didn't used to worry too much about learning. You could go straight from school into a job. That's all changed now." The college is trying to fill the gap by reaching out to potential students through leafletting, coffee mornings and open days. But the most successful recommendation is word of mouth — everyone I spoke to said they had come "because a friend said it was good." Those word-of-mouth recommendations have pushed the number of students up from 6,000 to 12,000 in three years, though the proportion of women in proving harder to raise.

The story of Bilston college started in 1982 when Wolverhampton decided to merge its further and higher education service into one open-access system for any age, from 16 to the grave. A two-day education conference on progress so far was held in the town last month. Interested observers who are considering whether to follow include Sheffield.

Wolverhampton is the front line of open-access education. Bilston is the flagship — the "College of the Proletariat" in Alan Birks's words. The college opened its doors in September 1984 on nine sites. Since then the number of students has doubled. Costs have risen from £4 million a year to £7 million, but Wolverhampton is paying only about £200,000 a year more.

The gap is filled by the EEC Social Fund which put up £50,000 for women's courses at Bilston which, by a little creative accounting, turned into the CADCAM centre's banks of microcomputers and the latest in computer-operated training lathes.

As well as Women into New Technology, there are women-only courses on supervision and management, art and design, and self-employment. More are planned on vehicle maintenance and construction. The only flop so far has been a science foundation course — a failure which women's course organiser Mary Higgins puts down to an over-traditional abstract format — and a lot of emotional problems among the students.

The aim is to start from the everyday and work up to the general. In the electronics course the women built a small burglar alarm — sign of the times on the council estates that surround the college. "We are trying to make it practical rather than theoretical so they end up with something useful to them at home," says electronics lecturer Colin Haywood.

The college ethos is one that gives top priority to equal opportunities for ethnic minorities, women and the disabled. A policy document says "antisexism means turning the world upside down." Objectives set out in the staff handbook include "the abandonment of antiquated and social-class based distinctions" between education and training; and "a rigorous debunking of exclusive, elitist theories of culture."

Car park signs reserving places for staff were abolished after a lot of conscience searching; security staff are non-uniformed youth workers. The watchwords are "trespassers will be enrolled" and "students mean jobs." For 25p, the jobless can have 21-hours' tuition on whatever course they like, to see what they want to do.

But some traditional roles are still firmly entrenched here. When I asked the women what their husbands thought of them attending the Women into New Technology course, none of them rebuked me.

Women doctors for rape

CLAIRE SANDERS

A group of female doctors in Northumbria are helping rape victims by taking internal examinations out of the police station.

"Years later, rape victims have come to us and complained about the police examination that took place after the rape. Some remembered it as being as traumatic as the rape itself," says Elaine Snaith of the Tyneside Rape Crisis Centre. It is a common complaint but, on Tyneside, the police have actually done something dramatic about it. There, now, all rape victims are examined by female doctors.

The Tyneside revolution began five years ago. At the time, all the police surgeons with the Northumbria force were male. It was Superintendent Rhona Cross, a down-to-earth and forceful police officer, who decided to make a change: and she assembled a group of women doctors who in future would take over responsibility for examining rape victims.

Cross decided to call in the women doctors after being much moved by an ITV documentary criticising police handling of rape cases. She was also responding to pressure from Snaith and the Rape Crisis Centre.

There are 44 women doctors on the police list who are prepared to examine victims of sexual assault on request. They cover Gateshead, Sunderland, north and south Tyneside and Newcastle. Most of the work falls on those living in the Newcastle area where a rota system operates.

The examination takes place in the casualty, gynaecology or paediatric departments of hospitals, rather than the police station as before. Cross explains that initially "some of the police surgeons were apprehensive about the ability of the women doctors to collect forensic evidence," and "sexual assault kits" which explain how to present medical evidence in court are available from the Northumbrian police.

Charlotte Wright, a doctor on the scheme, says: "We had to learn not only to examine someone from the point of view of caring for them and curing them, but also from the point of view of obtaining evidence. Tiny scratches which a doctor would normally ignore had to be noted as evidence. Swabs had to be taken as well as saliva and blood samples."

Another doctor on the Newcastle rota claims: "There is quite an art to writing the statement without putting in more than you have to. The police always want you to beef-up the briefing with information about how many sexual partners and so on.

From police expectation it is clear that some people in the past have been making sweeping medical statements such as 'this woman obviously had sexual intercourse on many occasions before.' But you just can't tell that from an examination."

According to Wright, the police are more willing to listen to "middle class female doctors" — reiterating what women from Rape Crisis have said for years. The women doctors also feel that they are now better qualified than most police surgeons to examine rape victims. While a police surgeon will see only one or two cases a year, the women doctors saw an average seven rape cases each in 1986.

As well as examining the rape victims, the doctors provide the telephone number of Rape Crisis, and offer the women contraceptive pills and advice on VD. Wright says: "I thought that mentioning VD would just upset someone more, but it is often something that the woman is extremely anxious about."

The doctors have also published guidelines on the better care of rape victims and have begun to identify patterns and trends in the incidence of sexual assault. Of the 272 cases they saw in 1986, 88 per cent of the victims were under 20 and 82 per cent were under the age of consent. Almost one third, 27 per cent, were under six years old.

"We really thought we would be dealing with mainly adult rape cases," says Wright. "In my first year I was brought an 18 month old child to examine. Many of us didn't feel qualified to see such cases, but now we've got specially trained members and we work closely with paediatricians. We have found that you cannot separate rape from child abuse — it is an extension of, or preliminary to, sexual abuse of vulnerable women."

This initiative has been praised in a Home Office circular and has also gained recognition from the women's movement. The local Rape Crisis centre calls the scheme a "shining example", and now encourages women to take rape cases to the police, which Superintendent Cross believes did not happen before.

According to Cross: "It seems so odd that the scheme should be unique. It is obvious that women should see a female doctor after being raped."

Playing fair

JOY MELVILLE

A charity in Liverpool is giving women a sporting chance.

"We once booked a squash court at the sports centre and when our group of women arrived to play, the men were still on court. I tapped on the door and one man came out, looked at his watch and said 'Give us two minutes, love.' I waited a few minutes, then tapped again, and he came out once more and said, 'Give us another five.' I said I was sorry, but we had booked the court and were losing time and he gave me a mouthful of abuse and said, 'I bet you can't even bloody play squash.' The assumption was that his game of squash was more important than ours."

"I walked straight onto the court and the other women with me thought I was a tough old boot. But if they had been there on their own, they would have felt a bit silly and intimidated and probably would never have got on court."

Sue Aldridge, the speaker, is coordinator of Liverpool's Women and Sport Project – formed in 1985 after a small group of women who lived in Toxteth started to discuss why women take so little part in sport.

Many had been hopeless at games at school; some felt that you had to be physically fit to take part; others were worried about what they would look like and that they would be laughed at by men. Sport was thought of as dominated by men, from football to snooker. Sports centres, after all, are run by men: even the photos on the walls are invariably of men boxing, running or displaying their muscles.

"We looked at the barriers and how we could break them down and get women interested in having a go at sport," says Sue, who was one of the original group. "Money constraints stop some women, so sessions had to be cheap; and there had to be a creche. We felt it important, too, to have women-only sessions, run by women – with no one watching. A lot of women will not put on a swimming costume, for instance; they're too self-conscious. Some thought they were going to have to wear designer leotards, or to be as good as Fatima Whitbread."

To begin with, the group approached the local sports centre and arranged to have women-only weight-training sessions for an hour twice a week – run by the sports teachers in the group, who gave their time voluntarily. It went so well that the group decided to have a pilot project and successfully applied to the Sports Council and the (now abolished) Merseyside county council for funding.

At present, the Sports Council pays the coordinator's salary, and the Manpower Services Commission provides the wages of eight part-time Community Programme workers. The MSC also pays a small part of the running costs, with the Sports Council paying the rest. Women and Sport is now a registered charity, with a management committee of seven that meets once a month and has a regular newsletter. Sessions are cheap or free and qualified nursery staff provide a free creche.

It was not easy to get the project off the ground. "When we first approached a sports centre, we were met with hostility," says Sue. "The first question was, 'How much is it is going to cost us?' and 'Why do you want only women?' We said we didn't like being watched and laughed at.

"It's a real hang-up. One woman rang up, for instance, and asked if there was anything she could come to. She said she was worried she would look foolish, adding, "You do know I am 17 stone?" I directed her to weight training, which would start to tone her up gradually, but my heart went out to her. We are not born with these hang-ups; we learn them from men's view of what women should be like."

Although the project started with weight-training, the weekly activities – held in sports centres or halls all round Merseyside – soon spread. They now include aerobics, badminton, swimming, Tai Chi, keep fit, self-defence, squash, netball, jogging and foot massage.

"Last summer we had a series of bike trips and we're developing more outdoor activities," says Sue. "We're having more weekends away, walking, camping and learning rock-climbing techniques in the quarries. A lot of women don't have a chance to go away. And we're not just talking about white women. Liverpool is a multiracial city and we have made links with the Chinese and with the women in the black community."

The aim of Women and Sport is to give women – from 16 to 60 – the confidence to take part. The scheme has been very successful. After a group had gone jogging with one of the women instructors, for instance, about twelve entered and completed the Liverpool Women's 10K (ten kilometre) Run. They now go running in every competition that is on.

There is a stream of similar stories. Talking to the dozen or so women who had turned up at a sports centre in Speke, near Liverpool, it was clear that without Women and Sport, they could not be there. "Well, if your kids were young, you really couldn't go anywhere," said one woman in her mid-twenties. "If you wanted to attend classes, it was just hard luck."

Women and Sport has further ambitions. "We have set up a working party on women's participation in sport," says Sue, "as we felt the council should have a policy. We would recommend: that all sports centre managers have a training course to look at needs of women and girls in sport; that women tutors are employed; and that all centres have a supervised creche."

"It really means a change of attitude. As far as I'm concerned, if one woman turns up, I think it's worthwhile. But a sports centre manager will think that a total flop. We will recommend that the package that Women and Sport gives should be available in all sports centres – though they'll say we're loony."

Pulling up the blinds

YASMIN ALIBHAI

A project in a London school teaches Asian girls self-assertion and feminism.

They were discussing sex and the English girl, the first time I visited the Asian girls project at the Elizabeth Garrett Anderson School in north London. Nine young girls, mostly from Bengali British families, were locked in amiable battle with Aqeela Alam, the group coordinator.

Alam asks: "In terms of the subjects you choose, the jobs you get, what happens to you ultimately in life, how is it different from white girls? Don't you think there is pressure on them to marry? It may not be arranged marriages, but they, too, are forced by society to think of themselves in terms of boys rather than making an independent career for themselves."

The discussion takes off, with voices and ideas scrambling over each other. The girls continue talking for two hours – about themselves, their conflicts and their position as young women in society. The spectre of the intransigent parent looms large.

The second time I visit the project is very different, Amina Patel, a lecturer in cultural studies, is running a video-making workshop in one corner of the school hall and in another corner young Asian girls practise Indian dancing. In an adjoining room, a small group grapples intensely with a personal problem which one of the girls brought in to disentangle.

The project, backed by the Inner London Education Youth Service, has been running for four years and many of the girls have been with it for most of the time. Frances Morrell, former leader of the Inner London Education Authority, has visited the school and praised the project.

Alam explains that the group was set up because, "The Asian girls at the school needed space to talk and to breathe – to feel stronger about their own culture and to express their feelings without fear of racist or sexist attacks. They needed to find out who they were, what they wanted to be and where they were going. These things were simply not being taken into account by teachers or often by parents, who themselves had to cope with terrible difficulties."

Alam is emphatic, strong and fiercely independent – a young Miss Brodie without the steel edges. Brought up in a single-parent family, she left home at 17. After a series of jobs in the social services she decided to work with Asian girls and women.

She has worked hard to get away from the "Yes Miss, No Miss" atmosphere. "Look at them now. They're oozing confidence. They don't even listen to me," she says proudly as her voice is drowned in a rising swell of noise. At times she baits the girls, to encourage them to test the ways of dealing with provocation.

She is well liked by the girls. "When you come here," says a slight girl called Roshna, "it's like a burden off your head. It's the only place you can come and really be yourself. Aqeela really understands us."

Roshna says, "The majority of us used to think you needed a man to live with, that you had to listen to your husband, cook for him and all that. Since this group, we feel more confident you can lead your own life, you don't have to depend on others as long as you have education."

The girls come from traditional homes and wear traditional clothes. But their behaviour is exuberant and self-confident – a far cry from the docile shrinking-violet image the British associate with Asian women.

Asma, a new recruit, is the exception, being non-traditional. She has short hair, wears jeans, chews gum, speak with a London accent and towers over her companions. She is, she says, an "Asian white girl, really westernised."

Her parents brought her up to be assimilated. "I thought all Asians were pathetic; stupid people in strange clothes." Earlier this year she left home and was "dragged by her social worker into the group."

Within ten minutes she formed a bond with the other girls. She says, "They've transformed me, I've got to realise about my culture and my religion. I'd always seen it from bad eyes, but it's *me.* I love my culture now, it's really important."

As the girls have become more combative, many people who initially approved of the project seem to have misgivings. Beryl

Loveridge, head of the Elizabeth Garrett Anderson school, gives clenched-teeth approval. She says the project "provides an opportunity for the girls to take part in an enormous range of activities that they couldn't before, because their parents may not have approved." But Loveridge adds: "the girls are attributing too much to one small project and not enough to the ethos of the entire school."

Alam says, "the school is all for the project because we do nice Indian dances," and she claims staff commitment is often only skin-deep. She comments, "Many teachers don't think Asian girls are worth bothering about. They think the girls don't concentrate because they are too preoccupied with getting married and having babies." A girl called Nazma told me, "We really need help because we're Asian. Some teachers think we're nothing but a bunch of bananas."

The project also has to come to terms with the fairly fixed futures that Asian parents have in mind for their children. Alam has visited many of the girls' families and has intervened to resolve one case of domestic violence. But I ask her if she is not disrupting the family life of these girls?

She replies, "What we haven't done is break conformity with the parents' wishes. What we do is look at our wishes and where they can go in terms of the parents' wishes. Most parents are not in opposition. They want their daughters to be educated and able to stand up for themselves – not battered. I work very hard with the parents too."

The emphasis on the value of the home cultures of the girls is especially important as young Asians often shed, conceal and resent their backgrounds in order to become more acceptable to their peers.

Loveridge recommends that the group "open its doors to the other girls in the school and share things with them." But for the Asian girls it seems equally important to organise as an *Asian* group where they can most comfortably be themselves.

But perhaps girls of *all* races and colours could benefit from this kind of training for life. Alam concludes: "I think that for young women there aren't many choices in life and the choices are even fewer for young Asian women. I think that is what I've shown them, and perhaps how they might stretch those choices."

Victims of crime

IAN SUTHERLAND

Strathclyde police's Female and Child Unit is welcomed by rape victim support groups and the community.

By common consent, Scotland does not exactly have an outstanding record in the matter of women's rights. All too often, the pattern has been of the depressing "one step forward – two steps back" variety. The problem is highlighted by the fate of legislation designed, at least in part, to mitigate the effects of violence against women. The Housing (Homeless Persons) Act only made it onto the statute book north of the border a year after it applied to England and Wales – the consequence of a relentless campaign by local authorities opposing the extension of the legislation. Once imposed, its implementation was obstructed at every turn in the Scots courts. Local sheriff courts can no longer deal with homeless cases, which must be heard in the Court of Session.

Similar problems have beset the Matrimonial Homes (Family Protection) (Scotland) Act, 1981, where a severe outbreak of catch-22 now applies. The courts have decided that an assaulted woman can only use the act if she is in the home at the time of application to the courts – who then say that since she is in the home, the situation clearly is neither intolerable nor actionable.

In such a comparatively dismal social and legal atmosphere, it may be a surprise to some to learn that one of the few rays of light around has been supplied by a Scottish police force. Perhaps even more surprisingly, Strathclyde's Female and Child Unit, now nearly two years old, has at least qualified support from rape crisis workers and feminist campaigners.

In his annual report for 1984, Strathclyde's then chief constable, Patrick Hamill, could claim that the introduction of specialist female and child units had, even on early indications, been well received. He went on to emphasise that their introduction was a response to a need to provide more support to female victims of crimes such as rape. South of the border, as late as February this year, the London-based Women Against Rape group complained in a letter to *The Guardian* that police were failing to address the problems of rape and attempted rape, by virtue of "priorities, policies, and practices which deter so many women from reporting offences." Angry views like this are now largely absent from the Scottish press.

Sandra Hood, Strathclyde's chief inspector responsible for training, is one of three women chief inspectors in the 6,700-strong force (which covers nearly half of Scotland's population is settings ranging from the city of Glasgow to the islands of the Inner Hebrides). Hood declares that she has always been concerned about the victims of crime, and she and her colleagues now claim that the detection rate in specialist areas like sexual offending (66.5 per cent in Strathclyde) is higher than the general rate (52.5 per cent), an important consideration at a time when police forces generally are under attack for falling detection levels.

The unit Hood now trains was formed in July 1984, with 60 female officers on full-time allocation, providing 24-hour coverage, seven days a week, in each of Strathclyde's 15 police divisions. The unit deals with rape, incest, all reports involving alleged indecency, non-accidental injury to children, wife assault, cot deaths and missing persons. Their prime function, says Sandra Hood, is to provide "special assistance to women and children – with care for the physical and psychological well being of victims."

Operating in plain clothes (uniform is donned only for direct public relations purposes), the unit's special assistance extends to sensitive handling of obtaining replacement clothing for victims (inevitably, clothing is vital evidence in sexual offences), the provision of transport and the arrangement of refreshments. Female officers – one designated to each victim – liaise between the victim and the CID, ensuring continuity in an inquiry.

The women officers of the Female and Child Unit are attached to Strathclyde CID's rank structure. Thus, viewed as appropriate use of police resources within crime investigation, the Strathclyde unit cannot be tagged with the accusation that, in progressing the 1984 initiative, they are furthering the "ghetto" role of women in the police.

Hood emphasises that female officers are selected for the unit's five-day training course because they have already displayed the qualities of good police officers. Selection is based on possession of tact, sympathy, and understanding. Service with the specialist unit is part of normal career progress, with women officers taking part for up to three years before resuming other aspects of police work.

Strathclyde police have a long history of positive community relations – an approach already developed in smaller forces before regionalisation in 1975. From the outset, the unit had identified with this tradition. Working from the viewpoint that "What's good for a woman is what's best for her," Sandra Hood and her colleagues recognise the importance of an integrated approach to the victims of sexual offences. Thus, rape crisis groups are brought into the police training schedule, along with family planning doctors, lawyers and social workers.

Recognition and use of existing community networks has, says Hood, created "a ripple effect – good for police and public." The victim now has access to a full range of services and support, official and informal. Groups outside the police force seem to agree with her.

Dr Elizabeth Wilson, a leading figure in Scotland's family planning services, regards the unit as "a huge step forward." She says the unit is even admired by women in some of the most deprived areas of Glasgow – such as the infamous Blackhill housing scheme, where the local police station has come under petrol bomb attack in the past. The way to a community's heart, it seems, may be through its women.

If any development and change is required, argues Dr Wilson, it is on the medical side of police operations. Ideally, a cadre of female doctors should be created, with specialist training to deal with rape or child abuse. Women are still apprehensive of medical men. But of the female police officers of the Female and Child Unit, she says: "They are interested and their special selection shows."

Clydeside's rape crisis campaigners also extend a welcome to the police initiative. "At least we've been consulted," said one rape crisis worker. With the unit providing a 24-hour service, campaigners feel that they would like to extend their own hours of availability. Rape victim support groups welcome their existing role in the training of selected police officers and stand ready to play an even more integral part.

Scotland will, sadly, continue to be a violent and abusive society towards women. History and cultural attitudes die hard – some local authorities continue to evade legal provision for women, the higher courts remain an exclusively male preserve and spending cuts diminish the ability of community-based groups such as Rape Crisis or Women's Aid to render effective support and assistance. Through the Female and Child Unit, Strathclyde's women can at least have some assurance that the force is with them.

Ethnic Minorities

Jobs for blacks

MADELEINE FULLERTON

A course in Leeds aims to redress racial disadvantage in employment.

Twelve black people in their twenties pore over piles of paper on office management and housing finance. "It makes me sick that I'm only on this course because I'm black," says one of them. He has been trying to get into housing management for years and it seems that "this is the only way." "It's tragic that a course like this is necessary," says Yvette, their course co-ordinator. "But it's a chance in a lifetime," says another trainee, and everyone agrees wholeheartedly.

The PATH course aims to redress racial disadvantage in employment by training black people for housing management within housing associations in west Yorkshire. Leeds city council, housing associations and the Community Relations Council decided positive action was needed following a report by the Commission for Racial Equality which showed that Asian and West Indians in Leeds wait longer for houses, receive poorer quality houses and form a disproportionate number on the transfer lists compared with whites. A report by the National Federation of Housing Associations in 1983 showed that many black people see housing associations as "remote, unresponsive white agencies at best out of touch with the communities they claim to serve, and at worst protecting white privilege and perpetuating racial disadvantage in housing and unemployment." Many housing associations, on the other hand, thought: "Black people had no real interest in either participation, employment or even in some cases, access to housing."

Section 37 of the Race Relations Act, 1976, allows training bodies to act positively in favour of people from ethnic minorities. This is why PATH was set up as an independent limited company to administer the training scheme which leads to the nationally recognised BEC General Certificate. Funding has been granted through the Rowntree Trust and city and county council grants. The Manpower Services Commission provides trainees' allowances, which are topped up by PATH to the agreed National Association of Local Government Officers' minimum of £60 a week. PATH is modelled on a similar well-established scheme in Liverpool which, despite opposition from the Militant controlled council, has helped many of its graduates into careers in housing management.

Few of the twelve Leeds trainees have educational qualifications and the pressures on the course are enormous. They work four days a week in housing associations learning the practical skills, and attend college for classes one day a week. They have twelve assignments to write and exams at the end of the year. Family life can suffer and single parents are struggling to pay childminding fees. So why did they come on the course in the first place?

"Not for the money," shouts Ben and everyone laughs loudly. Some were unemployed while others gave up better paid but dead-end jobs. But they feel passionately about housing issues and can give examples of unfairness in housing practice. Jonathan describes how a black friend married to a white woman applied for a house in a traditionally white area of the city. They were recently offered a house in Chapeltown – a black area – instead.

"Housing authorities can afford to employ just graduates now," says Rose, "but how many black people from the inner cities have the opportunity to get degrees?" All of them feel PATH offers a unique opportunity to enter white institutions where they can influence policy and help put an end to the disadvantage suffered by black people.

But while the housing associations agreed to cooperate with PATH, the people who work with the trainees on a day-to-day basis remain as prejudiced about black people as any other section of white society. On one occasion, a black worker was asked over the telephone to find people to fill a vacancy on a popular estate – but not a black family as they would lower the value of the area. All the trainees agreed the incident should be reported to senior management, but were divided over whether the officer should have been confronted immediately. Some thought they would have told her she was speaking to a black person and that her remarks were offensive, while others feel that in a crowded office, confrontation would only have antagonised fellow workers.

Some staff resent positive action and consider it unfair that black people are being offered training opportunities that they never had. There are also some supervisors who have unrealistic expectations of the trainees and offer very little guidance. While this may be because supervisors have no experience of training staff, Yvette suspects some staff want the scheme to fail out of a deep-rooted conviction that black people are not up to the job. Her suspicion grows whenever someone expresses surprise at how able and enthusiastic the trainees are. "Of course they're enthusiastic," she says, "few supervisors realise the amount of commitment demanded or how difficult it it to be the only black face in an organisation – PATH isn't an easy option."

At this point I ask, innocently, whether anyone has dropped out under all this pressure, and the whole group bristles. Jim says: "Sometimes we feel people are waiting for us to drop out, then they can say black people aren't worth all this money spent on them." Josie adds: "If this scheme is a flop, people like us will have less chance than ever – our failure will reflect on all black people." The group is very close; everyone is always ready to offer practical or emotional support to each other.

They do not believe they can change much on their own, but they are convinced they can change some white people's attitudes by showing them black people can do a first-rate job. "So many black people are ignorant," says Zahid. "They actually believe that because a person has dark skin they can't do the job – we've to prove them wrong." "All of us would rather have jobs on our own merits than through PATH," says Ben, and everyone nods vigorously.

They feel outraged that positive action is necessary, and insulted by practices such as ethnic monitoring. However, they do admit that under present conditions, housing authorities do need the information ethnic monitoring gives them in order to measure how fair their policies and practices are. Nor do they approve of some housing associations' ideas of building estates of larger houses designed for extended Asian families; "That's creating a South African style township – real segregation."

Next year, PATH will be launching a new course in Leeds to train black people for local government administration. PATH's reputation has grown and there are already four hundred applications for this. PATH also plans to set up training schemes for the voluntary and private sectors. The organisers feel confident that banks, building societies and insurance companies will be willing to participate if MSC and PATH are willing to pay trainees for them.

Meanwhile the positive action scheme in Merseyside is in its third year and a high proportion of its graduates have found permanent full-time posts in housing management. The idea is spreading and new positive action schemes are planned for several areas of the country. There is no guarantee that the Leeds trainees will find jobs, but they are all optimistic. "We'll go far," says Ben confidently, and again, everyone agrees.

Urdu for beginners

ADRIANA CAUDREY

English learners and Asian teachers find out about each other's worlds

Mushtaq Hussain dons dark glasses and takes a seat beside Bashir Ahmad. They smile cryptically and begin a comic dialogue in Urdu. Words like "Pakistan," "Lahore" and "Manchester" are the only clues in a completely uncrackable code. The other international touch is when a £10 note changes hands. Everyone laughs at *that*. But most of the students confess they missed the punchline.

The mystifying entertainment, taking place on a flagstoned roof garden in the centre of Oxford, is the light relief in a whole day of Urdu classes. (New vocabulary from the jokes is handed out at the next class.) This weekend session marks the start of a new term for second and third year Urdu students.

Oxford's Asian Language Development Project is the only one of its kind in the country. What distinguishes it from any others is that all its teachers are members of the local Asian community – they include factory workers, a city clerk and an assistant in an old people's home – none of whom has formal teaching qualifications. Their students are almost exclusively white, middle class professionals.

Among them are several teachers, a health visitor, a housing official, a youth worker, a police superintendent and an anthropologist. Most of them work in east Oxford, where there is a large Asian community, and the wish to be able to speak to clients and neighbours in their own language. Urdu, the national language of Pakistan, is also spoken in North India and in parts of South East Asia. It is the most widely used language among the Asian community in this country.

The project is the brainchild of Alison Shaw, an Urdu teacher, whose doctoral thesis was on Pakistani families in Oxford. She and two colleagues at the industrial branch of the Workers Educational Association ran a two-day pilot project in spoken Urdu four years ago. Four times as many people as expected wanted to enrol, so there was a clear demand. Alison applied for an Urban Aid Grant – 75 per cent from the Department of the Environment and 25 per cent from Oxford City Council – to set up evening classes.

Although the city council had only ranked the scheme ninth on its list of pet projects, it was the *only one* from Oxford to be picked by the DOE. Funding goes to Oxfordshire Council for Community Relations, which pays Alison Shaw in her role as project officer. (The WEA pays the teachers from student fees, which are £19 a head per term.) Alison, who is hyperenergetic and brainy, says their method of teaching is similar to that used for teaching English as a foreign language.

"Our methods are very different from those used to teach Urdu in Pakistan," she says. "There, they would start with the alphabet and then join the letters. That would be inappropriate for English learners who want to be able to speak, not to write, and don't have much time." Her mentor is Ralph Russell, chairman of the National Council for Urdu Teaching, and one-time reader in Urdu at London's School of Oriental and African Studies. She has used and developed his teaching materials, to help her train native speakers to become teachers.

Mushtaq Hussain, a smiling man with a full black beard, wearing a brown velvet jacket, is embarking on his second year as a teacher on the course. A worker at the Cowley car plant in east Oxford, whose first language is Punjabi, he says: "I was sitting in my brother's shop. I saw the paper that comes free from door to door and I noticed an advertisement saying 'Urdu speaker wanted,' " He contacted Alison Shaw. "I told her I am not highly educated in Urdu, but she said they only needed Urdu speakers." Like all the other prospective teachers Mushtaq went on Alison's training course – two nights a week for five weeks.

Mushtaq confides: "At first I was depressed because I thought I would be teaching educated people. What if they ask me a grammatical question and I can't answer it? They'll say: 'What sort of a teacher is he?' " The course "line" on this is that if a teacher doesn't know the answer, he promises to find it out after the lesson.

Mushtaq clearly had the respect and affection of his class. They settled down like eager schoolchildren as he agreed to read them a complicated story a second time. Then he went round the class asking questions. They were a brightly dressed group: pink ankle socks vied with blue ones, jade T-shirts were neck and neck with yellow ones and baggy white cotton trousers sat beside needle-striped ones. The students – predominantly women and mostly aged between 25 and 40 years – attend the course for a variety of reasons. But almost all of them meet Asian people in their work and want to have a better understanding of their language.

Terry Anley, a police superintendent, started the course when he was a chief inspector at Cowley Road police station, in the heart of the Asian community: "I suppose it must have been evident that there was a communication gap and that if we took a small step towards bridging it that would be constructive," he reflects. When he moved to Thames Valley police headquarters to become head of communications, his Urdu lessons helped him. "I've learned a lot about cultural differences," he says. "Inherent in the language is the importance of status in various sections of society."

His insights led him to authorise alterations to the wording of letters which the police write to Asian families. Instead of translating straight from English, they have introduced a new format to take account of Urdu protocol. He adds that one of the most important spin offs for him has been making friends and personal contacts in the Asian community.

Catherine Robertson, a health visitor in east Oxford, says that she has often had to use male members of a family to interpret between herself and female patients. She says: "I want to be able to communicate directly with the woman, otherwise she isn't getting the same service as an English woman." An anthropologist was learning the language partly so as to be able to communicate with elderly relatives of Indian friends.

The classes are a neat reversal of the more usual English as a second language approach. How often have Asian people been at the receiving end of shopping role plays? English students are being taught to buy provisions, in Urdu. That facility might endear them to the city's many Asian shopkeepers.

Nafisa Mirza, one of the teachers, a full-time assistant in an old people's home, stands behind a mock counter, with groceries around her and goes round the class asking students what they would like to buy. Luckily, the Urdu for "spoon" sounds rather like *jam jar;* "sugar" sounds like *genie.* So, when, unexpectedly, my turn comes, I have a way of remembering two things to buy.

Nafisa Mirza reckons that the classes help to foster understanding between the indigenous and the Asian communities. She said: "It's nice that English people want to learn an Asian language – it helps them to realise how a foreigner must find life in this country. When people come here, especially Asians, they can't speak a word of English. I don't think most English people realise how difficult their lives are over here." Teaching has clearly given people like Nafisa, Mushtaq and Bashir a confidence boost. "People like us can teach. You don't have to be highly educated to teach."

How to start again

MADELEINE FULLERTON

The Asian community can use its traditional skills to escape from unemployment

When the factories closed in the early 1980s, Mr Khan became just another member of Sparkbrook's army of long-term unemployed. Classified as "unskilled" by Birmingham's job centres, and with increasing debts, he thought setting up his own business was an impossible dream.

He went to the Ashram Community Service Project to ask for help now, just over a year later, he has two expanding businesses and hopes soon to employ other people. "We encourage people to look at and value the skills they do possess," says Ute Jaeckel, who co-ordinates the project. "Many have traditional skills such as weaving, craft work, rural and farm skills, and many come from families with generations of experience in trading, buying and selling."

Mr Khan decided to set up as a trader – importing and distributing rugs and prayer mats. With the help of Engin Hassan Mamouglu, one of the project's few paid workers, he discovered he could raise a bank loan of £1,000, a feasibility grant of £500 and claim £40 a week through the Enterprise Allowance Scheme. In addition to practical services such as free book-keeping and photocopying facilities, the project has offered emotional support.

"Living on £40 a week with a large family is impossible," he says. "We couldn't pay the mortgage for months and I needed somebody to keep me going." Engin advised him to import very small quantities at a time and now, with his bank loan increased up to £3,000, he has begun trading in shoes – taking up to 600 orders a month.

"I feel so free," he says, "so confident. Just to be busy and independent again is wonderful." Soon he hopes to rent premises through the Birmingham New Enterprise Workshop Scheme and develop his own shoe manufacturing business. Then he will buy second-hand machinery, and employ other people.

The Ashram project originated ten years ago when a group of Christians and Muslims decided to live together in the centre of Sparkbrook. Over the years they became increasingly involved in the life of the mainly Muslim community, and identified long-term unemployment and the resultant poverty as the most pressing problem for the families in the area.

One of the main aims of the project, which is now funded by Birmingham's Economic Development Committee, is to find ways to use the community's skills and match them with other wasted resources in the area such as derelict land and buildings. Ashram Acres is an example of this – wasteland in Sparkbrook has been transformed by volunteers into highly productive space where vegetables grow and farm animals flourish. This aspect of the project's work has been so successful that the city council gave an £87,000 grant to set up the Ashram Asian vegetables scheme which will eventually employ about 80 people paid through the Manpower Services Commission.

Meanwhile, on a smaller scale, one man has started a milk round, another is doing well as a painter and decorator and Engin Hassan plans to set up a resin workshop – encasing flowers from family celebrations or models of local mosques in resin and selling them as gifts for friends and relatives.

But occasionally, despite the project's best efforts, everything seems to work against the individual trying to return to employment. Mr Zafar ran his own knitting manufacturing and retail business which came to an abrupt end following a massive burglary. Though he was insured, the insurance company refused to pay, claiming they had told him to change the locks.

As a result, the bank withdrew its loan and after years of successful trading, he was out of business with five young children to support. He still has four knitting machines but his shop has fallen into disrepair. Despite Ashram's efforts, no bank or building society will lend him the £2,000 he needs to start again. The best advice they can give Mr Zafar is to sell his shop and start again in a New Enterprise Workshop where he can stay for up to a year. Unfortunately he cannot afford to have the necessary repairs carried out in order to sell. But here again, the Ashram project can offer practical help.

Urban Renewal money provides a worker to teach home maintenance skills to the long-term unemployed who cannot afford to carry out essential repairs to their homes. This is Mahmood, an electrician by trade, who has lived in Sparkbrook since he was nine years old. Mahmood hopes to take a group of his trainees to Mr Zafar's shop to tackle the work there—thus giving them practical experience and helping to solve Mr Zafar's problem at the same time. Without the project's help, Mr Zafar believes he would have given up all hope months ago.

Mahmood's home maintenance courses are popular partly because the new skills that increase self-sufficiency boost the community's battered self-esteem. Mr Shah, for example, believes he is too old ever to find paid employment again. He has been on two courses: "Now, instead of sitting at home doing nothing, I can do complicated jobs around my own house or help relatives with their problems." This work may not be paid, but discovering and developing new skills that can be helpful to others has given him renewed interest in life.

Many women possess traditional skills, but rarely perceive that they are marketable. Jill, who has lived in Ashram Community House for six years, runs business courses at the centre, and works with women in their homes helping them find the confidence to show their work to others. "We look at the obstacles in the way of women and try to find an acceptable way round them," she says.

Fatima urgently needs money but she does not want to leave home to work. For years she has taken in sewing work through an agent, but in her spare time she weaves with cotton and paints fabrics in traditional designs. She has recently begun to pass these skills on to other women at the centre, and the project has arranged for her work to be sold at craft fairs and twice-yearly exhibitions laid on by Ashram.

But as well as encouraging and giving practical help to women with special skills, the Ashram project also supports about 50 isolated home workers. They have to buy their own machines on hire purchase and pay the agent who brings them work a large part of their wages. Sometimes they earn as little as £2 for an eight-hour day.

Jill visits regularly, checking on health and safety standards and giving guidance on how to handle potentially dangerous substances. She also brings news of homework advertised at the job centre and information about what different firms pay. She tries to arrange direct contracts for the women, so they do not have to rely on an agent for their livelihood.

Meanwhile, money is a constant problem for anyone wishing to market their work. The community is interested in developing a credit union and the project has arranged a public meeting and invited speakers to discuss this. Credit unions can provide loans for people who are not eligible for bank loans. They are administered voluntarily and operate on the savings of their members.

But the Ashram project itself urgently needs funds. At present there are few paid workers and, as work opportunities expand, they are spreading themselves more and more thinly. If more funds cannot be found, meaningful work for many of Sparkbrook's long-term unemployed may again become an impossible dream.

Investigating racial attacks

STEVE PLATT

A panel attempts to deal with the alarming incidence of racial violence in Tower Hamlets

Superintendent P. Pridige, community liaison officer for the Metropolitan Police's H District, shuffled through his papers nervously. For the first time in the evening his easy and composed manner gave way to just a hint of frustration as his questioner refused to let the subject drop.

"This incident happened two or three months ago," said Abu Sayeed, senior community relations officer with the Tower Hamlets Association for Racial Equality. "It was reported within 90 seconds of the offence taking place to a police constable who was in the area at the time. He *spoke to* the youths who were responsible, so it's not as though the police don't know who they are. Why hasn't anything been done about it?"

The incident in question was a relatively minor racial assault on a black housing officer in the London Borough of Tower Hamlets. The local beat officer had taken details of the incident, but no one had been arrested. Abu Sayeed was now using the forum of Tower Hamlets' recently established Racial Incidents Panel to find out why.

The panel was set up last September to bring together councillors, community groups and the police in an attempt to deal with the alarming incidence of racial violence in London's East End. In particular, it was designed to provide an independent check on the way the police deal with racial incidents; to offer a means by which questions or criticism can be raised directly with police representatives; and so to encourage more people to report incidents.

Last year, 279 racial attacks were reported to the police in Tower Hamlets, down from 414 in 1984. Yet 495 assaults were dealt with by the Community Alliance for Police Accountability (CAPA), the local police monitoring group (only 16 of which resulted in arrests). Many Asians, say CAPA, don't bother reporting incidents to the police because they don't expect them to be properly investigated.

This, above all, was what prompted Ian Mikardo, the veteran Labour MP for the area, to throw his weight behind the idea of the Racial Incidents Panel. And it was his influence, exerted via senior officers at Scotland Yard, which persuaded the local police to participate.

That participation in itself makes the panel unique. In other areas the police have excused themselves from involvement in such bodies on the grounds that they fall outside the consultative procedures specified in the Police and Criminal Evidence Act. In Tower Hamlets, though, much as Superintendent Pridige might like the panel's work to be incorporated in that of the official police consultative group, the police have come to accept that the problem of racial violence necessitates a more flexible approach.

The meetings of the Racial Incidents Panel take a well-established form. The central feature is a written police report which lists all racial incidents notified during the previous month and provides details of what action has been taken in each case.

The police remarks on action taken vary from an unconvincing, "Local inquiries made with no further information being obtained," to quite detailed reports on major criminal investigations. They also reveal the now routine use of follow-up visits by home beat officers, who are sometimes most useful to the victims of racial violence when they go beyond their ordinary police duties.

"Housing office contacted concerning replacing broken window glass," said the report on one attack, earning the officer concerned unexpected plaudits from Asian members of the panel. "It was very kind of the police to get involved in this," said Abu Sayeed.

In an attempt to deal with the problem of racial violence as a whole (and get the windows fixed as well as arrest those who break them), the panel tries to bring together different departments and agencies. It encourages the involvement of social services and housing officials, particularly from the local race and housing team which works on estates in the area, as well as representatives of voluntary organisations, community groups, politicians and the police.

Inevitably, then, the panel deals with more than a mere catalogue of specific incidents. Among the issues to have been given special attention recently were those of racist graffiti and the concentration of racial attacks on particular estates. Impatient community representatives demanded effective joint action by the council and the police, and were dismissive of each organisation's implied blame of the other.

The growing problem of racist attacks at or outside schools has also come up at several panel meetings. After a series of attacks at the Morpeth school earlier this year, for instance, which culminated in a strike by 150 Bangladeshi children, the panel agreed upon a set of proposals to put to the education authority and the police.

Superintendent Pridige had a tough time justifying the police failure to stop the attacks, and his excuse that "if it happens inside the school, it is the head's responsibility," was given short shrift by panel members. Demands for increased police patrols, better liaison with the headteacher and the investigation of organised racist activity outside the school were all duly considered.

But the core of the panel's work remains the investigation of particular incidents. In addition to examining the police response in each reported case, panel members also bring up attacks which do not appear on the official police lists. Sometimes this may be because the police have not identified the assault as being racially motivated. Abu Sayeed raised one such case, which was later discovered to have been listed after all, of a doctor attending a call who was knocked unconscious by two youths yelling, "Paki bastard, why are you here?"

More usually, an attack will not appear on the police list because it has not been reported. Often the victims do not want further action to be taken, perhaps because they mistrust the police or are afraid of reprisals. "It is important that we know of these cases anyway," says Superintendent Pridige. "And if people are critical of the way the police respond they should come and say why."

Unfortunately for those who are committed to the panel as a means of increasing the reporting of racial attacks, some of the groups best placed to help achieve that objective have so far refused to take part in it. CAPA have never attended its meetings; and Kumar Murshid of the Federation of Bangladeshi Youth Organisations describes it as "a talking shop. We are prepared to have dialogue with the police, but it has to be meaningful and have some impact on policing. The panel can't bring about police accountability because it has no power, and until the police are accountable, Bengali people will not have confidence in them."

Ian Mikardo admits that the panel "is not yet meaningful to many community organisations." But he insists that it forces the police to do something about racial attacks when they are reported "because the panel is watching over them all the time."

"The panel will be beginning to achieve its objectives," he says, "when the number of cases of racial violence coming to our attention doubles—because that will represent a doubling of belief on the part of black people that something is finally being done to protect them from racists."

The small hill

IAN SUTHERLAND

A Glasgow project tackles the problems of the close Chinese community

Since the Chinese restaurant phenomenon came to Clydeside in the early 1960s, Glasgow's Garnethill has been home to approximately 1,000 Chinese—most from Hong Kong and still largely employed in the catering trade. The working day in the restaurant belt just down the hill in the city centre typically begins at lunch-time and ends in the small hours of the morning. Wages are low and working conditions poor. Despite a measure of tenement rehabilitation in Garnethill since the 1970s, housing conditions can be far from satisfactory.

Glasgow has a tradition of assimilating immigrant groups, although organised racism *does* exist, and may be growing, alongside a progressive history of immigrants moving from inner-city "ghetto" areas (Gorbals Jews before the second world war, for example) to lusher suburban pastures.

With a few exceptions, Garnethill's Chinese population seems intent on staying close to the inner city. Within this distinctive and close community, old ways die hard—leading to very real social and personal problems. Since 1985 the Garnethill-based San Jai Project (it translates literally as "the small hill," an apt description of the area's elevation above the shopping streets, has begun to tackle the problems of housing, poverty and isolation among Glasgow's Chinese residents. Eighteen months on, San Jai's small staff see cautious grounds for optimism.

San Jai was the brainchild of Zara Ross, National Children's Homes Scottish development officer, who in looking for new initiatives to replace the NCH emphasis on residential care, began to explore what might be of benefit to Glasgow's Indian and Pakistani communities. Finding this group relatively articulate and organised, NCH began to hold informal discussions with individual Chinese Glaswegians. "We found that there was a serious language problem," says Zara Ross, "and that the Chinese community was not aware of the services that are available to all citizens.

Knowledge of the opening of San Jai was spread by word of mouth. The aim has been to raise awareness among Chinese residents and to have a "ripple effect" of awareness among official agencies. "San Jai is looking both inward and outward," says Zara Ross, "and we can now provide assistance to social workers, the health board and the housing department." San Jai's foundation was boosted by the publication of a Commons select committee report on the needs of Britain's Chinese population, which helped get Scottish Office funding. The project now has an annual budget of £35,000.

Juliet Gallacher, herself a former Hong Kong schoolteacher married to a retired Scots colonial civil servant and now San Jai's family worker, says that until recently Garnethill's Chinese residents rarely claimed state benefits at all. "They came here to *work,*" she says, "and if they became unemployed, they sought support from relatives and friends still working." Elderly Chinese people rarely knew how to claim a pension.

"The early Chinese residents of Garnethill saw themselves as unlikely to remain in Glasgow," says Juliet Gallacher, "but their children want to stay." As this process develops, the demand for San Jai's advice and support has grown rapidly.

Health problems loom large in the centre's work. In a typical month, health inquiries can account for 50 out of the 200 referrals to the four-person agency. Young Garnethill women used to fly to Hong Kong to have their babies, with language problems and cultural barriers inhibiting involvement with local medical services. Glasgow now has a handful of Chinese GPs, but, ironically, these are second-generation Clydeside Chinese — and Glasgow's assimilation has been so successful that most don't speak either of the common Chinese languages of Cantonese and Hakka.

San Jai's health worker Teresa Liu, a Clydeside-trained nurse from Hong Kong, has instigated close liaison with inner-city health visitors. San Jai's first young mother's group will open shortly, with creche facilities in the project's Hill Street premises. Child and family problems form a big part of San Jai's caseload.

Teresa Liu arranges appointments with GPs and accompanies Chinese patients as "medical interpreter." "As a nurse, I can write Chinese instructions on a prescription bottle," she says. Teresa has found that Chinese patients won't approach a doctor unless they are very ill, and Chinese mothers will rather seek advice on baby-care from friends than a health visitor. Chinese mothers, faced with a sick child at nights and weekends, often don't realise that the NHS offers 24-hour cover.

Teresa Liu has recently produced simple leaflets listing common complaints side-by-side in English and Chinese, reducing the need for interpreters. But, she says, there is still a very big need for volunteer teachers of English to work in Chinese homes. "Many men, especially, work in an exclusively Chinese-speaking environment."

Elderly people, heavily committed to childcare where both parents work, can become increasingly isolated and housebound. "Ideally, we'd now like to encourage a group for elderly Chinese people," says Juliet Gallacher. Garnethill's first elderly Chinese person to enter local authority residential care is now coping successfully in a council house.

Community groups among Glasgow's Chinese residents are not always easy to foster. "The joke round here is that we'd need to change the times of the groups to 2am," says Juliet Gallacher wryly. In the absence of such facilities, Glasgow's restaurant workers all too easily drift into city centre casinos, which are all that stay open when the restaurants close their doors. The casino is social club, pub, news source and unofficial employment exchange. The darker side of casino life lies in the shadow operations of Glasgow's small but potent Chinese underworld, where the invisible and negative influence of the Tongs is ever present.

While the San Jai staff pick their way through the potential Garnethill minefields, the community is beginning to respond and appreciate their own service. On a typical Monday morning, San Jai is dealing with an elderly Chinese man who is not receiving a full supplementary pension, a worried woman disputing a demand (in official English) from the tax inspector and someone who needs an interpreter in order to sit their driving test.

Mr Chan (not his real name) has come for advice on obtaining a visa for Hong Kong. In the past, he says, the only way that a Glasgow Chinese could get a bill explained or a letter translated was to find a sympathetic student somewhere in town. That problem even led to the rates being paid twice as residents mistook a reminder for a second account. "They don't have enough workers here," says Mr Chan. But he also says: "Chinese people know the job gets done properly here. This is an *open* place."

In the past, says Juliet Gallacher, the Chinese in Glasgow were less than forceful and they've missed out. Strathclyde region is embarking on a major Urban Aid project to bring services closer to ethnic minorities. San Jai aims to ensure that Chinese Glasgow gets its share of the action. In the process, the "small hill" may begin to move outwards into the wider city.

Breaking the language barrier

KIRSTY MILNE

A new project helps people from ethnic minorities to overcome language difficulties.

"Multilingualism isn't a problem, it's a fact," Ann Corsellis insists. "It only becomes a problem when you don't do anything about it." She ought to know, having done a great deal about it since 1983, when she started the Community Interpreters Project under the auspices of the Institute of Linguists.

Her experience as a magistrate in Cambridge made her acutely aware of how poor interpreting across language barriers can generate misunderstanding and even injustice in the world of officialdom. When a French teenager was arrested on a shoplifting charge, a French-speaking court was relatively easy to assemble, but other languages presented more elaborate problems. On one occasion a colleague gave a judgment which he afterwards discovered had been relayed to the Asian defendant complete with an injunction to go home and pray and be a good Moslem.

The most notorious instance of how serious the consequences of inadequate interpreting can be is the textbook case of *Iqbal Begum v Regina* in 1981. A Pakistani woman apparently pleaded guilty to the murder of her husband—and was duly sentenced to life imprisonment. Not until four years later did it become clear that the interpreter her solicitor had used didn't speak Punjabi—her first language—and the defence had been based on a failure of communication.

Ann Corsellis was shocked that "professionals were making responsible decisions based on inaccurate information" and that people were paying for statutory services which they couldn't make proper use of, all because of language difficulties. Obviously what was needed was some way of recruiting and training interpreters to an agreed standard.

Ann Corsellis, who describes her appearance as that of "the archetypal Tory lady," has radical instincts. She went and talked to the Home Office, the Cambridgeshire police, probation service, courts, town hall and social services, all of whom said they would welcome a better system. So, funded by the Nuffield Foundation, she set out to provide a model for the recruitment and training of interpreters in Peterborough, where 14 per cent of the population are of non-English origin.

The range of languages spoken in the town is startlingly

eclectic. There are 6,000 Italians, most of whom came over after the war to work in the brickworks, and a sizeable Asian community, concentrated in the Gladstone district of the city. There, as one education worker put it, "English is a thousand miles away"; the languages that you hear are Urdu, Punjabi, Gujerati and Bengali.

Mr Bhatty's family are Moslems from Pakistan. His mother tongue is Punjabi and his English is very limited. Eighteen months ago his eldest son, whose formal education had been in Urdu, arrived from Pakistan to join the rest of the family. Not surprisingly, finding the right school for him in Peterborough has been a problem, and the local education welfare officer, Zulfikarsayeed, has kept in regular contact with Mr Bhatty.

This is where the Community Interpreters Project comes into its own. Even in the relatively ideal world of Peterborough local education authority, which makes a point of employing bilingual professionals, the multiplicity of Asian languages is such that the education welfare officer, whose first languages are Gujerati and Urdu, still needs to call out an interpreter to go with him. Thanks to the Community Interpreters Project, the education welfare office now has an index of interpreters in the languages they need.

Everyone on the list will have passed the Certificate in Community Interpretation, set up by the scheme and run by the Institute of Linguists. In addition to language and interpreting skills, students take an option on the legal system—or, as in this case, the social services (including education and local government). This modular approach allows them to specialise in the vocabulary for a particular type of interpreting and practise role playing with professionals from the agencies with whom they will be working.

The best interpreters, says Ann Corsellis, are "Quiet, self-possessed people—I don't mean shy—but modest." It's important they they should "allow people to be themselves," and resist the temptation to end up acting as a "culture broker." The interpreter must also be adept at assessing the appropriate interpreting techniques for different situations: consecutive translation for straightforward question and answer, simultaneous whispering if the speaker is in animated and continuous flow.

Through the interpreter, Gulam Farid, the education welfare officer, explains to Mr Bhatty plans for moving his son to a part-time course at Peterborough Regional College, where he will be mixing with students of his own age and offered back-up in Punjabi. "Can he still claim benefit?" Mr Bhatty wants to know. The interpreter happens to double as a welfare benefits advice officer, so he can give advice on this.

The interpreter must maintain a certain professional detachment at all times, even though this can be difficult; there is a syndrome well-known in court called "interpreter's arm," referring to the frantic grip of an over-anxious client. To cope with the ethical complexities of their profession, the interpreters have formed their own association—to which representatives of the service agencies are affiliated—and drawn up a code of conduct. But, as Ann Corsellis emphasises, "An interpreter is always second best. The best is a bilingual, bicultural professional."

The scheme is so obviously a success that the only question left is why nobody did it before. People like Mr Bhatty, who might otherwise be a prisoner of his own language, can have access to services which are theirs by right. And from the other end, the provision of a reliably trained interpreter is a great asset to officials in education, in the courts and the probation service. Ann Corsellis confirms that, "Every professional I have spoken to would like this facility to be available."

In the headquarters of the Cambridgeshire Constabulary at Huntingdon, details of each interpreter are stored so that police, courts and probation officers throughout the country can ring in if they need one. The police also plan to provide a leaflet to explain to a client that an interpreter is one the way.

The scheme now operates in Cambridge, Peterborough and Bedford, covering Gujerati, Urdu, Punjabi, French, Spanish, Italian, German and Cantonese. The most obvious omission from the agencies covered by the scheme up to now has been the NHS; but a pilot project is planned for Addenbrooke's hospital in Cambridge, where isolated groups of Vietnamese and Bengalis are in particular need of help.

What makes the Community Interpreters Project so remarkable is its willingness to grapple with the extraordinary linguistic diversity which exists in Britain today.

"What is needed," says Ann Corsellis, "is a little more competence and a little less sentiment." We are a multi-cultural society, but with honourable exceptions we are taking an inordinate length of time to wake up to the fact. A young nation like Australia, conscious of a history based on immigration, has a nationwide community interpreters network. Isn't it time our ageing nation had one too?

An Asian haven

MADELEINE FULLERTON

Community centres for Sikhs in Derby provide a retreat and help.

In a small terraced house in the heart of Derby's Asian community, a group of elderly Sikh men are discussing old times. The walls of the brightly decorated room are covered with photos of coach trips to historic places. There is a video, and a wide range of films, books and games. Downstairs, Asian welfare rights workers deal with the health, housing and social security problems of some 25 people a day.

Mr Singh Shoker, aged 85 and Mr Rattan Singh Sangha, 67, are the secretary and treasurer of Derby's Asian over-sixties' club. They have seen it develop from one small room in a church hall to a flourishing organisation with over 150 people attending three centres which stay open seven days a week.

"Many of us feel very lonely in our homes now," says Shoker. "At the centres we can discuss our old lives as farmers in the Punjab and talk to people who have been back to India." The centres are distributed around the inner city area where most of Derby's Asian elderly live. This means no one has to walk far for company, classes, activities and practical help. Disabled members are visited in their homes by other club members or by workers on the project.

Most of the club's users emigrated to Britain in their mid fifties and worked in Derby's heavy industry until they retired. Very few speak English and, when their children moved to larger houses in the suburbs, they preferred to remain in the small terraced houses they originally settled in, near friends, familiar shops, Gurdwaras and mosques. When the younger generation does not move away from home, the elderly face another problem; their families have expanded so much there is no room for them in the house during the day. Also, many consider it inappropriate for a man to be alone in a small terraced house with his daughter in law and this too drives the men out of their homes during the daytime while their sons are at work.

With very little money—most did not work long enough to qualify for pensions—and nowhere to go, the men used to congregate in the streets or parks where children laughed at their traditional dress, pushed them and threw stones. In bad weather they sought shelter in the local library, but since they could not read English newspapers they talked and were soon thrown back onto the streets. A survey carried out in 1981 revealed that many were not receiving even basic DHSS entitlements and virtually none received home help or any other aid from the local social services department.

People began to seek informal practical help with translation, interpreting and communication from trusted members of their community, including Hardial Singh Bains, a respected teacher. With his help, they applied for and received a grant from Age Concern to rent a room in a community centre where they could congregate daily. The club became a registered charity and they got urban aid funding to buy their own house and pay a full-time coordinator to develop new projects and activities. The city council gave them another building in the park and NACRO now funds five Asian workers who provide a translation and interpreting service, welfare rights surgeries at all three centres and home visits for the housebound.

But although workers have to help with correspondence and communication, users have always run the club themselves through an elected committee. "We tell our workers what we elderly people want," says Shoker. "I walk around the area, talk to people and find out who is disabled or housebound so we can visit and see if they need anything like home help or aids for the bath—or perhaps just someone to visit." "I look after the money," says Sangha. "I decide how much we can spend on videos, films, books, papers and games."

The club aims to provide a comprehensive welfare rights service. "Our people prefer to come to us for help," says Sangha. "At DHSS and social services they have to wait in a cold waiting room. No one understands them, people stare at their clothes, and anyway, they close early and don't open Saturdays and Sundays . . . At our centres there are no appointments but there are so many things to do and friends to talk to, people are happy to spend all day waiting if necessary."

Another aim of the project is to help people develop the skills they need to advocate on their own behalf. English classes are popular and information videos, translated welfare rights and health service leaflets as well as a library are all available at the club's main administrative centre. There is a newspaper translation service to keep people in touch with events in this country, keep fit classes and regular outings are arranged to places of interest with facilities for the disabled. Some users are currently making slides of their former way of life to show younger people.

But the social support the club provides is as important as practical help. In the past there was a ban on arguments about political developments in India. But at the centres, even those from families with opposing views enjoy settling down to talk about old times.

Bur Singh tells me, through an interpreter, that 75,000 Sikhs died for Britain in the first and second world wars: "Everyone here lost someone, a brother or a cousin and only we still remember them." He himself fought the Japanese on the Burma front: "When Prince Charles came to visit our club, we asked him why he has no Sikhs in his palace guard—he said he will see what he can do when he is king." "We don't see any practising Sikhs in the army now," adds Shoker. They all feel disappointed that practising Sikhs are no longer represented in the services: "It has always been our tradition you see," explains Bur Singh, "that, if there are three sons, one will become a soldier."

In view of this tradition of service the rejection they feel at the hands of modern British society is particularly confusing and hurtful. Their traditional dress is jeered at in the streets and their needs overlooked by the statutory agencies set up to help the elderly. Their centre in the park has suffered most from racist attacks—probably because it is the most isolated. Windows have been broken and indelible graffiti—"Asian bastards, fuck you"—scrawled on the walls. But despite this, at least 40 people now meet every day in the once derelict city council building. The most memorable incident was when white youths blocked the entrances with snow one winter evening imprisoning elderly men for some hours before they could attract help. Since that time a phone has been installed. The attacks are dying down as the Sikhs' presence gradually becomes accepted.

Members are especially proud of people from their community who are visibly successful. The club's coordinator, Jarnail Singh Birring, may be married to an Englishwoman and dress in western style, but what has really earned him trust and respect is his success as a weightlifter. He runs his own sports club and has won five national championships. His appointment lasts until 1989 when urban aid funding runs out. Unfortunately the NACRO workers are appointed for one year only. This means that no sooner has a worker become experienced and trusted by club users than he or she must be replaced by someone unknown.

"We also have financial problems," says Hardial: "Our urban aid funding was fixed three years ago but we are expanding all the time. The amount fixed for the phone bill was enough then but now more and more people come to us for help it is far too little."

He hopes social services will take over funding so the posts can become permanent and the project can build on what it has already achieved—but so far there are no promises from social services.

A black stair to yuppiedom

KIRSTY MILNE

A self-help course in London trains blacks to set up their own businesses.

It's six thirty on a drizzling summer evening in the City. Outside the City of London Polytechnic, tired tourists are trooping home from Tower Hill. Inside, 40 aspiring entrepreneurs, hungry but committed, are intent on a session called "How to present your case to the bank manager," conducted by a representative from National Westminster's small business section.

It could be an evening class on any business training course. The difference is that the 40 faces in the lecture room are all black; the lecturers, cool and authoritative in suits and ties, are black; and the session is part of a unique course run by Britain's first Ethnic Minority Business Development Unit.

The EMBDU was established 18 months ago to offer training for black and Asian people aiming to set up in business. The prototype came—inevitably—from the United States, where more than 30 universities run special units aimed at helping ethnic minorities break into business. Something along the same lines was obviously needed in Britain, where ethnic minorities, particularly Afro-Caribbeans, are under-represented in the self-employment figures.

According to the 1984 Labour Force Survey, only 4.6 per cent among economically active Afro-Caribbeans and 16.7 per cent among Asians are self-employed; there are 256,000 Asian businessmen in the UK but only 20,000 Afro-Caribbeans. A survey carried out by Hackney council in the early 1980s suggested that as many as 74 per cent of viable business proposals put to banks by black businessmen were being turned down.

Cosmos Charles, director of the unit, says that his students encounter all the obstacles familiar to anyone trying to start up a small business; they need to know, among other things, about book-keeping, management, how to draw up a business plan, how to raise a loan. But, he says, they also have to grapple with the consequences of direct and indirect racism; specifically, "bank managers who assume that if someone is black they can't run a business," or customers who feel that any product made by a black person is inferior. He is also anxious that his students should not automatically find themselves fulfilling the occupational stereotypes of their ethnic group; for Asians, running shops and restaurants; for Afro-Caribbeans, working as hairdressers and mechanics.

Most of those attending the class are Afro-Caribbeans. Cosmos

Charles points out that in the Asian community business skills are often learned naturally at an early age; it is not uncommon to find an Asian child "in the family shop with a box on his head at eight o'clock in the morning." But, in the Afro-Caribbean community, "there just isn't the same tradition."

He is worried, however, about the lack of Bangladeshi students; the unit has recently appointed a lecturer who speaks Bengali and Sylheti, but Cosmos Charles feels they may need to do more outreach work to make contact with the isolated Bangladeshi community. The EMBDU has also found it difficult—again presumably for cultural reasons—to attract Asian women; Cosmos Charles accepts that it may be necessary to offer separate courses for them.

The basic business training course offered by the EMBDU is carefully designed to make it practical for tired students to cope with at the end of their working day. A questionnaire is issued at the start of each course to find out what topics individuals want to cover, and there is another at the finish to canvass their reactions. A conscious decision was taken to hold classes in the City of London Polytechnic on the grounds that a location in the City gave added status and professionalism to the course. For the same reason, students pay a registration fee; nominal, but a gesture of commitment to the course.

The students in class, armed with cardboard folders and brief-cases, are a heterogeneous collection: sharp-suited or impeccably cool in baseball caps and trainers. Someone swans in late, black polo-neck, white raincoat, filofax, straight out the *The Face*. Concentration is fierce. But, beyond the official talk of cash-flow forecasts and business plans, you can sense the palpable presence of bank managers, loans from the family and mortgages out in the real world.

It is time for the teabreak, and a sense of community emerges. There are rueful smiles, anecdotal evidence of the intransigence of bank managers and the insecurity of profit margins. Those already in business are shyly consulted by those who are still just turning over an idea; there is a definite hierarchy. One girl wants to sell hand-printed T-shirts, convinced that there is a market for them in Nigeria and Ghana but not so sure where to get the money from to start selling. A musician, who has his own recording studio and *knows* that image is everything, confides that he didn't much want to come on the course at first but has since been won over: "I've hardly missed a session . . . more and more people are turning up each time."

Meanwhile, two Asian partners, just about to open a news-agent shop in Dalston, are trying to pin down the Nat West man on the question of bank loans. Informal access to this kind of contact and help is obviously one of the most valuable assets that the unit has to offer. As if to illustrate the point, during the lecture Cosmos Charles silently handed my next-door neighbour a letter from Hackney Economic Development Unit saying that his grant application was in the pipeline. And only a few days before he had negotiated a maze of bureaucracy to help another student find a grant to start up as a travel agent in Croydon. He is keen to bring former students together in a Business Club.

Funding for the EMBDU comes from the Inner London Education Authority and the department of education and science, and the home office, but principally from the latter. It was officially opened in June 1986 by the then home office minister, David Waddington, and you can see why his department might be happy to endorse the project. The EMBDU embodies two of the government's favourite themes: encouraging employment in small businesses, and being seen to do something about the economic imbalance against ethnic minorities in the inner cities.

Handicap

Home visits for the deaf

HILARY SESTA

An audiological unit provides a unique service to Manchester patients.

Of the ten million hearing-impaired people in this country, only two and a half million are supplied with hearing aids, and one third of these do not use them when they get them.

These are some of the facts that emerged when "Breaking The Sound Barrier," a campaign to help the elderly hard of hearing, was launched this week by the Royal Institute for the Deaf, Age Concern and the British Association of the Hard of Hearing. Six out of ten people over 70 suffer from some sort of hearing loss, but many refuse to admit to difficulty, and for those who do, the service is patchy.

In some parts of the country, such patients can wait a staggering two-and-a-half years for their first diagnostic appointment. "An elderly person may die before receiving an aid," says the RNID. There are too few physiology measurement technicians, and they do not have to meet a statutory training requirement to be employed by the NHS. The withdrawal of central funding has caused a chronic shortage of hearing therapists which may lead to a return to the over-the-counter method of supply, with scant rehabilitation and further underuse of hearing aids.

However, flying in the face of such difficulties, the audiological unit at the Withington Hospital gives a uniquely caring service to its patients in south Manchester, many of them elderly. Their service includes a home counselling scheme which has radically increased hearing aid use. In 1983, they surveyed a group of 437 patients who had been supplied with hearing aids in 1980, and of whom 149 had received counselling. They found that the percentage of non-users of the aids dropped by 50 per cent in the counselled group.

At the Withington, Denzil Brooks, the principal phycisist and Dorothy Johnson, the hearing therapist, head a team of highly trained technicians and volunteers, working with the ear, nose and throat consultants.

Brooks says, "It is not enough just to give people hearing aids. These must be carefully prescribed, with adequate care before and after supply. Without that, they will probably end up in the sideboard drawer."

His scheme consists of both pre-fitting and post-fitting counselling. The pre-fitting visit is carried out by the professionals. It is unique and crucial to the success of the project. "A visit to a hospital is a worrying experience, especially for the elderly," Brooks says. "The home visit establishes a personal relationship. When the patient comes to have his hearing aid fitted he will be less anxious, and therefore more alert and receptive and likely to succeed with the aid."

First, the patient is sent a questionnaire with a personal letter, not a hospital *pro forma*. The letter explains: "It will help us in providing the highest possible level of service . . . assisting you to better hearing." The answers show the person's attitude to his hearing impairment, the difficulties it is causing him, and his expectations of a hearing aid.

The team starts work most days by 8.30. On a visiting day, after sorting out their papers, Brooks and Johnson go to see their first patient, discussing the case in the car. "Alfred Grant" is 80 and lives alone in a council house. Brooks says: "His answers are a little too positive. He may be over-estimating himself."

As they arrive, the net curtains move a little, and the front door is opened before the bell is rung. A spruce elderly man stands smiling in the hall, which is shiny with new paint. He introduces a neighbour—patients are asked to have someone else present who can later go over anything that might not have been understood; a friend, relative or sometimes one of the volunteers.

Dorothy asks Alfred some general questions, enunciating carefully. He describes his previous work with the water board, his involvement with local clubs, now curtailed because of his bad hearing and the four operations he has had in the past year.

The time has come to show him a hearing aid, similar to the one he will be issued with. Dorothy asks him whether he can hear the clock ticking. He says, "No." She puts the aid gently in his ear. "Is that comfortable? she asks. "Yes." "Now can you hear the clock ticking?" He smiles at us: "Yes, fancy that."

Next she gives instructions in the use of the aid that will be supplied. "Be careful to wear it for six weeks at home before going out with it. Remember, six weeks," she repeats patiently. "Otherwise loud sounds will surprise you." She rattles paper by the ear that has the aid in it. "Now isn't that loud? Imagine how traffic will sound for the first time. It wouldn't be a good idea to wear it outside too soon. You might get a shock, blame the aid, and not bother to wear it again."

Outside, they look at Alfred's audiogram; the prognosis is that he will need two aids. If so, he will get them, as do many of Withington's patients.

"I ask the region for what I need," says Brooks, "I budget carefully. The counselling scheme does not cost a lot and I save money by seeing people in their own homes. Then there is the saving from the low wastage of hearing aids. Our service cannot be bettered anywhere in the public sector. Or, he adds, "the private one. Their technicians carry out home visits, but their motives are different to ours."

The next patient is an 83 year old widow. She suffers from tinnitus (ringing in the ears) in addition to her deafness and fears that she may have a brain tumour. As there are no other symptoms, this is unlikely, but it is noted that she will need extra visits to show her how the hearing aid will help the tinnitus.

More patients follow. All are given the basic instructions, but with particular attention to special needs. A younger woman will need a modified aid because she works in a noisy canteen. Another patient suffers from tinnitus and keeps the wireless on all day "to drown out the other sounds."

Their work includes lecturing to professionals, including GPs, district nurses and care assistants, publicising the need for people to come for treatment early. And they recruit and train the volunteers who do much of the post-fitting counselling.

Some of the volunteers are recruited from former patients, who have overcome problems with hearing aids. They have husband and wife teams, one of whom has normal hearing. Each may spot things the other misses. In the main, volunteers tackle smaller problems, such as difficulties in inserting the ear mould or changing batteries. But it is these problems which have led to non-use in the past, or taken up hospital time. They also monitor the amount of time the aid is used by a patient, report regularly to the unit, and request more skilled help if necessary. The patients are also seen by the professionals at carefully judged intervals.

Isobel Mander has worked as a volunteer for three years. Now retired, she likes to keep occupied, also attending history of art classes, and lecturing herself, at pre-retirement classes. Many of her visits are to elderly people living alone, who feel vulnerable. She says, "even those living in sheltered housing, can feel isolated. One lady of 90 told me she was scared she wouldn't hear a fire alarm. A lot of people I help do get over simple problems. Some don't succeed though, and I used to feel it was my fault. But Miss Johnson told me that we can't ever achieve 100 per cent success. And I've never heard of any of them say anything but good about the unit."

Meeting the social market

LINDA LENNARD

A factory is making goods to supply the unmet needs of the disabled.

Just off the Holloway Road in north London, is what looks like an ordinary factory building. But that is all that is ordinary about it. Inside, work on projects ranging from low-energy self-build housing to kits for teaching hydraulics and a light-weight wheelchair for use in hospitals is going on. One of the more ambitious products being developed is a gym for people with disabilities.

The gym has been designed by a former acrobat, Jon McGrath. Twenty six years ago, he broke his neck doing a high-diving stunt into a swimming pool. Now a part-time tutor in remedial exercises, he is working with the London Innovation Network which runs the building, to develop his idea. Working out exercises to overcome his own disability, he became irritated at the degree of dependence to which disabled people are subjected when they try to use an ordinary gym. So he designed his own which people with disabilities can use without having to be helped out of their wheelchairs.

At the London Innovation Network's building, the gym project is one of a range being explored to meet the network's twin aims of helping develop "socially useful" products, and creating worthwhile jobs. The idea of socially useful production is based on the belief that conventional market forces ignore a huge "social market" of unmet needs for both products and services. It requires involving the public, as consumers, in the design and development of useful products. At the network's building, products for use by people with disabilities form a hefty chunk of the projects under way. In the field of disability, more than in other areas, there is a sharp mis-match between what is technically achievable and what is ultimately available to the consumers. So people with disabilities have become more disadvantaged as their needs have been ignored by commercial manufacturers. It is rare for them to be asked what *they* want.

"The most interesting thing about the network is the way that anyone can come in with an idea," according to Mary Moore, the publicity worker. When someone does come in with an idea, the next stage is for them to attend a "design surgery" with people involved in industrial design, marketing and so on. Marketing is defined as assessing need and technical feasibility, rather than sales promotion. A decision is then taken as to whether a prototype should be produced. If the idea goes ahead, a project group is set up involving people with relevant skills. Consumers are involved informally in the design and assessment—the aim is eventually to have a panel of consumers who can be called upon.

It is up to the originator how much they want to be involved. This also depends on their skills and knowledge. A new-style walking frame has, for instance, been developed by a group of physiotherapists in Islington, who are well-placed both to do trials and to assess development with consumers.

Other ideas being developed include an adjustable changing bed for older disabled children, tactile toys for blind children, adjustable seating for disabled schoolchildren, and a pocket vibrating device to alert deaf people to the doorbell or telephone. The idea for the last in this list came from a local resident whose father was deaf.

Amongst other projects—not in the disability field—is a new type of workstation for teaching technology which has just gone into production, storage play equipment for playgroups, and a kit for teaching hydraulics—both of which are about to go into production. The new wheelchair access bus (see below), now being used on a number of routes by London Region Transport, was originally developed by the network.

In the area of service provision, the network has been running a Mobile Repair Service for some time. It is non-profitmaking and carries out essential electrical and plumbing repairs for elderly and disabled people. With the price of commercial repairs often prohibitive, such a service can be of vital importance. The basic charge is £1 plus the cost of materials. It complements the direct labour services of local authorities. It fits into the network's aim of creating employment—the people carrying out the work are skilled—and, although the workforce is tiny at present, the intention is to expand and provide more permanent jobs for skilled workers.

Mobile's advantages are not only financial as far as the consumers are concerned. They can get to know the permanent staff over a period of time, building up a feeling of trust which is of immense value to people living alone. It also means that the staff can pick up on other problems confronting their clients, putting them in touch with other agencies such as the social services department. A support group has been set up involving consumers using the service and representatives of agencies such as Age Concern, Islington Disablement Association and Pensioner's Link, which meets regularly.

Originally funded with start-up money from the Greater London Enterprise Board, the future of the Mobile Service is uncertain as it is waiting to hear if long-term funding will be made available through the Inner City Partnership scheme. Considerable interest is being shown in the service from other parts of the country.

When the stage of developing actual products is reached, cooperatives are contacted to see if they have the right machinery, skills, and production capacity. But often they don't, so commercial manufacturers are also explored. According to Mary Moore, there is enormous potential here for Economic Development Units of local authorities to become more involved.

Contracts are drawn up between the eventual manufacturer and the network to protect the originator and provide a return for the network. The contracts also have to cover matters such as guaranteeing a minimum production run. This is to prevent manufacturers acquiring an idea and then simply sitting on it. The conditions of work in the company concerned are also taken into account.

Obviously a tension can exist between the manufactuer's need to make a profit and the network's aim of producing socially useful products. But it can make sense even within narrow economic terms. Frequently ignored, when the calculation is made, are the costs of *not* providing such products and services: the costs of unemployment, and the costs of people suffering through lack of appropriate goods and services to the extent of becoming institutionalised. The notion of the social market has wide ramifications. By looking at the real things people want at a time of high unemployment, a model is being tested for meeting different sorts of need, all at once.

Befriending in Belfast

CHRIS MOFFAT

A new project is helping to relieve the isolation trapping so many handicapped young people.

"Leonard and I went out together to the leisure centre. We were playing snooker. It was a good match. Then I went to Leonard's house. I had a cup of tea and a bun. It was nice. Then I went home. It was a great day." An ordinary friendly get-together? Yes, but with a difference.

Jim, who wrote this account of his first day out with Leonard, is a student at one of Belfast's social education centres. He is 28 and suffers from Down's syndrome. Leonard, who is in his early twenties, is a member of Belfast Voluntary Welfare Society's mental handicap volunteer project. He and Jim have been together with the project for nearly three years.

The befriending scheme is Northern Ireland's first. Begun in 1982, it now has some 30 volunteers match up with mentally handicapped young people, mostly in their twenties, who have been referred by social workers in north and west Belfast.

Tommy O'Reilly, who is coordinator of the scheme, believes that volunteers get as much out of the project as the young mentally handicapped people. However, he stresses that the volunteer's commitment is vitally important. "We ask for a minimum commitment of three months. Most relationships last for a year, although some go on longer."

For Leonard and Jim, a typical weekly outing now is a visit to the local leisure centre for a game of badminton. Leonard usually calls at Jim's house half an hour early to allow time for a game or two of snooker. They are well known at the leisure centre and get onto the court for a mere 10p. After their match, they buy a drink from the vending machine in the foyer, chat, and then go back to Jim's house for a few more games of snooker and a cup of coffee. Says Leonard, "This also provides an opportunity for Jim's mother to let me know how she feels things are going and if there are any things she'd like me to change or do."

The most obvious benefit for parents of mentally handicapped people, apart from the relief support, is the satisfaction of knowing that their son or daughter is going out through choice and having an enjoyable time in safety. But the coordinator believes volunteers can also open parents' eyes to their handicapped children's potential.

Frank had always been driven everywhere by car by his parents because they were afraid to let him use public transport by himself. His volunteer friend, Joe, always uses the bus and one of his tasks was to teach Frank how to cope with public transport on his own. One day, Joe phoned Frank to say he couldn't call for him as usual. Frank went out and caught the bus by himself and later returned safely, again by bus. His parents were amazed and delighted with his new-found independence.

One of the advantages of the one-to-one approach is that volunteers can help handicapped people to master everyday social skills, like using money, going shopping and going to leisure centres and discos. Appropriate tasks are usually worked out by social workers and staff at the day centres. But the scheme aims to do more than simply help to develop social skills. Tommy O'Reilly argues that just by introducing handicapped people to their family and friends, volunteers can widen their range of social contacts.

Handicapped people themselves clearly appreciate the opportunity to make social contacts and get out more often. "It's great to get out and meet new friends," says Jenny, who has knowm her volunteer, Rita, for six months. "She brings me out to discos and the pictures and to the Opera House to see plays and that. She is a friend. She brings me down to the town. I wouldn't go down there if I didn't have a volunteer."

Besides relieving the isolation which traps so many handicapped young people, the project aims to encourage them to participate in "ordinary" social activities as individuals in their own right.

Frank had always been interested in car magazines and accessories, so Joe now takes him to car maintenance classes. Gradually, Frank is picking up some useful information about cars; but, just as important, he is getting to know and be accepted by a circle of friends and acquaintances who share a common interest.

Just how much preparation and training volunteers should receive is an issue which has aroused much soul-searching in the Belfast project. A highly favourable official recommended more training for volunteers and suggested they should spend at least a week in a social education centre. But the project has successfully moved away from the social education and day centres. If volunteers receive too much training," says O'Reilly, "handicapped people think of them as staff and the unique attributes which they bring to the project are lost."

It is not always easy for volunteers to get the right balance between finding stimulating social activities and providing genuine companionship. Most of them value the opportunity for regular appraisal and support from the coordinator and the handicapped person's social worker. Andrea, a volunteer who has been with Sonya for two years, says, "Sometimes it is hard to know where to go and often we end up at home. She likes to play with my puppy and chat to my parents. I'd like to do more, but sometimes she's withdrawn and a bit giggly. She used to phone me up, but now she waits until I phone her. You have to play it by ear."

It is common for volunteers to be anxious about the impact they are having. "Some volunteers do find it difficult," says Aidan Murray, a social worker who has used and supported the scheme from the beginning. "They come back and ask, what *does* this handicapped person enjoy doing? It's not easy. All you can say is, try something else. It takes time. That is why we try to discourage people who might see it as a short-term commitment."

Most of the volunteers are recruited by advertisements in the local papers and because the project is funded by a grant from the Community Volunteering Scheme, they are meant to be unemployed. Most of those who apply are quite young and many have already been involved in voluntary work. Often an important motive is the opportunity to gain experience which will help secure a place on a social work course, or a job in social services. However, unemployed people don't necessarily make the best or most committed volunteers, and under present fundings, a high turnover of volunteers is almost inevitable.

"I'm grateful that the scheme is there," says Aidan Murray. "But I have to balance its usefulness against the possibility of a volunteer dropping out after three or six months. It can be devastating for handicapped people if a volunteer leaves without warning. And how do you explain to them that someone might only want to be their special friend for a few months?"

However, there are now carefully worked out procedures for replacing volunteers who leave. And even where handicapped people have been disappointed by the departure of a volunteer, the gains in wider social and educational opportunities invariably far outweigh any temporary setback.

Moreover, most of the befriending relationships which have survived have become genuine and lasting friendships in their own right. As Leonard says, "Jim and I have both helped each other over sticky patches. I try to get to the volunteer support meetings, but I don't really need their support. I think the Belfast Voluntary Welfare Society now acknowledge that I am responsible."

A means of independence

JOY MELVILLE

Volunteers work with the disabled to help them live independently at home.

Hazel Gibson has cerebral palsy. Twenty nine out of her 35 years have been spent in a residential home where, seven years ago, she met and married her husband Ron, who has muscular dystrophy.

With both Hazel and Ron in wheelchairs, and Hazel having very limited, but constant spastic movements, and difficulty in speaking, the idea of them living on their own seemed totally unrealistic. Yet both badly wanted to. Six years ago they met a disabled person who was able to live at home through the Independent Living Scheme, run by Community Service Volunteers based in London, whereby volunteers work in the home, giving continual assistance.

"We thought, that we could do that," says Ron. "But it took four and a half years' pressure before we actually got out—setting it all up, persuading the council it was cheaper for us to live outside, and finding suitable accommodation."

For 15 months now, they have been living in a house in Deptford, south London, helped by two volunteers who do alternate 24-hour shifts—though not all the users of the scheme require that level of help. They are both delighted with the result.

"It's the freedom of choice," says Hazel. "We are in charge of our own lives. We can do things that people like you take for granted, like getting up, or having a meal, at the time we *want* to. No more being told you can't have a bath, you can't do this or that."

Didn't she find it hard, after 29 years in residential care, to cope on the outside? It's a very protected environment and not everyone has the mental independence to want to try coping on their own—a factor more important then the degree of disability. "A residential home can switch your brain off," she admits, "and it did affect me. I keep forgetting I am not there, but in my own home, and can decide what to eat and when to have a bath."

Hazel and Ron contacted the scheme themselves, but it can also be done by recommendation. It's important that those who apply like young people. The young volunteers are there to help, to be friends, not supervisors. "They aren't trained," says Ron. "*We* train them in the way we want things done. We teach them how to dress us and how to bathe us—and in some cases, how to cook. They do the things that we would normally do ourselves, like feed the cat and the dog."

On an average morning, says Hazel, "they get us up, make breakfast, do a bit of housework, put the washing machine on for me, do a bit of ironing and shopping, help get lunch. With cooking, we tell them how we want them to do it. It's nice company; we hardly saw anybody in the home."

Fiona Dawe, the coordinator of the ILS scheme, which has been in operation since the beginning of 1982, says it was deliberate policy to keep the control and expertise in the hands of the disabled themselves. "It's really an exchange of expertise. The volunteers are mostly aged between 17 and 22, and they, too, are learning to be independent. They live in—usually being placed for between four to six months, although they may stay up to a year—and the disabled, or 'users' of the scheme as we call them, help the volunteers to get over homesickness, and teach them skills. The scheme is as much about volunteers as it is about disabled people needing help.

"There is no training, because the philosphy of the scheme is that the volunteeer learns on the job. Because our policy is never to reject a volunteer, we have a long interview with them about who they are and why they want to do the job. We take up references and try to place volunteers where their personality and skills can be best used.

"We don't introduce the volunteer to the person they will be working with before they start: first impressions can be erroneous and they could get cold feet. And the volunteers themselves might not look particularly promising. But we are very honest and make sure expectations on both sides are realistic. Most of the users are severely physically handicapped; others have a mental handicap and need to learn independent skills. We brief the volunteers not to go in and take over, but to do what the user wants them to do. Most users don't want trained personnel, they want to get away from people knowing what is best for them. They prefer to train the volunteer in the way most appropriate for them."

The scheme originally got off the ground by means of a three-year DHSS grant, but the aim—now virtually achieved—was to make it self-financing. It costs a disabled person £68 a month per volunteer; the volunteer gets free board and lodging and some pocket money. The scheme now has some partnerships with local authorities—such as in Avon, Hereford, Birmingham and Islington—whereby the authority gives a grant to pay for volunteers to work with their clients.

Volunteers usually work as one of a pair or trio. They are initially interviewed by the volunteer director working with the project in that area, who explains the scheme. They are supervised regularly, but for on-the-spot help the volunteer can always turn to the disabled person's social worker. There are about 250 to 300 volunteers working on the scheme at any one time, which sounds a lot, but CSV—now up to capacity for users—desperately needs many more. Without an advertising budget, it can only find them through giving talks at schools and colleges and word-of-mouth recommendation.

Daniel Janes, 19 years old, is one of the volunteers working with Hazel and Ron. He has been with them since June, working during his vacation from university, where he is studying behavioural sciences. Quiet and soft spoken, he admits he's done nothing like this before. "You learn as you go along," he says, "and Ron and Hazel are very tolerant of my mistakes. It hasn't been difficult or upsetting at all. It's such great fun working here, we're very light-hearted most of the time."

"I suppose before I came here I had some sort of fairly textbook, academic understanding, but if you are living with disabled people, this increases. Obviously, there are things you are doing for them; but I much prefer to think that I am doing things *with* them. When we are cooking, for instance, I am the person who turns the gas oven down and Hazel is the one telling me to."

After a month, CSV asks both parties for a report and everyone involved has a chance to discuss any problems. Most important of all, to Daniel, was being able to talk openly to Ron and Hazel. "It's a mutual relationship," says Hazel, and Ron adds: "Some of the volunteers we have met we are probably going to know for the rest of our lives."

One of these is Grant Davis, who came originally as a volunteer and now drops in frequently to help Hazel with painting. "Hazel has the ideas, which are based on her experiences, and I draw or paint them," he says. I looked at a poster showing not a person, but a gremlin in a wheelchair. "I did that because I don't look normal myself, because of my movement," says Hazel. "Nobody shows pictures of people like me. I look like a gremlin and people tend to treat me like one." Another poster, showing the disabled like mushrooms in the dark, is based on her fight for independence. "There are many people in residential homes who shouldn't be there," she says.

Ron and Hazel, thanks to their volunteers, have at last found independence. "Our only future problem is finding the money to pay for it," says Ron. "But if they tried to take us back to a home now, we'd kick and scream."

Facing up to it

IAN SUTHERLAND

A centre in east Scotland provides guidance and support for disfigured people.

In the United States disfigured people are said to be joining pseudo-therapeutic support groups with such names as "Freaks Anonymous" or "Ugly Clubs." The very idea makes Britain's internationally known campaigner for disfigured people, Doreen Trust, wince in horror. At the UK's first and only Disfigurement Guidance Centre, opened last year in the small Fife town of Cupar, Trust's over-riding emphasis is on treating disfigured people as individuals or, especially in the case of disfigured children, as members of a family.

"Approaches like the 'Ugly Clubs' mean that disfigured people are simply reinforcing their alienation and isolation from society," says Doreen's husband and campaign partner Peter Trust. "They have a better chance of surviving and leading a good life in society on their own." The new Fife centre—the culmination of a 25-year campaign by the Trusts to improve services to disfigured people—is sponsored by Fife Regional Council and supported increasingly by charitable effort.

Precise figures on how many people in Britain have their lives marred by facial disfigurement are hard to come by. What is certain is that traffic accidents are increasing, industrial accidents are rising—along with growing street violence and accidents in the home. Premature and handicapped children, who may also have facial disfigurement—are more likely to survive thanks to developing medical techniques and technology. It is small wonder that even before the Cupar centre was opened, 6,000 letters and perhaps 1,000 callers a year were making their way to Doreen Trust's east Scotland base.

"Your face," says Doreen Trust, herself facially disfigured from birth "is your identity." Perhaps the most chilling example in her recent files concerns the Glasgow man who has learned the hard way not to try and buy chips after 8 o'clock at night. His prominent facial scar marks him out to the neds spilling out of the local pubs as a "hard man." On Clydeside, "taking on a hard man" is an individual and group virility symbol. No kind of a hard man at all, this wretched individual came by his branding disfigurement in a road accident at the age of five.

Historically—and especially since disfigurement cosmetics became available on the NHS in the mid-1970s—facial disfigurement has been, literally, covered up. As with the grotesque US "Freaks Anonymous" type of response to the problem of disfigurement, undue recourse to cosmetic disguise also receives somewhat short shrift as the Fife centre's work gets into its stride. "We find that only perhaps 20 people out of 100 are really helped by cosmetic use," argues Doreen Trust. She is dismissive of the commercial cosmetics companies who have a vested financial interest in promoting this traditional approach. The Disfigurement Guidance Centre's message is simple, and is being increasingly widely disseminated in newsletters and in a forthcoming range of disfigurement handbooks intended for medical practitioners, disfigurement victims and their families and voluntary groups: "Don't use cosmetics until you can cope with life."

Cosmetics are not simply evasion of reality; they can actually prove dangerous. Doreen Trust has had recent experience of a Scottish missionary couple's daughter who had been made to wear heavy make-up from early childhood. She was with her parents in Peru during a serious earthquake, and afraid to be ever seen outside without her almost obsessive disguise, the girl remained in the house, taking 45 minutes to apply the camouflage, risking being buried alive while everyone around fled to safety. Thanks to the Cupar centre, she is learning the first steps in coping without the ritual of covering her blemished face. "If you use cosmetics all the time," says Doreen Trust wearily, "you're a prisoner of your face."

With council premises available since last year, the Trusts and their growing band of voluntary helpers are beginning to use their now comparatively secure base to develop education aimed at the non-disfigured majority. A modest MSC programme, with the enthusiastic involvement of the local education department, is touring a specially produced puppet show round Fife schools. In these moral pantomimes, the ugly sisters and the hideous witches don't lose out. They don't triumph either. The puppets with their eyes in the wrong place of an oversized and misplaced mouth just live normal lives among normal people.

Rather than see the Fife puppet programme develop into a national theatre, Peter Trust argues that the development of localised theatre-education companies is the road ahead. A video is planned and will become available for use elsewhere in the UK. The Cupar premises—already overcrowded a year after commissioning—do, however, provide the nucleus of a wider educational programme, and seminars and courses are being run for students from various disciplines. "Strangely enough," says Doreen Trust, "we don't get that much demand from social work educators."

Amid the development work, the personalised service—which earned Doreen Trust an MBE in last summer's Birthday Honours

List—relentlessly carries on. The demand for advice and counselling from disfigured people and their friends and families seems limitless. When Doreen Trust made a recent appearance on a children's TV show recently and offered telephone counselling to any young person who felt they had a disfigurement problem, the Cupar phones didn't stop ringing for 48 hours. A single radio spot has been known to bring in 2,000 callers.

If there is one miserable item of baggage that comes with Doreen Trust's clients on their journey north, it has got to be guilt: "What have I done to deserve this?" The guilt, and the concomitant anger, infuses their families too. The birth of a disfigured child can wreck a marriage. The level of blame and accusation can be massively irrational, if not downright superstitious. After a lifetime coping with her own and other people's disfigurements, Doreen has become as expert a family therapist as she has become an adviser on the appropriate use of cosmetics. "It's never too late to take a chance," says Doreen Trust, citing the recent referral of a woman in her sixties who had worn make-up since her early teenage years, and whose husband had never seen her without the elaborately applied make-up.

But although money remains short (before the present official support and recognition, Doreen Trust had virtually become personally bankrupt as she stomped Britain campaigning for the acceptance and integration of disfigured people) and MSC staffing is, necessarily, temporary, dawn is beginning to break.

General Secretary Gorbachev doesn't seem to need to use cosmetics on *his* birthmark and he seems to have ditched Ronald Reagan (who the satirists insist *does* wear make-up) in the world-wide popularity stakes. The achievement of actually setting up Fife's disfigurement project and the award of Doreen Trust's public honour are a milestone for people who have lived—some of them literally—in the shadows.

Learning from handicap

MADELEINE FULLERTON

A nursery encourages parents and other children to help handicapped children realise greater potential.

"Why don't your legs work? You're all wrong," said one child to a three year old with cerebral palsy.

"There's nothing wrong with me or my legs," retorted the handicapped child, "my brain just can't get the right messages to them." The first child was quite satisfied with this explanation.

Every afternoon parents bring their handicapped and ordinary children to the opportunity group at Charnwood Nursery in Stockport. There is no limit to the numbers and they are all welcome from birth. Both children's and parent's attitudes to physical and mental handicap have been transformed by attending the nursery.

Linda joined the opportunity group when her eldest child Sarah was born with Down's syndrome. When Sarah was born, Linda and her husband were devastated and left her in the hospital. "I'd only ever seen mentally handicapped people in large groups—outings from institutions, all behaving strangely and wearing odd clothes. We knew we couldn't cope with someone like that so we tried to forget we'd ever had the baby."

But Linda's GP told her to talk to Grace Wyatt at Charnwood Nursery. Grace, who retired in April after 30 years of pioneering the integration of handicapped and ordinary children from birth, showed Linda and her husband how children with many different handicaps can learn from and teach ordinary children.

Linda collected her daughter from the hospital and named her Sarah. Sarah is now a lively three year old who tears around the nursery trying her hand at everything from sand and water to singing and playing instruments.

During the years when the local authority was pouring money into special education, Grace noisily defended parents who wanted their handicapped children to continue their education in ordinary schools. She soon earned herself the reputation of a meddling do gooder. But in the face of all opposition, Grace remained convinced that it is wrong to segregate handicapped children.

"All disabled children and their parents suffer from the medical model of handicap," she explains, "the doctor's assessment still rules their lives." The doctor measures the child against some model of the "perfect" and finds the child a failure. Parents and children receive the message: "you are not normal, you are not whole."

"Of course people are shocked when they see a child with no eyes or suffering terrible fits, just as one is shocked by the sight of blood. People shouldn't be ashamed that these things hurt them deeply. The crucial question is what do we do about it? Do we accept the fact and perceive that person's intrinsic value, or do we measure such children against the ideals of health, wealth and achievement worshipped by our society?"

Grace insists that parents of handicapped children, particularly mothers, become depressed and isolated because they are only presented with the medical model of handicap. Once the mother becomes depressed, the child becomes understimulated and performs nowhere near his or her real potential. Thus by the time these children are old enough for special school at five, antisocial and bizarre behaviour may become established which everyone just assumes to be part of the handicap.

"We don't demand anything of parents," says Brenda Kyle, who took over from Grace in April. "But when they want emotional or practical help we are always here."

All the staff believe that ordinary children are the best educators—they provide good models of speech, movement and activity and in return the handicapped children help them learn patience, compassion and some understanding.

By the age of three, most children are ready to move from the opportunity group towards more independence—two or three morning sessions a week without their parents. Looking around the busy nursery it is almost impossible to tell which children are handicapped and which are not. There are none of the awkward postures or unusual behaviour such as rocking or head banging that single out the understimulated or institutionalised child. "Some people think we demand too much of them" says Grace. "We've never allowed any wheel chairs here and nearly all the children are expected to climb the stairs and play in the garden like everyone else." It sounds tough, but Charnwood does provide a safe and sheltered environment for children to learn to cope with their difficulties.

Charnwood has four teachers, one nursery nurse and numerous volunteers—including some handicapped ones. All the staff believe in bringing resources from the community into the nursery and Grace thinks parents themselves make the best volunteers. Parents also help with the toy library at weekends. One hundred and fifty families with handicapped children belong to this, and it has to be maintained and the toys mended.

Charnwood is a registered charity but the local authority does provide £15,000 a year to help maintain equipment for the handicapped children. Ordinary children pay £2 a day, if parents can afford it. Staff and parents themselves have to raise the rest of the money needed.

The Education Act, 1981, supported the idea of integrating handicapped children into ordinary schools and Grace now feels her status in the educational world has suddenly risen. But most of the staff feel they remain unpopular with both ordinary and special schools because they encourage militant and demanding parents. They argue that once parents have become accustomed to the idea of integration and witnessed the benefits for their children, they are not going to accept sudden segregation at the age of five.

A doctor once called Grace an "evil woman" in front of parents and children for encouraging parents to shun the skilled and professional help their children would receive at special schools.

"But," argues Grace, "what have the special schools really got to offer?" Children's classes are constantly interrupted by one therapy or another so they never have a chance to reach their full potential or to learn anything ordinary children are learning.

Charnwood does employ a part-time physiotherapist, but one of her roles is to teach parents how to do the therapy at home—something Grace believes the special schools, with their emphasis on professional expertise, would never dream of. Special education leads parents to believe that only trained people can cope with their children. Recognising that parents have to cope most of the time anyway, and will certainly have to cope after the children 18, Charnwood emphasises the need for professionals to work with them.

"Children who go to special schools," says Grace, "know they are handicapped." Once children know this, they begin to believe they cannot do things, that they need special treatment. Special schools encourage this mentality and make children even less able to cope with the demands of the outside world.

An arm and a leg

AMANDA MITCHISON

Volunteers act as limbs to allow disabled people to live independent lives.

In a specially converted Islington house, four volunteers—the collective 16 arms and legs of Gurmeet Caspa and Melvin Kinnear—live in two apartments upstairs, and are on buzzer call. Gurmeet and Melvin are both quadriplegic, but because of their helpers they can hold down full-time jobs. Gurmeet is a scriptwriter and film producer, and Melvin works in an organisation for the disabled.

Sarah Cleveland, one of Melvin's volunteers, turns him over at seven in the morning, gets him up a bit later, prepares whatever he wants for breakfast and drives him to work, where she stays in the background with a book or some knitting. Melvin will call her over if he wants a coffee, or needs something opened or taken from the filing cabinet. For two days, Sarah will accompany Melvin wherever he goes, doing what he asks, but being as unobtrusive as possible. Sarah said, "I don't make decisions for him, even over things like making the bed or opening the curtains. I don't just do it automatically. In fact that is the most difficult thing, if you see something that you think needs doing, you don't go and do it. It is up to him."

Melvin and Gurmeet are two of twelve disabled people in the Independent Living Scheme, run by Islington council and Community Service Volunteers. The scheme, which was set up in 1978, provides disabled people with living accommodation and two voluntary helpers, who will stay with them for four to six months. As far as possible, volunteers and users are matched, and both have project troubleshooters who see them regularly. According to Deborah Livingston, who is in charge of CSV recruitment, most of the volunteers are around 20 years old—some come before or just after going to college, others want to gain professional experience and some come from abroad to improve their English while doing voluntary work.

In general, CSVs used to be predominantly white and middle class, but Deborah said: "We now have working class people and way over the national average of black volunteers, though very few Asians." Deborah believes the pressures of unemployment-—the need to start on a career as soon as possible—has made recruitment more difficult. Total numbers of volunteers have been falling. ILS is also hampered by shortage of funds—in Islington the scheme has been told to limit its users to twelve. However, independent living is catching on, and other London boroughs, including Wandsworth, Haringey and Lambeth, are financing similar schemes.

The aim is to give volunteers experience and to allow people with disabilities to lead independent lives, no longer at the mercy of institutions or condescension. According to Melvin: "The whole philosophy behind it is that, although severely disabled people require a lot of care, that doesn't mean that they are not independent and can't make their own decisions. Basic lack of services in society means relying on the good will of someone else. You are always asking people to do you favours."

Melvin was crippled when he was 16, and never intended to remain in an institution all his life. For six years he lived in King Henry's Walk, an Islington residential home which helped hatch the independent living scheme. Melvin said, "Even though mine was a really good hostel, it was still always a type of gilded cage. Living in an institution is demoralising, and it undermines your confidence eventually. You find yourself getting really cut off."

The relationship between the volunteer and user is thought to become too intense if they remain together for more than six months. But after four months, commented Melvin, the helper is only just beginning to get very good at the physical skills of looking after him. "The volunteers do two days on and two days off, and during that time they are going to see me in very different situations: at work, in a meeting, in a social setting. They have got to understand that, when I am out for a drink with some friends, I am not going to relate to them in the same way as I would if it's just me and the volunteer, driving along in my car chatting. They might easily feel put out. They can't necessarily always expect to join in."

Melvin and Gurmeet said they would, ideally, prefer to have paid helpers, rather than volunteers from whom you could not ask so much. Age could also be a problem; most CSVs are around 20 while their users are older. Gurmeet, who is 34, commented that he spent much more time with his volunteers than with his friends. He said, "The problem is that they are getting younger and we are getting older." He has just finished a film with Faye Dunaway called *Raspberry Ripple,* and groused slightly about having been sent a young volunteer once who was thought a good match because "she wanted to become an actress."

To get into the independent living scheme as a user requires initiative and persistence—it took Melvin and Gurmeet three years to arrange housing. Eventually they convinced a housing association to convert an old house, using financing from a special project grant. Islington and Hackney (where Melvin was previously a resident) pay the expenses of their CSVs—including accommodation and household bills, in addition to pocket money of £15 a week.

Hugh, another user who is a victim of cerebral palsy, has a very open character and gets on well with his CSVs. He thought that the user/volunteer relationship had to be reciprocal with you getting back what you put in. He found that the friendships he had formed with CSVs had really begun after they had finished their term with him. Hugh lives with his girlfriend, who is a social worker, and although the scheme makes it possible for the couple to lead independent lives, it creates an additional problem for the volunteers. "If you live with someone it's a completely different ball game. The CSV has not only to consider the user but also the other person in the relationship. For example, how much he should talk to the girlfriend?"

Hugh is now secretary of the local tenants' association. He believes: "No matter what you want to do, as long as you have a volunteer and you are able to give precise instructions, you have no disability." Taking this philosophy to its logical conclusion, he has become part of a new link scheme in Haringey for families with a disabled person—thanks to his CSV arms and legs—and has joined as a helper.

Clubland for the old

MADELEINE FULLERTON

Handicapped pensioners in Tyneside are helped by more able-bodied club members.

Every Friday, Jim Williams, aged 76, sits in a wheelchair outside a church hall in Whitley Bay gazing into space. As two community transport buses approach he jumps up to wheel 25 severely handicapped old people down the ramps and up into the building.

Members of the Friday club love to see the startled faces of passers-by as he leaps from his chair to help them and several tell me how the hall's caretaker went home and told his wife he had witnessed a miracle.

The Friday club is different from most pensioners' clubs because the organisers are able-bodied people in their seventies. Jim is a retired union official and his wife Peggy, 77 years old, a retired cook. Neither of them gave much thought to the problems of the handicapped elderly until they retired and saw close friends becoming ill and losing their independence. Now they feel committed to doing all they can to help the housebound elderly for as long as they remain active. "We're nearly the same age as most of these people—older than some," says Peggy. "We can imagine what it must feel like when your mind is active but your body won't work for you any more. We aim to offer people a good day out once a week with plenty of laughs." They also arrange outings, parties and concerts and provide support at home when any member is sick or in trouble.

Jenny, 73, deals with most of the club's correspondence. This morning she greets the members with packs of butter from the EEC butter mountain, given to her by Age Concern pensioners' club. Anne, another helper, is also in her seventies; her handicapped husband used to be a member of the group. Alone now, she is still strong enough to offer physical help to others. Tessa, too, though tiny and frail at 77, still manages to help people to the toilet and push wheelchairs, while Alan, by far the youngest at 62, is able to help with any heavy lifting.

They all feel they have a great deal in common with the members. Like them, several are lonely since their partners died and children moved far away. Helpers and members are all local, so being close in age, they share a lot of memories. "We look forward to Fridays as much as they do," says Anne. "We enjoy a good laugh and a natter—we're good friends you see."

The club members appreciate this and see the helpers as able-bodied friends and equals rather than as traditional volunteers. "Younger people want to organise you," says Mrs Freeman, aged 86. "We just want a relaxing day away from our own four walls—chatting with friends. They understand that here."

Crippled by arthritis, she lives alone and can only go out in a wheelchair. Her sons live far away and her husband is dead. All her life Mrs Freeman has played the piano for local choirs and concerts. Now she is almost deaf and unable to play a single note. "I wish every day was a Friday," she says. "Every other day in the week I try to keep myself occupied watching TV and reading . . . it's all too easy to give up."

Betty, at 89, has been blind for 15 years. "There is no privacy when you're blind," she says. "To think, I've looked after other people all my life—nursed my husband for six years." Since he died she has lived alone near her son. "If a letter comes through the door I have to wait till someone comes in to read it to me—and it could be a bill or anything—it's very worrying." Betty sees the helpers as friends and feels they understand her problems—perhaps because they could find themselves in the same boat.

"Younger people never believe it's going to happen to them—however kind they are, they think they're different from us. I suppose if anyone had told me I'd lose my independence like this, I'd never have believed them either."

Margaret, also blind and living with an invalid husband, reminds Betty of the time when Peggy, a volunteer, was carrying the Christmas dinner she'd cooked for the club party, and tripped and fell at the entrance, breaking her wrist. She spent Christmas in hospital, but both agree it could have been a lot worse at her age. "You just exist if you don't get out sometimes," says Margaret. She enjoys coming to the club to play braille dominoes and bingo, as well as to chat to friends. And 92 year old Mrs Brady finds the outing helps her to sleep. "Fridays, I go out, come home tired and sleep all night. The other days are all the same—you lose track of night and day and can't sleep at all."

Like most of the others, Lily's children have moved far away. Confined to a wheelchair, she finds life in a private old people's home just as lonely as living on her own. "There's no one with any sense left there—this is the only time I can get away from the place and have an intelligent conversation."

When they are asked what they actually do each Friday, Lily says, "Nothing much—have a good giggle." "Play bingo for chocolate biscuits," says someone else, and Tessa adds: "We just spoil ourselves." Some of them bake cakes or bring in sweets to share. Planning outings, concerts and parties takes up a good deal of time too.

People hear about the club through talks given by helpers, through home helps, wardens, social workers and churches. One woman came because Jenny told her daughter about the club on the Newcastle metro. Inevitably, people die—five since November—which upsets the group, but new members are always welcome.

The club recently got a grant from "New Horizons," which funds projects where elderly people organise themselves to help each other. Members also agreed amongst themselves to pay £1 a week for tea, coffee, biscuits and lunch. However, costs still work out higher than income. Buses from Community Transport cost £16 a week and rent for the hall, including their own store cupboard, is £12 a week. Outings cost nearly £400 a year. Jim spends a lot of time writing round asking for grants and other people raise money by speaking to local organisations about the group. Peggy makes cakes, dolls and baby clothes to sell at fairs and jumble sales—she buys the materials herself and all the profits go into the club.

All the helpers expect to become members themselves in a few years and trust that there will still be able-bodied elderly people willing to take over their present role.

Coping with a disabled child

AMANDA MITCHISON

A London charity has successfully linked parents of the disabled.

"You feel that you are the only one to have a disabled child. My befriender was absolutely marvellous, very helpful. I'm just an ordinary working class girl from Ireland and she was just another ordinary girl. She said it doesn't get easy or easier, you just learn to copc."

Deborah, whose three year old daughter Tracey has a mild case of cerebral palsy, is part of a parent support link project set up three years ago by KIDS, a London-based charity for disabled children and their families. Deborah's befriender is a trained volunteer, who has a seven year old spastic child, more severely handicapped than Tracey. Deborah has no family in London and felt "left out on a limb." With the befriender she could finally unburden her feelings of isolation and helplessness and come to terms with her daughter's disability.

Deborah says: "I was on the verge of a breakdown, up to that stage I wouldn't go out. I couldn't answer the phone. You feel it is your baby, and you've let her down. I couldn't talk about Tracey without crying. I couldn't make a fuss of my other baby without feeling guilty. I even used to go to the clinic at 9.20 in the morning rather than 9.30 so the other mothers wouldn't see her come in with her bad leg. But I felt very well after talking to my befriender. Now when I take Tracey out, I don't even think about it. And if she plays up in the street, I smack her like a normal child."

Martin and Amy, who have two year old twins with cerebral palsy, use the parent support link for practical advice "to cope with the professionals. That's what really wears you down." Their befriender, who has got her spastic son accepted into ordinary education, has advised them to start applying to schools now, and to follow up the assessment procedure with regular phone calls to the local authorities. "She kept us genned up about our rights, about how to and who to harass without having to go through endless grey pamphlets on the Education Act, 1981," says Martin. The couple also ask their befriender about "silly things, for instance teasing in the playground. When we have problems we think let's phone up the link. It really does fill a gap."

According to Martin, "When they find their child is disabled, people do go into deep shock, and it's very difficult to listen to anyone who hasn't had the same experience. You'll hear a lot of doctors saying 'we think this sort of organisation is very bad and harmful.' But things like this need doing. People are left completely in the dark, they imagine monsters, they have no idea."

Medical opposition to self-help groups is based on the fear that unqualified advisers will adopt the role of professionals. But, in the KIDS scheme, the befrienders are trained to provide only appropriate support and not to take on the role of doctors or social workers. The scheme is managed part-time by Caroline Woollett, a social worker, and Naomi Dale, a clinical psychologist, both of whom are based at the KIDS centre in Hampstead. They link up the parents and keep in contact with befrienders and befriended—or "new"—parents.

The project pays for two part-time salaries, a few hours of secretarial help, the volunteer's expenses and a share of the upkeep of the KIDS centre building. There have been problems financing the scheme, but next year's funding (£14,000) is to be provided jointly by King Edward's Hospital Fund and the DHSS.

Since the KIDS project was set up three years ago, it has provided 25 links. The befrienders are predominantly white, articulate, middle class mothers who use other facilities at the KIDS centre. Caroline Woollett says that for the latest batch of new befrienders, she went out of her way to take on working class parents who were less eager recruits. Ideally, befrienders and befriended parents should come from similar cultural backgrounds, and have children with the same disabilities. In many cases, KIDS has not been able to find appropriate befrienders, and parents have been refused help or had to wait.

Caroline Woollett notes that there is also a problem publicising the link scheme and that "the more isolated the parents, the more likely that we won't get through to them." For example, Deborah did not hear about the KIDS charity or the link scheme until Tracey was three. She says she is disgusted that neo natal clinics do not automatically provide leaflets and information on charities such as KIDS.

Parent support schemes set up without the type of professional back-up services provided at KIDS have tended to disintegrate, partly because social workers and health visitors are unwilling to refer patients, and partly because the befriender relationship can be problematic and requires professional support.

KIDS parent befrienders attend a weekend course of discussions and workshops on how to listen to others and share experiences without misleading or being invasive. Befrienders are taught to avoid judgemental comments, inappropriate reassurance and technical advice on child development or medical matters. The course also includes advice on cases of child abuse and a therapy session, where befrienders recount something secret or deeply personal. One befriender, who refers to the exercise as "the emotional bit" says she made close friends on the course and believes she is now a better listener.

The course is designed to prepare befrienders for the most intense types of relationship. However, many "new" parents have practical queries and may only want to meet befrienders once, or talk to them on the phone. Also, despite claims by parents of older disabled children that they would have liked a link befriender early on, the parents of newly diagnosed or newly born disabled children do not tend to use the service immediately. As Caroline Woollett says: "They find the idea of meeting another parent with a child in the same condition a bit frightening. They haven't quite faced the thought that their child has this condition."

Jeanette, who has a Down's syndrome child and has befriended seven new parents, says some families just want reassurance and ask about the development of her son—at what age he started to walk and talk, for instance. Other parents were worried by small things they wouldn't dare ask the doctors about. Jeanette has reassured mothers in cases concerning a baby's cry or the shape of their teeth, where the characteristics of disabled children can differ from the norm. She finds that talking to new parents reminds her of the grief and shock she initially felt, but adds that "it doesn't stir up the pain."

According to Jeanette, "The main thing is to listen. The difficulties are that one's own opinions and attitudes are not necessarily the same." Jeanette remembered one woman who had thought that nobody noticed her child had Down's syndrome. If she had not been a befriender she would have told the mother she was fooling herself. "But," Jeanette said, "I hadn't to be bossy, I had to say, 'Oh yes . . .' She will have time to find out the truth in her own time."

Living dangerously

AMANDA MITCHISON

An umbrella organisation in the north east raises money for charity by putting on dare-devil stunts.

On a cold, gusty morning Margaret Burdus looks up at 90 feet of uninviting Northern sky and steel girder to the spot where her son is about to be lowered over the side of the Tyne bridge and hoisted down on a rope. It would be a frightening experience for any mother; but for Margaret Burdus it is especially so, because four years ago David Burdus's spine was shattered in a motor bike accident that has put him in a wheelchair.

Burdus is to abseil off Newcastle's Tyne Bridge to raise money for the Aidan Charitable Trust, the north east's new umbrella fund-raising body. The abseil, which several insurance companies refused to cover, is a typical outdoor, danger-defying Aidan Trust event.

The marines ease Burdus over the bridge parapet and his tiny figure, with a pale face and trussed-up spindly legs, wobbles slowly downwards in a harness. Below on the quayside Mrs Burdus refuses the offer of binoculars. The audience shuffles queasily and even the watching crowd from St Charles's junior fourth form and a plump, vivacious clown in flippers, flannel tights and silver lurex gloves fall silent.

A third of the way down, Burdus is overcome with exhilaration and stops to wave to the audience below. He then glides down the rest of the rope, gives a camera call about seven feet off the ground, and is helped down onto his wheelchair.

The Burdus family coming up to embrace him, discover to their chagrin that he'll repeat the drop to give the Tyne Tees Television crew a worm's eye view—he is having a great time, more so than his audience who, now the suspense has slackened, are feeling the cold.

The stunt finishes with a chorus of cheers from the junior fourths, orchestrated by the clown, with collection box in hand. A pinstriped man from Joshua Tetley & Son, the brewers, presents Burdus with a poster-size cheque for £30,000 for the trust, and he will also collect over £500 from sponsors.

The abseil was nothing on the 8,000 foot tandem free-fall parachute Burdus did last year. That stunt brought in £5,000, enough to buy him "reciprocating braces," a type of mechanical walking calipers. He says, "I was holding onto the instructor like a baby kangaroo. Because of my legs dangling out we turned turtle. I couldn't see anything. It was tremendous," he sighs.

After the parachute jump, Burdus became the coordinator of the Aidan Trust's special appeals unit, which helps handicapped people raise funds for special equipment. He is now running appeals for an electrically powered wheelchair, a computer with extra large print out, and an electronic braille machine that can send messages by telephone. Sponsored wheelchair pushes and walks in calipers will be held to raise funds. Burdus believes that his sponsorship events encourage others to join in. It also helps to dispel the helpless image of the handicapped.

All the trust's fund-raising sponsorship events are meant to be fun, of the sporting, student fraternity type. They include beginners' skiing trips, road races, commando assault courses, adventure weekends, fashion shows, and glorified pub crawls. In a booklet which begins: "Have you ever wished to throw yourself from an aircraft? *Now is your chance!*", the trust advertises free parachuting weekends for beginners in Northumberland, one of Europe's "most hazard-free and picturesque drop zones."

The Aidan trust are planning an October "jail break," where

participants pretend to escape from a north east pub and are sponsored for the distance they can travel free of charge in 24 hours. Escapers are expected to cadge lifts from haulage firms and negotiate freebies. The organisers claim that sponsorship per mile could be lucrative—three local lads in a jail break for charity three years ago are rumoured to have got from Sunderland to Alcatraz.

Using such original methods, the trust raised £70,000 last year. John Hudspeth, Aidan's director, aims to bring that up to half a million in 1987. About £50,000 will come from a payroll deduction scheme, and the trust also aims to recruit in schools and colleges and among probate solicitors—who will be sent personalised letters and invited to seminar briefings.

The organisation, which has only five paid full-time staff, relies heavily on volunteers. Running costs are covered by Tetleys, whose monocled huntsman in a red hacking jacket is on the Aidan brochures and posters. (The Tetley logo jars slightly with the youthful dynamic image of the trust, whose patron is the rock star Sting.)

Tetley owns over 100 pubs in the north east. And pubs and clubs, according to Hudspeth, are where 60 per cent of spontaneous (or as he calls it "frictional") fund-raising for charity happens. Local people like pubs. The north east, with its open-hearted, generous people, is a gold mine for charity, Hudspeth believes. Yet only one national charity—"Keep Britain Warm"—is based there. Because of its Tetley's connection, Hudspeth argues, the trust can mobilise dispersed fund raising and be "frictional yet structured."

Hudspeth also believes that an umbrella local organisation can reach a public which may be prejudiced against charities such as the mentally ill or handicapped. Aidan's contributors know their money is going to be used locally.

Grant allocations are decided by a board of trustees, representing a cross-section of the community. Grants are usually small scale, under a £1,000, and are meant to cover a capital outlay, such as a piece of equipment. Small local organisations are generally preferred to national charities, which have easier access to alternative funds and tend to employ slicker presentation. Burdus says, "One application we got was terrible and full of grammar mistakes and looked as if it was written on a hand-made typewriter, with the print everywhere . . . but in the end we gave them what they wanted."

Aidan grants are "not for animals and not for the third world," says Hudspeth. Aidan has had no grant applications for help to AIDS victims, and a word processor for a North Tyneside gay and lesbian group was turned down. Hudspeth says, "We say the benefit is mainly for people who are disabled, and gays and lesbians are certainly not disabled. They should be able to propel their own funds rather than be aided by the community." He is only too aware that Aidan's public image could be soured by just one controversial grant; the trustees are likely to stick to safe donations.

It would be little wonder if, a year from now, the quayside crowd aren't blowing their hands and stamping their feet at the Cairngorm ski-lifts waiting for a small blond Geordie to charge down the White Lady, brandishing a Tetley's brewery banner.

Bobsleighing, hang-gliding, waterskiing, potholing . . . there are still plenty of pyrotechnic sports to test Burdus's ingenuity and courage.

Removing the barriers

STEVE PLATT

At a Workability Day held in a Hackney sports centre disabled people are encouraged—and helped—to apply for jobs with the council.

Dave Griffiths lied to get his job as a social worker with Hackney council because he didn't think that they would employ him if he told the truth. He was right. When his falsehood was discovered, twelve months after he started the job, the council intended to sack him. Only a petition in his support from fellow workers—and the threat of strike action—saved him from the dole queue.

Now, eight years later, Dave is manning Hackney social services department's stall at the council's Workability Day—an initiative to encourage more people with disabilities to apply for council jobs. He is telling an inquirer at the stall that the things he found it necessary to lie about back in 1979 are not considered a positive asset in applicants for many jobs with Hackney social services.

Dave has Usher's syndrome, a progressive condition which has caused hearing loss and left him partially sighted, with night blindness and tunnel vision. He kept the disability secret from the council and his colleagues until his deteriorating eyesight made it impossible for him to pretend any longer.

Although his workmates rallied to his support and the council was persuaded to keep him on, he says that it was not until 1983, when Hackney set up a disability unit and adopted a new, more positive, policy towards the employment of people with disabilities, that he felt truly able to "come out."

Now Dave talks persuasively to visitors at the exhibition about how Hackney council regards people with disabilities as "a source of strength, not weakness." "Disabilities can be a positive advantage in a lot of jobs," he says, "especially in the social services, where it helps you to understand the problems faced by the people you're working for. The council isn't doing anyone a favour by trying to get them to apply for these jobs. They want to employ them because they are strong candidates.

The same message comes from Linda Laurie and Jane Nation, the joint heads of Hackney's disability unit, which organised Workability Day. "People with disabilities have a staggering range of skills and potential," says Jane Nation. "But it isn't being tapped." "It's not enough just to adopt an equal opportunities policy," adds Linda Laurie. "You have to go out and say to people, "We recognise you've got skills and we want to use them'."

Both women, who themselves have mobility difficulties, say that disability is given a low priority in equal opportunities policies. "Events such as this help to raise the profile," says Jane Nation. "And they also deal with the argument of a lot of employers that it is very hard to find people with disabilities to apply for jobs. By doing this sort of outreach work we can encourage people to come forward who might not otherwise consider applying for jobs with the council."

Held in a wheelchair-accessible sports centre at the rear of Hackney town hall, Workability Day consists primarily of a large exhibition involving every council department. Current job vacancies are displayed (in large print) around stalls which also provide additional information about the jobs on offer and the work of each department. Around 50 council employees are on hand to deal with inquiries and offer advice and assistance.

But what makes the day more than just a big job shop is the attention that has been given to meeting the needs of disabled visitors. "We have tried to remove the barriers which normally put off people with disabilities," says Jane Nation.

These barriers are both physical and attitudinal, so as much attention has been paid to the way those staffimg the exhibition present themselves as to the accessibility of the materials and information on display. Everyone has attended voluntary disability awareness training sessions to prepare them for the day.

"Often it is the little things that are important," says Linda Laurie. "Sitting down to talk to people in wheelchairs, asking if people need help, not assuming it." She says the process of educating council officers is almost as important as getting people with disabilities to apply for jobs.

Going round the exhibition with several visitors, each of whom has a different disability, I see the educational process in action. One council employee becomes visibly embarrassed when he has to ask a visitor with a speech difficulty to repeat himself for the fourth time. "Was that rude?" he asks a disabled colleague later. "No, but it would have been if you had pretended you understood what he said when you didn't," comes the reply.

Dave Griffiths has less need than most for education on how to relate to people with disabilities. When Gina Walker, who is almost blind, nervously approaches him for information about a luncheon club supervisor's job, he immediately puts her at ease with jokes about their shared disability. "I'm constantly walking into old ladies in the street," he tells her. "I keep knocking them over. They think I'm mugging them—until they see the white stick."

Before Gina leaves, Dave has helped her to fill in application forms for two social services jobs. He has advised her on the sort of visual aids that are available to help her do the jobs and on the support she would get if offered one of them. And, with other council workers, he has encouraged her to apply for two clerical posts in the housing department, after first arranging for her to listen to the job descriptions on special tapes.

"You experience a lot of failure if you're disabled," says Dave, "so your confidence is undermined. One of the most important things we can do today is give people the confidence to apply for jobs, and know that their applications will be treated fairly." Before speaking to Gina he had spent over an hour talking to a man with spina bifida. "He has a degree and he has done four years' youth work, but he is completely insecure about applying for a job. It would be worth sitting here all day just to get him to put in an application."

Another visitor, Marie Bryant, who is in a wheelchair, tells me that the Workability Day staff have struck the right balance by being "friendly but not condescending." She says the exhibition is "very well presented and informative. It makes a nice change not to have to keep looking upwards to read notices—they're at my level for once." Other visitors appreciate the presence of interpreters and signers, the braille tapes and visual aids, or the recognition given to the different needs of people from Hackney's ethnic communities.

Despite the positive response, however, the disability unit staff are disappointed by what they regard as a poor attendance—about 150 people, less than half the number at the first

Workability Day last year. Chris Harrison, the unit's outreach and liaison worker, points out that a year ago the event had novelty value, but that most of the people attending this time were seriously seeking employment. Others say that a limited budget—just £5,000—made it impossible to advertise widely or to lay on proper transport facilities.

Even so, the day is an undoubted success. Most council departments have taken applications for jobs. Many visitors have registered to be sent details of jobs which may come up in the future. The ILEA careers office stand has arranged further interviews for a number of people. And at least one local private employer has called in to see what he can do to employ more people with disabilities. There is talk that next year the event might be widened to include the voluntary sector and other employers.

As I leave, it strikes me how *normal* disability is, but how abnormal society makes it seem. One person in ten in the UK—at least five million people—has some form of disability. Half of the rest will become seriously disabled in their old age. As Marie Bryant put it, "The able bodied have a lot of places where they can go to look for work, so I don't think the occasional event like this for people with disabilities is too much to expect. We've got just as much right to work for our local council as anyone else."

Caring for the cared-for

JANET HADLEY

A new scheme in London trains volunteers to befriend and protect the rights of mentally handicapped hospital patients.

Jimmy is 48 years old and has Down's syndrome. He has no family and, since the age of 13, he has lived at St Lawrence's hospital, Caterham, in Surrey. He is typical of thousands of mentally handicapped people who are being shifted, in increasing numbers, out of the big Victorian institutions and "into the community." Last autumn, after 34 years living on a mental handicap hospital ward, he moved into a privately run residential home in Ross-on-Wye, Hereford.

But in Jimmy's case, someone outside the hospital was watching vigilantly over the plans to resettle him—his volunteer "advocate" David.

"When I heard last August that Jimmy was on the list for resettlement I had hoped that it would be into a home nearby," says David, a bluff Territorial Army enthusiast who works in a firm of chartered accountants. He explains that Jimmy did not come from the Croydon area originally so the borough could not provide accommodation and he had to go further afield.

Jimmy and David had been friends for more than two years, and once a week David would help Jimmy across the busy road between the hospital and the nearby pub, where they'd have a few drinks. The discussion, says David, was mainly about the state of Jimmy's radio batteries—a topic which preoccupies him greatly.

Being an advocate for a mentally handicapped hospital patient is much more than being a friend. With the training of the Advocacy Alliance charity behind him, David's job was also to stand up for Jimmy's rights and interests.

David tried to ensure that the home in Ross-on-Wye was the right place for Jimmy. He questioned Jimmy and also sought a detailed explanation from Dr Geoffrey Harris, the consultant in charge of the resettlement programme. "I wasn't going to let anything happen to Jimmy that was against his best interest," says David.

The Advocacy Alliance was set up in 1981, by charities for the ill and handicapped: Mencap, Mind, The Spastics Society, the Leonard Cheshire Foundation and One-to-One. The scheme has recruited advocates for three of the big Surrey mental handicap hospitals which for decades have taken in London's patients: St Ebba's at Epsom, Normansfield at Kingston, and St Lawrence's.

The advocates range from 20 to 70 years old and come from many different backgrounds. Some are retired but the majority of advocates are white collar employees, and two thirds are women.

The charity gives would-be advocates an eight-week training course, one evening a week. On the course they learn about legal rights and welfare benefits, and are given a chance to reassess social attitudes and expectations towards the mentally handicapped. They also meet advocates and their patients.

About half those who begin the course drop out. But almost all of those who befriend a patient have stayed with advocacy and have only stopped when they have moved out of the area.

Advocates hold regular consultations with each other and tend to devote much time and thought to their patients. At the advocates meetings away from the hospital, they chat about outings, clothes shopping, fear of dogs, visits home and even holidays abroad. At one of their meetings I heard them grumbling about patients' poor personal hygiene and the frustrations of trying to get them speech therapy. Relations with ward staff seem good, at least from the patients' point of view. One advocate said of the nurses: "they'd never dare do anything that'd upset *me*."

Only seven St Lawrence's patients have ever had advocates. At the two other Surrey hospitals the alliance operates on a slightly bigger scale but patients there are not being moved out as fast as at St Lawrence's which is due to close in 1994.

Jimmy was one of about 250 patients who have moved out of St Lawrence's since the beginning of 1985. Most are going into private residential homes, paid for by the £150 a week DHSS board and lodging allowance, which is topped up by a health service grant to cover costs equivalent to the patient's upkeep in hospital.

When they leave the hospital, patients are given a twelve week trial period. So far only three patients have had to return to St Lawrence's.

One of these was 28 year old Vicki who had been in hospital since she was six months old, when an attack of spinal meningitis left her severely mentally retarded. Her legs are in calipers and she also has a withered arm.

Vicki's advocate, Sandra, had "serious misgivings," when she heard that Vicki was to go to a "family home" in Sussex. The home was run by a young couple, who themselves had a young handicapped child and were proposing to take in simultaneously six mentally handicapped adults.

Sandra, a mother of five, felt she had a very close affinity with Vicki partly because they were both Roman Catholics. She had taken her regularly to her home, and even on a pilgrimage to Yugoslavia. Over a period of three years Vicki was transformed from a monosyllabic, withdrawn patient into an affectionate garrulous young woman, with a strong sense of her own identity.

In contrast to David, who felt he had some authority to challenge the hospital's views, Sandra was persuaded to let Vicki move: "they said she must be given a chance." But Vicki missed the *dolce vita* of St Lawrence's, with its discos, outings, and the freedom to roam the corridors. At the new home she went just twice a week to the day centre, the rest of the time she was in her bedroom or confined to one room.

Sandra was advised not to visit Vicki for a few weeks, then she got a phone call, asking her to come down. Vicki had become remote and obsessional, wetting and biting herself, and threatening to remove her clothes. It was four months before the hospital took Vicki back.

Sandra regrets Vicki's suffering and says that next time she will be more outspoken. Dr Harris suggests that advocates can sometimes get "too attached," yet he believes that the befriending side of advocacy is its most valuable aspect. He is disappointed that after four years, the scheme is still so small.

For a mentally handicapped person who has lived for years in a long-stay hospital, moving out is quite an undertaking. Despite the shortage of facilities and support in the community, some do settle happily, often not far from their old hospital. But for others, resettlement is a traumatic event. The need for advocates—articulate allies committed to the needs of the individual, not the system, can hardly be greater than at this precarious moment.

Health

Relaxing practices

JACI STEPHEN

A Cambridgeshire scheme helps people cope with the symptoms of work stress and tension.

On a freezing winter's night, the floor of a small room in Addenbrooke's Hospital, Cambridge, is lined with bodies, seemingly in an advanced state of rigor mortis. The rise and fall of hushed breath fills the air like a dirty phone-call over long distance; a few bones creak. "Tense your buttocks . . . hold them as tight as you can . . ." comes a voice through the constipated silence, ". . . and relax." More creaking of bones. A dozen people are doing tensing and relaxing exercises in a new scheme to develop relaxation classes within GP practices, health centres and places associated with community health education throughout the Cambridge Health District.

"There is a growing body of research which substantiates that relaxation techniques are effective in treating physical and mental problems," says Marion Howell, the health education officer. "Relaxation groups have a number of advantages: several people can be helped at the same time, problems are generalised and shared and, most importantly, people are reassured that they are not alone in their problem."

The Cambridge project is intended to offer a viable alternative to drug therapy and the possibility of a reduction in demand on the conventional mental health services. It is directed towards those outside contact with the psychiatric service and aims to meet needs before any psychiatric intervention is necessary.

The seeds for the scheme were planted back in 1981 at Barnwell Health Centre, a new, purpose-build facility with six GPs and over 30 staff. Some of the GPs were aware that the needs of patients (particularly those with handicap, long-term illness, or socially induced stress) could not always be met by standard treatment, and they now saw the possibility of patients being a "resource for each other in providing a supportive network." As a result, a group-work organiser was funded for two years to develop a range of patient self-help groups and patient participation organisations.

Gill Westland, deputy head occupational therapist at Fulbourn Hospital, Cambridge, met with the group organiser in 1981, with a view to exploring the role of occupational therapy for mental health within the wider community, rather than just that within the hospital. At this time, Westland could offer one session a week of creative therapy, small group psychotherapy, relaxation, and social skills. She had also had experience of working with psychiatric day patients.

Many of the frequent attenders at Barnwell Health Centre were women who recieved regular prescriptions for antidepressants and anxiolytics. The question was: were they getting the kind of support they needed? If not, what form of support would be most acceptable to them, involving both doctors and the occupational therapist working together? Then came the idea of starting a relaxation group for women.

At this stage, the group focused on specific problems: women aged between 30 and 50 who suffered from mild anxiety and/or depression, headaches, lethargy, nausea, weight problems, unnecessarily dependent upon drugs and experiencing difficulty to in social intercourse. The group would introduce members to simple relaxation techniques, help them to talk about the stresses and strains of their everyday lives and, in doing so, learn from each other. There would also be the opportunity for social contact, thereby encouraging members to develop their own supportive social networks such as self-help groups, which would be run with minimal professional involvement.

In 1984, the idea was taken up by the Cambridge Health Authority and Cambridge Social Services, working as joint development teams. This sub-group aimed to extend the service into other primary health care settings. At the beginning of 1984, the first training course for group leaders was established: in a ten-week course (two hours per session, once a week), training would be given free of charge, in return for which the leader would offer a ten-week relaxation course in a primary health care setting. Any GP practice willing to set up a class would be welcome to do so.

"We sent letters to all the GPs in the Cambridge Health District," says Jane Whitehead, a locum for Marion Howell, "Over 80 in all. We had just eleven positive replies. It's only natural that many GPs are going to be cautious, though now there's a growing confidence."

By the summer of 1984, there were six relaxation groups within GP practices, at Histon, Bourn, Soham, East Barnwell, Hurst Park Avenue and Hills Road. Now there are also classes at a community school and at Addenbrooke's Hospital. The Health Authority has committed a further £4,000 for 1986/7, much of which will go towards the training of group leaders.

There is no attendance charge, and all the classes are oversubscribed. "At present there are more women than men, possibly because many people think of it in terms of an antenatal class. We are trying to encourage more men though," says Whitehead. The members come from all walks of life, but work stress is the most common reason for joining a class. Often this shows itself in physical symptoms—breathlessness, insomnia, loss of appetite.

"I've come because I want to improve my lifestyle and my family's lifestyle—something that it's easier to do if I'm relaxed," says one hopeful at the Addenbrooke's class. "My doctor recommended I try a relaxtion class as a possible cure for insomnia," says another.

Frank Weir, co-leader of the group, explains the structure of the course, the techniques of which are based on tensing and relaxing groups of muscles. "You have to learn to be in tune with your body and what it's telling you, develop an in-built relaxation mechanism. We'll learn to adapt the method to everyday situations, recognise tensions and then do something about it." Guided fantasies and music are on the agenda, together with an examination of general lifestyle; looking at areas where stress can be avoided; looking at different methods of coping with stress; food; routines we get into.

There is no overwhelming evidence to prove that prescriptions for antidepressants and so on have been drastically reduced since Cambridge launched its scheme. Until extensive research takes place, it will be impossible to assess the value of the classes other than on an individual basis. Of the people who have attended so far, however, some individuals have said they rely less on drugs, and others have experienced a reduction in general aches and pains. The attendance itself shows that there is a demand for such groups.

For Gill Westland, there are two central issues underlying the whole question of relaxation: first, taking more responsibility and recognising the personal control over their lives that individuals can have, and second, demanding a different quality of life for themselves. In contributing to change in the public's attitude towards visiting their doctor, she feels relaxation techniques are making a positive contribution to preventive medicine.

Watch your diet

DOROTHY WADE

The BMA this week spoke out against alternative medicine, but one GP at least is in favour of it.

A quiet revolution in medicine could be taking place, almost unnoticed, in a sleepy corner of West Sussex. One hundred patients in a Worthing medical practice are being treated for a range of complaints—from depression to arthritis to epilepsy to multiple sclerosis—by individually tailored diets.

There are no rash instructions to throw out all pills. Instead, patients are being advised to cut out certain foods, usually staples of our western diet, such as wheat and dairy products, in the interests of their health. As a result, many of them are gradually putting aside their painkillers and their anti-depressants, declaring that they haven't felt better in years.

The man responsible for this apparent success is no dubious merchant of miracle cures. He is a sober, Scottish GP, the son of a sober retired Scottish professor, with two years experience of hospital medicine in Glasgow and seven years of general practice in Worthing behind him.

Dr James Anderson is convinced that many, indeed most, of the ailments that we commonly suffer from are the result of eating food that we are allergic to. Varying our diet to exclude or cut down the foods that irritate us can often do more, he believes, to improve complaints such as sinusitis, migraine and asthma than any amount of pharmaceutial drugs.

In this belief he is not alone. Prestigious consultants have debated the effects and mechanisms of food allergies in academic journals, and private doctors offer expensive "desensitizing" treatments in Harley Street clinics. But only Anderson is offering this type of treatment on the NHS.

To test his convictions, he has hand-picked a group of 100—eventually to be expanded to 500—people from his Worthing practice. He has deliberately chosen people who have found little relief from chronic complaints in conventional medicine, and who are broadminded enough to try out novel treatment which cannot be found in the textbooks.

The group includes men and women, and ranges from a 12 year old child with a history of backache and headaches, to a 72 year old man with emphysema. Some patients are seriously ill; others complain of being continually rundown with symptoms such as bad temper, fatigue, depression, chronic influenza—like joint pains, or even catarrh. Anderson believes that by treating symptoms like these early, he may be forestalling more serious illness such as arthritic disease or sinusitis.

At the beginning of the treatment, he takes a patient's blood sample and sends it to the York Alternative Medical Centre. There it is tested against 43 commonly eaten foods and ten chemicals (including additives) to discover what the patient is allergic to. The patient is presented with a list of their reactions to different foods in four columns; severe, moderate, mild and no reaction. Anderson then helps the patient to devise a diet using food from the "mild" and "no" reaction columns, and some from the "moderate" column.

Very often people say that they find an improvement in their condition almost immediately. After six months Anderson sends them a questionnaire to see if they have stuck to the diet and to ask them to assess the effects. Of the 36 questionnaires he has studied so far, 28 patients believe the treatment was successful, while eight say it failed.

Significantly, the younger the patients are, the more they appear to respond to their new diet. Six of the eight overall "failures" were 60 years old or over. Four of the eight "failures" noticed some improvement in their symptoms, and only one felt worse. Many also found other benefits from the diet: "I feel more alert." "I can relax more and I don't lose my temper so easily," were typical replies.

The results are encouraging enough for Dr Anderson to continue with the experiement he began in 1984, when a conference on general allergies on the Isle of Wight sparked off his interest.

The conference coincided with two personal problems: his own ill-health, and frustration with his work as a GP. Ironically, the rich conference fare—steak, red wine, roast beef—seemed to be making the sinusitis he had suffered from for years, worse than usual. He had a terrible headache and felt completely exhausted and depressed. After the conference he started to experiment and found that he could control his sinusitis by cutting out some foods and eating less of others.

The physician, having healed himself, now began to look at his general practice. For some years he had been increasingly disillusioned with the doctor's role of dishing out tranquillisers and antibiotics to people who would often return again and again with the same complaint.

"As a conventional doctor I was usually thinking, "What the hell am I going to do with Mrs Jones when she comes back next Tuesday . . . I would keep seeing people again and again until either of us reached the end of our tether." At one stage he was ready to drop medicine altogether, had not food allergies awakened his interest. "Medicine is a primitive art in most respects and that is why I was open to any investigation or technique for looking at disease."

One investigation that he studied was work being done by Professor Jonathan Brostoff, an immunologist at the Middlesex Hospital, London. Brostoff had discovered an allergic reaction to food that could be the key to all sorts of symptoms, from abdominal pain to learning problems.

He found that when we eat, clusters of food allergens and antibodies, called immune complexes, are produced and move freely thoughout the body. Some people can metabolise these complexes normally; others cannot—the complexes lodge themselves in various organs or joints of the body and cause inflammation. This work, although not widely known in the medical profession, seemed to confirm Anderson's hunches. Immune complexes could be seen as a root of illness.

Dr Anderson has no qualms about carrying out his work on the NHS; it is merely an extension of what he believes to be the GP's duties of caring for his patients and, if possible, preventing them from becoming seriously ill. Initially, the patients require a lot of help and guidance. But eventually he believes his system would prove economic as the rate of return visits to the GP slowed down. Those he has already treated also tend to take less time off work and to use fewer drugs.

Anderson is the first to admit that only doctors in a professional middle-class area like Worthing can allow themselves the luxury of trying to find "the root of illness." He is well aware that in Glasgow such work would have been impossible. "There the GPs are too busy rescuing people from alcoholism and chronic bronchitis to look into the mechanisms that cause bronchitis."

He also makes no claim to being an expert in the field of immunology. "I see myself as a very middle-of-the-road doctor whose main problem is his conscience. I have an interest in the science, but I'd rather be doing the practical work of getting people better. I want to provoke more interest in professionals, especially those working within the NHS, who can look at this type of work without financial bias."

A growing venture

DAVID WHITE

A market garden provides horticultural therapy and a thriving business.

Hillside market garden, a few miles north of Dorchester, looks like any other market garden. And in most respects it is. It is a commercially run horticulture business with a healthy turnover of some £10,000 a year.

But in one respect Hillside is different. Everyone who works there, apart from the supervisory staff, suffers from some form of mental illness or mental handicap.

Hillside is attached to the Herrison psychiatric hospital. It is one of a growing number of schemes in Britain which provide "horticultural therapy" for psychiatric patients. Broadly, horticultural therapy means the use of outdoor activities to encourage people to take more control of their lives.

Horticultural therapy started in the United States, where a National Council for Therapy and Rehabilitation through Horticulture was set up in 1973. Since then, it has spread to Britain. A Society for Horticultural Therapy was established in 1978, and by 1979, there were some 50 schemes, ranging from city farms to market gardens, offering some sort of horticultural therapy. And in 1980, the Federation to Promote Horticulture for Disabled People was formed, largely through the efforts of horticulturalists at Bath university, to provide an information exchange and talking shop for people involved in horticultural therapy schemes.

The value of horticulture lies in the variety of its tasks, says Nick Saynor, the manager of Hillside. "Horticulture is the most useful sort of therapy because of the huge range of skills involved. Anything from picking up stones to micro-propagation."

Nick Saynor has built up the Hillside project from scratch. He was appointed in 1972 to design a therapeutic farm for the patients at the Herrison hospital. The hospital had had a farm of its own since Victorian times. But increasing mechanisation reduced its usefulness as a form of occupational therapy.

On top of this, there was government pressure to sell off hospital farmland. So the hospital farm closed in 1975. However, the hospital management committee and the health authority still wanted some sort of farm activity to provide occupational therapy. The answer was a therapeutic farm.

There have been two major changes to the scheme since then. The therapeutic farm has evolved into a market garden. The original idea was to keep livestock, but this proved "precarious." Increasingly, the farm concentrated on agriculture and horticulture. This process was accelerated when a horticulturalist, Stephen Harris, joined the scheme in 1987.

A few years ago, the project was renamed the Hillside market garden. This freed it from association with the Herrison hospital; even today, psychiatric hospitals still carry a stigma. It also recognised that the project had become a free-standing commercial venture.

"We would use the word 'realistic' rather than 'commercial'," Nick Saynor says. "We feel that what they produce should be sold at the going price." Hillside sells most of what it grows in the farm shop. The rest goes to retailers and wholesalers. Occasionally, produce will be sold cheaply to old people's homes.

The other major change is in the people who are referred to Hillside. The therapeutic farm began with four elderly inpatients tending a quarter of an acre of land. Today there are 25 people at work on 16 acres, but only five of these are inpatients.

This reflects the government's policy of moving psychiatric patients out of hospitals and into the community. The majority of people at Hillside now live either in sheltered accommodation or lodgings (as part of the resettlement programme) or at home.

Hillside now attracts a variety of referrals: a wide range of people with a wide range of problems. Patients have included a chartered accountant, a lorry driver and a journalist. Problems range from depression to schizophrenia.

Referrals can come from the hospital, the community psychiatric services or the social services. Patients are interviewed, then put on a month's trial. Not all of them are suitable. "We don't want a runner, and we don't want a high suicidal risk," Nick Saynor says. Hillside takes about one in six of the people referred to it. "The ratio is narrowing, though, as people get to know what we do."

The aim is not merely to keep patients occupied, but to encourage them to develop skills. "You've got to find what their level is and then try to improve it until you get to the level where a limit is reached."

This is the real purpose of Hillside; to ease patients, as gently as possible, back into the world of work. To this end, it tries to make the work as realistic and as credible as possible. With some success. Nick Saynor sees three pointers to this: "First, they tell their friends they're going to a proper job when they come to Hillside. Second, they get all hot and bothered when their produce doesn't sell. Third, they turn up. They don't have to come, unless there's a court order."

The real test, however, is results. Does Hillside get people back into normal circulation? Unfortunately, results are difficult to measure.

An assessment has been carried out by Susan Woodward, the occupational therapist who was appointed to Hillside in 1982. She studied the progress of ten patients between 1982 and 1984, assessing them on work skills, social skills, health and anti-social behaviour.

Her findings, however, were inconclusive. She found that, generally, the work skills of patients deteriorated, while their social skills improved marginally. However, there was a marked improvement in one of their social skills – initiative. And the health of all of them improved.

As Susan Woodward herself admits, her sample was too small. And most of the patients had problems which were either serious or long-term; problems which a short period at Hillside would be unlikely to solve. Evidence of improvement therefore is bound to be anecdotal. But often this evidence is not always detectable. Nick Saynor cites the case of a 16 year old boy who had been referred to Hillside. The staff soon despaired of helping him. He was too destructive, they decided. But at a case conference, his local doctor remarked that since the boy had been coming to Hillside, he had heard no reports of threats or assaults by the boy against his neighbours. In short, his behaviour at Hillside had not changed, but his behaviour at home had.

Others, who might have been inpatients, avoid this by referral to Hillside: "This place has stopped people being readmitted, or even admitted in the first place," Nick Saynor says. "They short-circuit the system by coming here."

In this sense, horticultural therapy is obviously cost-effective. "One of the basic reasons horticultural therapy schemes are growing is that they are economical in a climate of perpetual cuts," Nick Saynor says.

All that is needed for a horticultural therapy scheme is five acres of ground, some greenhouses (often patients need to work under cover, because extremes of temperature can interact with drugs) and the right team. The demand for such schemes is growing daily. Nick Saynor sees a rapidly expanding grey area of need – the "unemployables." These are young people, with nothing much wrong with them, who nevertheless are unlikely to hold down jobs. They will need the sort of stability a place like Hillside can offer. For, as Stephen Harris puts it, "Hillside gives people roots."

Help for helplines

JOY MELVILLE

Nonprofessionals setting up support groups for AIDS sufferers can find that they, too, need help.

Anyone with AIDS needs all the support they can get. And in many areas the voluntary sector has been faster than statutory bodies in setting up initiatives to help. Take Merseyside, for instance.

Merseyside now has four voluntary support groups or helplines: the Liverpool Aids Advisory Group; Mersey Aids Line; Aids Information Line, Crewe; and Halton Aids Information and Support Group. Two other voluntary support groups, at Warrington and Chester, are in the pipeline.

Dominic Davies of Mersey Aids Prevention Unit, acts as co-ordinator and consultant to new AIDS support groups. He admires the enthusiasm of those who want to help – mainly, in this country, gay men and heterosexual women – but warns new groups intending to set up that they could face major pitfalls. "They may have no professional background," he says, "and therefore don't always appreciate the level of training and skills needed to provide emotional support to someone who is going through a major crisis in their life. Enthusiasm is not enough: accredited counsellors have 900 hours of training behind them.

"People say, 'What can we do?' and the first thing they think of is the phone line. But it is not easy to get a phone installed in an office. And they may also not realise how time-consuming it is to run one. Volunteers tend to do too much too soon, like running a service for twelve hours a day with five or six helpers."

In his experience, another problem is when a volunteer suggests to a caller that he or she comes in for a chat. But the caller may live some distance away and want to come in after work in the evening. And if they are upset, they may stay for three or four hours. Then, after this one visit, the caller inevitably gets worried again and needs more personal reassurance and the group members find that they are doing too much and simply can't cope, or they may sympathetically give their home phone number to someone, only to get constant calls in the middle of the night.

A further difficulty is finding premises. If you have a single room with one or two phones in it, and then at some future stage decide that you would like to expand and see people with AIDS, where can you put them? It is not just a question of space in the one room, but also of confidentiality. And if members want to hold training sessions or group meetings, where will they sit?

Some of the Mersey groups have had to battle with problems like these. All of them have different histories.

The Liverpool Aids Advisory Group, which started up last December, is based in a very active church community advice centre in the Liverpool suburb of Aintree. Those at the centre noticed an increasing number of inquiries about AIDS and a number of staff volunteered to set up an AIDS helpline.

They had no professional background, outside the basic training programme provided by the centre. But they now run a small office with two phone lines, manned twelve hours a day, Mondays to Fridays, and two hours on Saturdays. They have information leaflets and there are plans to offer face-to-face support in the future.

The Aids Information Line at Crewe was set up for an experimental six months, from 6.30pm to 8.30pm on Wednesdays only, by health authority staff. Dominic Davies feels that this is woefully inadequate. "It's the wrong time of the evening, and the volunteers themselves have no training in listening skills. If they get someone who is suicidal ringing in, they may not be skilled enough to support that person."

The Halton Aids Information and Support Group, which started in January this year, offers clients more time: 9am to 5pm, Mondays to Fridays. Run by Manpower Services Commission staff on a Community Programme project, as part of the health authority's health promotions unit, it has four part-time and seven volunteers.

The Mersey Aids Line, set up in 1984, is the second oldest AIDS support group in the country. Its history shows the difficulties such groups face.

After the Terrence Higgins Trust was formed, some concerned people in Merseyside got together and asked members of the trust to go up there to advise on starting a group. About 30 people attended, but a group of that size would have been too unwieldy, so the number was limited to about twelve, with an executive committee of seven. This included a consultant in sexually transmitted diseases, a lecturer and a taxi driver.

Joyce Radley, JP, a health visitor employed by Liverpool Health Authority, was recently appointed chairman of the group. "We weren't funded by anyone," she says. "But Lesbian Line, which operated within the structure of Friend, Merseyside, offered us free use of their phone line one evening a week. We wanted to have our own premises and money for this was slowly raised by the gay community, who held dances, discos, fun runs and similar activities. We are manning the phone lines and training ourselves, working with Dr Peter Carey, a genitourinary consultant at the Royal Liverpool Hospital."

This first group has now trained two further groups. Training, which amounts to 28 hours, covers telephone techniques (like being able to talk about safe sex in language the listener understands) and education about AIDS. "We try to let the participants discover their own prejudices," says Joyce Radley, "and discuss their experience of bereavement and their reactions to sexuality and whether they are comfortable about their own sexuality. It is a very intense and draining course and at the end only those who are committed will carry on."

But she emphasises that group members are careful not to claim that they are counsellors – just telephone volunteers who recognise callers' needs, support them and direct them to specialist help, if they require it. The next step is training people to befriend people with AIDS in their own homes – offering them emotional and practical help.

In April this year, the regional health authority gave the group a room on the third floor of a building in Liverpool – "hardly ideal for anyone who has AIDS," says Joyce Radley, wryly, "as some would find it very difficult to climb the stairs. The address is kept confidential, as there is still too much of a stigma attached to AIDS for clients to visit openly."

The phone helpline for people concerned about AIDS is run on Mondays, Wednesdays and Fridays, with Tuesday evenings set aside for those tested for the virus and found positive to meet and support each other.

Telephone inquiries range from the general ("Could you tell me what the symptoms of AIDS are?") to the particular ("Is anal sex safe if you don't come?" – that is, is penetration without ejaculation safe?). Women who have been on "singles" holidays and had brief affairs ring in; so do mothers who want to talk about their sons who have AIDS and the isolation they feel in their grief, and the stigma. This year, an increasing number of worried heterosexuals have been calling.

Dominic Davies, who is an AIDS counsellor himself, says that AIDS patients "may need to talk over their death and the funeral arrangements and prepare their partners and family members for this. There may be a lot of anger that they have unjustifiably caught this disease through a normal human function like having sex."

The answer is to have even more support groups. But it is not an undertaking to be entered into casually. Group members must be adequately trained – or they may create more problems than they solve.

The potter's belly

JAMES STEPHENSON

A health food shop in the Potteries entices the elderly to look after themselves in more ways than one.

Situated in the heart of pie, chips and pottery country, conveniently near to a local bus station, the Senior Health Shop in Stoke on Trent is part of a self-health project, designed to help older people to look after their health.

Stripped pine chairs, Laura Ashley tablecloths, potted plants, and trellised walls catch the eye – it looks at first sight like a quaint tea shop. The intended effect is to lure the hesitant elderly into the shop. So successful has this been that a notice had to be placed in the window to deter the increasing numbers of under-age eaters.

"There was nothing quite like this, so everything we do is extra," is how Betty Ball describes the difference that the shop has made to the lives of the over-fifties in Stoke. The shop she manages is at present, in the words of the Beth Johnson Foundation's research officer, Dr Miriam Bernard, a "shop front for a whole operation."

Opened in August last year, it provides information on a whole range of subjects and services of interest to older people. Where appropriate, referral is made to other organisations, like the North Staffordshire Bereavement Centre. It is funded jointly by the Beth Johnson Foundation, based in Stoke on Trent, and the ECC under the Second Programme to Combat Poverty.

On offer inside the shop is a simple menu, including baked potatoes, salads, flapjacks and camomile and rosehip tea, and at the foot of the menu is a reminder that free blood pressure checks can be had without appointment.

Regular visitors are encouraged to monitor their weight on a set of scales. An impressive array of computer equipment gives general advice – almost irrespective of the different answers given to the various questions about eating habits and lifestyle. Pessimistic forecasts that old people would be reluctant to handle the equipment have been proved wrong, and it is not uncommon for a group to cluster around the screen comparing notes.

Up Date, the quarterly bulletin of the project, reports that: "Once people are settled with a drink and a snack, they become relaxed enough to take an interest in the surrounding racks of leaflets and health education material." The food plays a multiple role, and as well as providing a social focus it is part of the attempt to re-educate, and recipe sheets for the meals provided are available.

The shop provides an initial introduction to the three other elements of the scheme for self-health care in old age. Peer health counselling involves the training of people, enabling them to lead discussions and gentle exercise groups with others of their own age. The director of the Beth Johnson Foundation, Arthur Creber, stresses the need to help a generation which tends to be deferential towards medical expertise "to cope with their own doctors," and avoid feeling "demeaned and dismissed" by them.

The foundation also runs courses on handling stress and a "look after yourself course" based at a nearby centre. Healthy food is available here, too, from a canteen which welcomes newcomers with the slogan: "Nice to see you, to see you nice."

Miriam Bernard stresses the fluidity of the organisation of these events. It is common for visitors to become volunteers, and for volunteers to participate in activities.

It had been hoped to have these activities on the same site as the shop, but rents in the town centre proved too expensive. The only element of the project currently based at the shop is Careline, and this is partly funded by the Opportunities for Volunteering Scheme. Two volunteers operate the phoneline from a small room, "more a box than an office." They call about 30 mainly housebound people each day to ensure that they are all right.

Callers undertake a preliminary visit to ensure that the elderly can reach a telephone, and establish face-to-face contact. Key numbers, of a relation or a neighbour, are also provided in case the call is not answered. On this occasion Sybil was talking to a woman who was feeling a bit subdued after finishing an overly morbid Catherine Cookson novel.

The driving force behind the whole project is the Beth Johnson Foundation. Its five full-time staff operate from a double-fronted Georgian house. Set up in 1972 with the bequest of a local pottery heiress, the foundation has as its aim the improvement of the quality of older people's lives. It is an objective pursued through a policy of innovative development, monitoring, research and education.

The Senior Health Shop has had its problems, principal amongst them the early resignation of the shop's first manager. But it is now running smoothly, with between 250 and 400 attendances a month. About half of these are first timers, who happened to be in the area, underlining the importance of the shop as a link to the larger project. Six-day opening allows the shop to accommodate those in their fifties and early sixties, who are still at work. Plans are afoot to expand.

The project has attracted the attention of the junior health minister Edwina Currie, who expressed interest in visiting the shop. Presumably to witness the subversion of her stereotypical view of northern eating habits.

Citizens to the rescue

JENNY ROGERS

A project in Brighton teaches ordinary people to save lives.

A few years ago, Martyn, a keen sportsman living in Brighton, decided to take one of the special two-hour "Heart Guard" courses available locally. He went along, hoping perhaps that he would never have to use the simple but dramatic life-saving techniques of resuscitaion that would be taught. That was on Wednesday. On Saturday he was at the scene of a spectacular collision involving two of his team mates. One was concussed, but otherwise all right. The other had already turned blue. He looked dead.

"I didn't really stop to worry about it," says Martyn. "I just swung straight into the routine. I checked that he wasn't breathing and didn't have a pulse. I opened his airway, gave mouth-to-mouth, then compressions. After about a minute, to my immense relief he started breathing again. A few minutes later, he was coming round." It was about ten minutres before the ambulance arrived. Without Martyn's help, one healthy young man, now completely recovered, would certainly have died. A pulseless, non-breathing casualty will be irreversibly brain damaged after only three or four minutes unless cardio-pulmonary resusciation maintains or re-starts circulation.

This young man owes his life, not just to his rescuer, but also to the flair, persistence and long-sightedness of the Brighton cardiologist, Dr Douglas Chamberlain and his colleagues at the Royal Sussex Hospital who started the Heart Guard project eight years ago and have seen it grow to the point where it has now trained 30,000 people.

As a local initiative in community health education it would be remarkable enough. But Heart Guard has also provided the model for the new national "Save a Life Campaign" which begins this month. It will link six BBC television programmes with St John's Ambulance, the Red Cross, St Andrew and the Royal Life Saving Society in serving hundreds of new local projects nationwide.

Heart Guard runs on a lot of hard work and a slender budget. Funded originally by the British Heart Foundation, then sustained briefly by the health authority, it is now self-financing. The only salaried personnel are the director, George Ellis, and his half-time assistant. People who attend courses are politely asked to donate £1.00. The rest of the £13,000 a year it costs to keep the project going is prised skilfully and quietly out of local businesses and with noisy panache through sponsored events out of the community at large.

The instructors are all volunteers. Of the 40 regulars, roughly half are ambulancemen and there are three nurses. But even the lay instructors often work in paramedical jobs. One, for instance, runs an old people's home. Many have had a life-long commitment to first-aid with Red Cross or St John's certificates to prove it. Why do they do it?

Dave Fletcher is an ambulanceman, and one of the stalwarts of the scheme. His response was simple and heartfelt: "So often, you can get to an incident and you find someone dead who could have survived. It especially hurts to see a child or young person who should have had years ahead of them – and what needed to be done was so simple, anyone could learn it."

Heart Guard has proved that anyone can learn what is involved in saving life in an emergency. The two-hour course ruthlessly dispenses with anything redolent of the Elastoplast-and-bandage image of conventional first aid. It is aimed fair and square at what to do to keep a casualty alive until more skilled help arrives.

Heart Guard runs 30 courses a month, many now aimed at particular groups: in schools, women's institutes, industry and offices. The course I visited was being held in a local hospital. Our group included porters, physiotherapists, cleaners and nurses.

After an opening pep talk by Derek Emery (also an ambulanceman), we split into four groups each with its own tutor and manikin – a life-sized doll with a flexible airway, inflatable lungs and a sternum (breast bone). One by one, we practised the routine of assessing the casualty, opening the airway, giving mouth-to-mouth and chest compressions. We rolled each other into the recovery position again and again until Dorothy, our tutor (a shop assistant who regularly gives up her day off for Heart Guard), was satisfied that we were doing it properly. Finally, we were called together for questions and a demonstration of the Heimlich manoeuvre, an effective (but still controversial) treatment for choking.

Heart Guard makes this kind of teaching look easy, but it is not. Pummelling the manikin, or rolling round on the floor being prodded by strangers is likely to lead, at the very least, to the kind of embarrassment which it takes skill to deflect. People with false teeth may find it difficult to make a proper seal round the stiff plastic of the manikin's mouth. (They are reassured and offered tactful help later.) Some trainees have come forward because they have been helpless bystanders at an incident where someone they loved has died. Often the unstated reason for attending is to confront their guilt. All this can make for tricky teaching. "There's often someone who cries," says Dave Fletcher, "but that's all right. We can cope."

To find out how people use the knowledge they have acquired, Heart Guard gives all its trainees an incident form and begs them to send it back if they are ever involved in using what they have learnt. We know that at least 26 saved lives are directly attributable to the project. However, this must just be the recorded peak of a much larger mass which remains stubbornly hidden. While some people are straightforwardly pleased and proud of what they have done, others modestly decline the "hero" role. Many feel doubts and discomfort after giving resuscitation. Did I do it right? Was there something I forgot? Could I be officially rebuked if I made a mistake? Then, too, some incidents are indeed life-threatening, but because the first aid was successful, never reach hospital records.

All the ambulancemen teaching on the project have tales of incidents where bystanders gave the right help, but then "just melted away." Only last week, a crew was called to a woman who had collapsed unconscious in the street after drinking too much. She had been correctly propped on her side in the recovery position by a member of the public who had called and then waited for the ambulance, but had then disappeared. This kind of action (potentially life-saving as it protects the patient's airway) is most unusual elsewhere, but is becoming increasingly common in Brighton. Who is to say whether this bystander was actually a Heart Guard graduate, or just someone to whom the knowledge had percolated in a community where "citizen life-saving" is so much in the air?

Other gains may be even less tangible but equally valuable: having the confidence to call an ambulance sooner rather than later with possible heart attack cases; calming panicking people at road accidents; realising that it is always best to do *something*.

If bald statistics are hard to gather, even less is known for sure about the feelings of either rescuer or rescued. Martyn, whose experience I quoted at the beginning of this piece, describes the unexpected confusion it created on both sides. "I was rather pleased with myself for a while," he says. "This rapidly changed to total embarrassment when his family contacted me with expressions of thanks, undying gratitude and offers of money. Since he and I were acquainted, I met him on one or two occasions later. We found it a considerable strain even to carry on a conversation together, since this matter of his believing I'd saved his life seemed to lie like a lead weight between us. Maybe this accounts for the old Chinese superstition that if you save someone you are responsible for them for the rest of their life."

Heart Guard will be seizing every opportunity offered by the national campaign to push on to its next 30,000 trainees. So will the 18 or so similar projects (for instance in Oxford, Wakefield and the City of London) now up and running. The campaign has a national office, but success will depend, as it has in Brighton, on the vigour and dedication of a handful of people, mostly volunteers, who can apply energy and commitment to a cause which could, directly or indirectly, save many lives.

Beating the addiction

JENNY CUFFE

Ex-addicts can offer counselling which really speaks to drug abusers.

There's one kind of person a drug user doesn't meet very often – if at all. That's the user who has beaten his addiction. The government's anti-drug campaign reinforces the image of a no-hoper who'll be hooked for life. The message that's rarely heard is that it is perfectly possible to come off drugs, given the right sort of help. And if that help is offered, not by social workers and drug professionals but by people who've been addicts themselves, it's more likely to be effective.

This is the philosophy of Druglink, a counselling service and referral agency in Hemel Hempstead. Like thousands of other local projects, it's financed by a patchwork of government grants, charities and fund-raising events, and manned mainly by volunteers. But the essence of Druglink is that those volunteers are only one step away from the people they support and, instead of offering a particular method of rehabilitation to all clients, they work out a different scheme suited to the needs of each one. It is this which has singled the project out for praise from one of the country's leading experts in drug addiction, Dr Betty Tylden, a psychiatrist who has researched the problem since it became widespread in the early sixties.

The heart of Druglink is a small white house just off the busy A41 on the edge of the town. The traffic on the main road is nothing to the flow of people through its narrow hallway: volunteer helpers on their way to and from visits to clients, probation officers and the man in charge of it all – Stuart Ware – trying to answer a pressing query before rushing off to an appointment at County Hall. Ware is the Drug Prevention Officer for Hertfordshire County Council. He got Druglink off the ground 18 months ago, and it opened officially last October when Dacorum District Council found the house. Since then it has helped 172 clients (54 on illegal drugs, 48 on tranquillisers, and 70 on alcohol).

Although a professional himself, Stuart Ware is fiercely critical of others in the field. The heroin explosion, he says, has opened up a growing market for careerists, and some of those involved in drug prevention and treatment earn very high salaries. They tend, he says, to have a "case" mentality in their dealings with people, "an open case, close case, them and us approach." "What we're trying to do at Druglink," he explains, "is develop a community where those who are being treated have a feeling they belong. And we encourage those who've tried drugs themselves to turn round and help."

Listening to volunteer Sue Golebiowski talk to a client called Kevin on the phone is like listening to a conversation between close friends. He's been prescribed Librium to help cope with his withdrawal symptoms, and is worried that he'll get hooked on that instead. Sue talked to him for a long time, giving bits of advice between lots of support and encouragement. It's two years since she came off heroin and she says for her it was extremely easy because she knew it was that or "doing the big one" – killing herself. A friend sat with her through three days of acute physical discomfort – sickness, sweating, muscular pains; then she gradually felt herself get better.

Graham Hardinge is Druglink's only full-time field worker. Like Sue, he's a former heroin addict, led to drugs through a sense of despondency about a world he saw as increasingly violent and senseless. He tried several types of treatment, including a spell in psychiatric hospital, before succeeding in coming off drugs completely. That experience makes him sympathetic to clients who try and fail, and he'll continue to support them if they return to drugs. But it's the success stories that give him most satisfaction.

Take Robert, for instance. When he first approached Druglink, he wanted to go it alone, and when Graham visited him the next day he was already into the first stage of withdrawal and feeling very rough. Graham phoned his employers to let them know he'd be off work for a while, and asked his doctor for a medical certificate – saying he had influenza. Later he brought round books and cassettes and kept Robert company through a week of sleeplessness and mental distress till the symptoms eased. When he'd recovered, Robert took a holiday abroad and is now back at work leading a full and happy life without the crutch of heroin.

Addiction to hard drugs isn't the only problem area for the Hemel Hempstead team. They also tackle alcohol abuse and addiction to tranquillisers. The latter is Veronica Wall's field of operation, and I joined her on a visit to Yvonne, a housewife who was first prescribed Valium and anti-depressants 16 years ago after being diagnosed as agoraphobic.

A friend told Yvonne about Druglink when she was on the verge of mental illness. She'd tried to cut her dosage too quickly, and was suffering acute pains, sickness, breathing difficulties and palpitations. Worse still, she was having irrational fears. "I couldn't part with anything – not even rubbish. There was one day I was so bad that when the dustmen called I threw myself at the dustbin like a frenzied woman; I couldn't let them empty it." Veronica was able to offer Yvonne friendship, someone she could share her experiences with. Now she's managed to overcome her fears – she had a grand clear out recently of all the unnecessary possessions she'd gathered around herself – and she's also conquering the agoraphobia.

In Hertfordshire, the problem of drug and alcohol abuse is kept in the public eye by the efforts of the county's Deputy Lieutenant, Elizabeth Cory-Wright. A forceful personality, with connections in the Conservative Party, she uses her manor house near Hitchin as the headquarters of a personal campaign to help drug users. She believes that what they most need is a sense of being valued and loved, and that the support and understanding of relatives can be a major factor in rehabilitation. She has visited 10 Downing Street to urge Mrs Thatcher to put more money into voluntary projects like the one at Hemel Hempstead, and self-help groups for the families of addicts. Overcoming her political allegiances, she accuses the government of being ill-advised in their use of funds. Their publicity campaign is, in her view, more likely to do harm than good – a message reiterated by Graham Hardinge, who thinks it appeals to young people's fantasies of an anti-hero defying parents and teachers and getting his own back on society.

Mrs Cory-Wright also has strong opinions about the medical profession and the role they can play in tackling drug abuse. Doctors are often reluctant to help users because they risk being harassed.

One of the factors behind Druglink's success is the cooperation of local doctors. Stuart Ware has spent hours winning them over to his side, and he now has a list of 50 GPS in the Hemel area to whom he can refer clients. In turn, he can sort out the clients who are likely to misuse their perscriptions from the ones who are genuine.

Another sign of expansion is the local authority's promise of a second house, to be used as a short-stay detoxification unit for up to four people. Stuart Ware welcomes the chance to increase the opportunities for rehabilitation within the community. But he doesn't count withdrawal from drugs as the only mark of success. Even if a user comes off drugs, you can never guarantee it is forever. He feels that Druglink has done its job well every time a user is persuaded to change from hard to soft drugs, or to reduce his drug intake. That's success enough.

Save the workers

JACKIE WILLS

A mobile health and safety service visits small factories and offices in the south of England.

John worked for a small flooring company which subcontracted work from factory and shop refitters, laying tiles and sealing floors. He was given no mask, told nothing about the solvents he used and every night when he went home his breath reeked of chemicals. He became so worried about his health that he quit after six months.

Next year, under the new regulations in amendments to the Health and Safety at Work Act, 1974, John's former boss will be legally obliged to carry out medical checks on his workers and tell them about the effects of the substances they are using. But where will a family firm like this—where a handful of employees work from a front parlour—find the resources to comply with the law?

In the south of England a new health service for companies who cannot afford to run their own in-house medical service was set up in June this year. The Southern Counties Occupational Health Service is the first of its kind in the country and has been established by the University of Surrey Robens Institute of Industrial and Environmental Health.

The service provides companies with "health packages" for their workforce which include blood and urine analysis, eye and hearing tests, stress management lessons, fitness and coronary risk assessments, air sampling and hygiene and safety surveys in the workplace. For female employees the team can also carry out cervical smears, breast examinations and mammographies.

Dr Leslie Hawkins, who heads SCOHS, says that his team has carried out examinations on builders who clear asbestos and work in highly polluted sites. His team has also checked labourers excavating contaminated soil for the Channel Tunnel at Dover.

Occupational health schemes can be adapted to any industry and SCOHS states that the service is also available to voluntary organisations. In offices, the hazards to workers are different—VDUs, stress and the "sick building" syndrome where employees regularly go down with a mystery bug. Eye tests for VDU users and pre-employment medical interviews are also provided for office-based employers.

Long-term monitoring is also critical in order to build up information about the effects of dangerous substances. Thousands of casual workers in the building trade are especially at risk. According to Judy Baker-Rogers, an occupational health nurse on the scheme, "The construction industry gets away with murder."

Baker-Rogers's job not only involves taking biological samples and carrying out lung tests. She also has to sell the service to managements who have perhaps been forced unwillingly to confront the problem of their work-force's well-being by the health and safety executive.

Hawkins claims: "Large commercial organisations which could be employing several thousand people don't have any occupational health service at all, not even a nurse. It is not a priority for spending. Even big organisations, like banks, tend not to want to spend money on staff welfare.

"One of the difficulties is demonstrating its cost benefits. It is like an insurance really, and in the long term it will save them money but you can't put a figure on it."

On the other hand, employees are generally receptive to the service and have often been calling for improvements to their working environments. They do, however, often remain more resistant to changes in working practice. Baker-Rogers says: "We protect the individual all the time. I get them to sign consent forms so that any tests we do can go back to the management, but the forms only get passed on if the employee agrees."

Hawkins intends to build up a database from the work conducted for small and medium-sized companies, to monitor occupational health risks in companies with between 20 and 50 employees. He says: "A large number of small firms do handle all sorts of material that large firms do not. If we can put together a lot of small firms doing the same sort of work, eventually we will be able to build up a database to make some meaningful use of the links between health problems and handling different substances."

But Hawkins already keeps some health statistics on tap: stress, he says, costs industry 3 per cent of gross national product and mental disorders are responsible for the loss of 55 million working days a year, and 15 per cent of sickness absence. Illness loses 360 million working days a year in the UK and can cost companies 10 per cent of their annual wage bill.

Occupational health has not been a top priority in cautious, recession-conscious Britain, which lags well behind Finland, Sweden and Germany. And public bodies are not leading the way—the police, and many ambulance services and fire brigades have no occupational health scheme. Meanwhile, most local authorities have only a nurse and a part-time doctor to cover thousands of employees.

Baker-Rogers believes: "This is how occupational health will go now, groups like us will be taking it out to the country because companies won't be able to afford to employ their own nurse full-time, but can cope with having a contract with us or just use us for statutory medicals."

Moving with the times

SUSANNAH KIRKMAN

A travelling day hospital provides accessible psychogeriatric care for patients in the Portsmouth area.

"It's a day I look forward to," said silver-haired Joan, with a smile. "You meet people and talk about different things, forget your own ailments. It's homely—not like hospital."

Joan has been coming to the psychogeriatric travelling day

hospital for almost a year. As she explained, she has suffered from "terrible periods of depression," since her husband died three years ago. After his death, she gave up their flat and moved into a warden-controlled block where she knew no one. Until then, she had enjoyed her yearly holidays abroad, but she gradually became afraid to leave her flat.

She was admitted to St James's Hospital, Portsmouth, for psychiatric treatment. Six weeks later, she was able to return home but continued to attend the day centre at St James's. Eventually, she was completely discharged. However, Joan soon began to feel depressed and isolated again.

This time, she was referred to the travelling day hospital in Waterlooville, just outside Portsmouth, which caters for depressed and lonely old people. Instead of the hour-long ambulance trip into Portsmouth, Joan now has a short ride in a minibus to Sandringham House, the old people's home which the peripatetic hospital team uses every Thursday.

Cutting transport time is only one of the advantages of the travelling hospital, according to Caroline Austin, the nurse in charge. "Patients are more willing to come here," she said. "If you say the name 'St James's', it puts them off." Although St James's has been modernised inside, it looks forbidding from the outside; the Victorian asylum image is hard to shake off. Many people still feel there's a stigma attached to attending the old hospital.

The travelling hospital, which visits four different centres in the Portsmouth area every week, is welcoming and informal. As the old people arrive at Waterlooville, they're given a cup of tea by Richard, the volunteer worker, who's a redundant polytechnic lecturer. It is christian names all round and Caroline and her assistant, Natalie Haddigan, who's wearing a glamorous tailored suit, are not in starchy uniforms. The large sunny room has plenty of easy chairs which tone with the carpet and curtains.

This morning, a retired policeman is giving a talk on security in the home. John dozes off in a corner, but the other old people listen attentively, chuckling appreciatively at the policeman's jokes. Afterwards, there's a chance for discussion and questions. Caroline encourages some of the quieter patients to have their say. Halfway through Mary's long monologue on her daughter's illness, Caroline gently steers her back to the point.

The relationship between the old people and the staff is warm and relaxed. Joan describes the nurses as "charming" and Natalie admits, "You get very attached to the patients. They're just like friends, really." None of the four groups has more than 15 old people, so it's easy for staff and patients to get to know each other. Attendance is also excellent, and the nurses have a chance to visit reluctant patients on Tuesday and Wednesday afternoons, which are reserved for home visits.

Before lunch, which is prepared and served by local voluntary services, there's a game to help staff and patients to remember each other's names. Everyone sits in a circle and plays catch with a large ball. As they throw the ball, they have to call out the name of the persons it's meant for. There's applause as 89 year old Barbara leans right out of her chair for a difficult catch. Shyly, she confesses that she used to be a champion tennis player, but since she injured her knee, she has found even walking a struggle.

According to Caroline, frustration at failing health and faculties is one of the main causes of depression among her elderly patients. Tom, for instance, a big gentle man, shows a dramatic improvement in the summer when he can get out into his garden. Others, like Fred and Barbara, became withdrawn and isolated after the death of partners or friends. "The more they shut themselves away, the less confident they become; it's a vicious circle," Caroline said. At first, Barbara was very wary of attending the travelling hospital but she enjoys coming now. "It's somewhere to break the monotony," she said. "It helps to get out."

The team, which includes an occupational therapist, two hospital consultants and a clerical assistant, sometimes arranges trips out to bingo and other activities for patients during the rest of the week. "But we try to persuade them to make some arrangements themselves so they don't get totally dependent on us," Caroline added.

The nurses also help by counselling recently bereaved patients in their own homes. If patients are living with relatives, members of the hospital team can visit to give the families support and help them to understand the patients' difficulties.

A particular problem for old people can be the agonising decision to give up their own homes, which have become too large and difficult for them to manage, and here the travelling staff can also help. The team's social worker is to counsel Fred on selling his house. "Patients want you to make the decision for them," Caroline said. "But you have to let them know that they won't be forced into anything, otherwise they lose their trust in you."

The travelling day hospital's very popularity can be a difficulty. Some of the patients grew too attached to it and didn't want to leave. "We've had to 'wean' people who'd been coming here for four years. But what can you move them onto?" Caroline asked. Alternative provision in the area is fairly limited.

Activities at the travelling day hospital are specially designed to prepare the patients to cope with an ordinary social life again. In the afternoons, there are word games and current affairs quizzes to improve their attention and concentration.

While the old people are having a rest, one of the travelling hospital's doctors, Dr Irfan Sheikh, who also has a practice in Waterlooville, calls in to discuss the patients with Caroline and Natalie. Many of the old people have been referred to the travelling hospital by Dr Sheikh. "It's very useful," he said. "A lot of my patients are not that ill, but they're not well enough to be left alone. They need something more than a social services day centre. Because they've come here, patients who would have been in and out of hospital several times have been all right." Dr Sheikh has found that the hospital admission rate for his elderly patients has gone down enormously since the travelling day hospital started in 1982.

Dr Padmini Samaratunga, one of St James's consultants in charge of the travelling hospital, agrees that it has prevented many hospital admissions. "If we can offer them support most people don't need to come into hospital," she said.

Apart from the savings on hospital beds, transport is cheaper too. An ambulance trip from Waterlooville to St James's can cost around £35, while the minibus trip is only about 60p a mile. Follow-up of patients is better because nurses can visit patients and their relatives in their own homes: it's also easier for consultants to meet relatives at the travelling hospital, instead of expecting them to come out to St James's.

Dr Samaratunga is convinced that the travelling day hospital offers patients a better service because it provides specialised care for those with depression. Unlike the St James's day centres, the travelling day hospital has no confused or demented patients. "If you mix a very confused person with a very depressed person, the depressed person will get even more depressed," Dr Samaratunga said.

Taking care of the carers

JOY MELVILLE

A centre in Wallasey provides support, advice and laundry facilities for carers.

"When you come in here, you do have a bit of company," says John Breckell, a spruce 81 year old, who is sitting in the comfortable main room of the Carers Care Centre in Wallasey. "It's saved my life, I can tell you," he insists to Sadie Reynolds, aged 66, another occupant of the room. "I would have cut my throat long before." Sadie looks concerned "Oh, you don't want to do that," she says. "You can always come down to my house and have a chat."

Carers who come to the centre get the chance of meeting others in the same situation, who are sometimes even worse off than they are. "I thought I was badly done to," says Sadie, "but then I heard some of the stories of the others who come here."

At home, carers feel they can't complain, but, says John, "at the centre you feel there is somebody you can moan to. Well, perhaps a bit more than a moan, a jolly good cry at times." Sadie agrees: "It makes you sleep better after, thinking about what people have talked about, holidays and things.

John looked after his wife, who had chronic arthritis, for 15 years on his own before the centre opened last September. "I had never been used to housework, and I got no help from anyone. And because nobody seemed to want to know, you felt as though you were begging for charity if you asked anybody for anything. It was a 22-hour day. But when I came in here they said, 'Come in and have a cup of tea.' And I thought, 'What have I met here?" Sadie, too, recalls getting no sleep, coping at home with a husband who had terminal cancer and was blind.

Apart from giving carers a place to meet each other, as at the coffee mornings, the centre has two functions.

The first is to give out information—particularly on welfare rights like attendance allowances, as staff find many carers are not getting the benefits to which they are entitled. The centre acts as a referral point, telling carers where to go for help and, if necessary, assisting them in filling out forms and so on.

Also on the information side, a series of weekend talks has just been started on subjects related to caring—like stress, lifting, incontinence—in conjunction with the social services. There is, too, a small selection of aids for the disabled on show.

Secondly, trained staff will do the carers' laundry in a launderette specifically designed to cope with incontinents' linen. "I had to do terrible laundry and I couldn't do it," says Sadie. "It really pulled me down. This place has been a lifeline to me." Because of the strain, carers can be in a worse state of health than the cared-for.

The idea for such a centre originally came from the general secretary of the Wallasey Council for Voluntary Services, Irene Rayner, who considered not enough was being done for the carers. In 1984 the WCVS successfully applied for a grant of £35,000, which allowed them to buy and refurbish premises for the centre. It then sponsored a Community Programme scheme which pays for staff salaries and certain stipulated costs. This runs out at the end of July, though an extension has been applied for.

The centre is the only project of its kind at the moment, but other care programmes are considering similar centres based on the Wallasey model. It is run by two full-time staff—Ted Collier and Val Higginson—and twelve part-timers and is open every day, including Sundays since laundry needs don't stop at the weekend.

"This laundry is very important," says Ted Collier. "If carers do it at home, apart from the work, there's the question of hygiene. Their machines aren't capable of the high temperatures necessary with incontinence. They come in here with their black bags full, though more and more are asking us to collect and deliver." The normal charge is 75p for a washload—which includes drying, collection and delivery in the Wallasey area (transport otherwise is 25p extra). Charges can be waived or reduced if a person cannot afford it.

To ensure that the service is not misused by people who don't really need it, carers must be referred by a professional, like a GP or home help. "We also have referrals from health visitors about elderly and infirm people who are living alone and not able to do their own laundry," says Ted Collier. "We call them lone carers. At the moment, we have one aged 94. We also have a 96 year old looking after a 94 year old. Our oldest 'cared-for' person is 101."

Coming in to ask about the laundry is sometimes a cover for other problems, and only if the person feels confident will he or she reveal the true issue. "We say, 'Come and have a cup of tea,' and eventually they tell us what they have really come in for," says Val Higginson.

"One man told us he was caring for a friend and only later admitted that it was his wife. Another man, whose wife had had a stroke, came to us about the laundry and we found out he was absolutely petrified. He had no home help and it turned out he couldn't cook. We helped him shop and buy some boil-in-the-bag meals to start with."

"Everyone has a different problem. When one woman first came in she did not even know what a commode was and was using a bucket. Faeces were on the carpet, everywhere."

"We don't take over. We don't say, 'I will do it for you.' We like carers to try for themselves. They are quite happy to have a go when you tell them who to contact. Of course, if someone is distraught, and quite a few are, then we will do the necessary contacting."

Even though the centre is to help carers, sometimes those they are caring for come to the centre too. I watched while Elaine, a middle-aged woman confined to a wheelchair after an accident, was helped in over the doorstep. As her husband works every day, she gets lonely and she is finding it hard to come to terms with being disabled. "I hate to be dependent on people," she says. "I did not know I could get an orthopaedic chair till I came here; and I am having a stair rail put up. We didn't know anything of this. My husband would still be lifting me in to have a shower. I can be independent in the bath now. And you know if you have a worry the staff will listen."

Carers often continue to come in even when the person they have cared for has died. "You still have problems of your own," says Sadie, whose husband died recently. "The terms of my husband's will nearly broke my heart and the centre is helping me to battle on. I've got no family to help me as I lost my only son and you can't ask neighbours." A bereaved carer is often devastatingly lonely, the death making an extra big gap in their life.

The centre has helped 180 carers since last September, and many others come in briefly. "You go to other places for help and they treat you like a piece of cardboard," said one. "Here it's unbelievable—they actually listen to you."

Education

Children who tell tales

SUSANNAH KIRKMAN

A scheme in Dorset involves children and parents in introducing pre-school children to books and school.

Every Monday lunchtime, a procession of some 25 mothers with their toddlers streams into St Leonard's School in Blandford, Dorset. They are part of a storybook project—each mother helps a nine or ten year old pupil to write a book designed for her own pre-school child.

The project, part of a national writing scheme funded by the Schools' Curriculum Development Council, aims to encourage parents to participate in their children's education, and to build better community links.

The parents and toddlers have lunch with pupils in the school canteen and, after lunch, the parents and pupils settle down to work—the adults contorted over the child-sized desks. Meanwhile, the toddlers and their baby brothers and sisters are cared for next door by a group of twelve and 13 year olds.

Some of the toddlers are also in the room with their mothers to offer advice. Three year old Frances likes worms and snails, so Peggy, aged ten, is writing a story about garden insects and Frances is cutting out some pink worms which will slide between the pages.

Jo Grant, who is helping two girls to write a book about magic for her four year old daughter, now feels happier about the child starting school. "It's taken on a completely different meaning for her; she finds it thrilling coming to the big boys' and girls' school."

Debby Morgan, a young mother with four children under six, believes that the project also gives parents more confidence to help their own children with school work. "It's nice to get down and do some work with a positive results at the end of it," she says. "It is easy to forget that there is anything beyond your home and children."

Parents also appreciate the benefits for the children who

write the books. As Debby claims: "Instead of striving to gain the attention of the teacher, they have the undivided attention of one adult." Parents build up a close relationship with the pupils they're working with, occasionally meeting outside school to discuss their book.

Simon Adorian, a teacher at St Leonard's who started up the project last year, believes that "parents should be involved with children's learning, not just making coffee and being deferential. The project has included parents who are not specially confident or literate, and some of the parents who have offered most to the children haven't been competent writers themselves."

The recruitment system is partly responsible for the wide range of participants; Adorian advertises the scheme through local play-groups. The response has been enthusiastic, partly in response to a dearth of state-run nurseries in the area, and also because of parents' concern to get their young children off to a good start.

Eight parents were on the planning committee which set up the project, and, after an initial explanatory session, the scheme is completely in the hands of the parents and pupils, with Adorian remaining in the background making occasional cups of coffee. The books, which are written over ten weeks, represent a term's work in English for the children.

According to Adorian: "If you hand over the responsibility to children and parents, you will always be surprised at how much they can achieve. Mr Baker's benchmarks don't come into it, and teachers are not necessarily the fount of all wisdom. There are other strategies which parents know and can pass on to children."

He believes the insight and motivation that pupils gain through writing for an audience are more important than the end product— but many of last year's books are actually very lively, colourful and imaginatively designed.

Also, the project represents a constructive way of giving power to parents. "We hear so much about negative parental involvement these days—vetoing sex education, removing a school from ILEA control—but we want to use parents in a positive way, as partners in their children's learning."

Learning in style

ADRIANA CAUDREY

A Jacobean mansion provides a culture lesson for West Bromwich schoolchildren.

"We're in a heritage capsule," declares Kevin Callan, dramatically. The principal of Ingestre Hall Arts Centre, near Stafford, is addressing spellbound fourth and fifth formers from Hill Top High School in West Bromwich. For the past week these 40 inner-city schoolchildren have been living in the rose-brick Jacobean mansion—seat of the Earls of Shrewsbury and for a short time the Glyndebourne of the midlands—while intensively studying art, drama or music.

Are they overawed by the rarified setting and the emphasis on art? On the last day of the week-long course 14 art students—or "artists" as Callan calls them—give the principal their reactions. "I feel really at home here," says Lisa. "Everywhere you look there's art all around you," says Sarah, full of appreciation. Another girl observes that everyone has quietened down: "Maybe because the place so old everyone respects it."

These responses tell Callan that once again the Ingestre experiment has worked. Each year, 2,500 pupils from schools within the Sandwell metropolitan area spend a week at the hall and depart changed by the experience. Originally Callan had wondered: "how does a child who says 'we am' and lives in darkest West Bromwich respond to this place?" "They respond to it intuitively," he now says.

For one week the teenagers live an all-pervading aesthetic experience. They rehearse their plays in an elegant wood-panelled library. They relax in a drawing-room packed with ancestral portraits and stone busts. They sleep in grand dormitories and congregate in a great hall with minstrel galleries and plush furniture. They are treated informally by their tutors and are encouraged—perhaps for the first time—to be creative.

The arts centre really began in 1961 when the impoverished 21st Earl of Shrewsbury decided to sell his ancestral home—having tried, briefly, to turn it into a second Glyndebourne. West Bromwich Council—now Sandwell metropolitan authority—bought the house for £10,000 for use as an arts centre. Some felt it should be used for advanced students, but radical educationalists decided it should be for children from the Black Country.

The centre was launched in 1962, and Callan became principal three years later. Many of the schoolchildren currently on his arts courses have parents who were also his pupils. Also, many of the youngsters who played music for first time here, have returned year after year—through their twenties—to take part in music, art and drama weekends.

Youngsters from schools, further education colleges and sixth form colleges throughout the five towns served by Sandwell come to Ingestre. They pay £2.75 a day for board and tuition and £1.90 for the coach trip. Sandwell does, however, provide extra subsidies for those who cannot afford the fees. Young people at higher education colleges also come to the hall for arts courses. Those earning wages pay £11.45 a day.

The youngsters at Ingestre can choose to do either music, drama or art. In all these disciplines the emphasis is on producing something from scratch. The youngsters never work from prepared material—whether a text, tune or composition. Instead, they are encouraged to use their originality and to bounce ideas off each other. There are three resident tutors—one for each discipline. And the pupils are usually accompanied by two of their own teachers, who have a pastoral role.

Sue Reynolds, the art tutor with paint still on her hands, says: "Here you don't have to be a teacher with a 'capital T,' although there are times when you have to show them you can be." She points out: "There is pressure on time. You've got to achieve an end product and let them all find their own level." This week's art group have been painting faces, with a food theme.

Diane Cantillon, the drama tutor, says: "At the beginning the youngsters are very hesitant about putting forward any of their ideas, then they start to pick up on each other's ideas." Dressed in a suitably dramatic calf-length blue cardigan, black skirt and pink gym shoes, she crouches over the lighting controls behind the wood panelling in the library, while the six drama students rehearse their production.

Then Diane gives them their final instructions: "Remember—concentration and communication." The drama is all their own work. Using their imagination and improvising together they came up with a plot and themes. The starting point was a set of paper masks which they made on their first day. These later formed the basis for mythical figures and forces.

On the last day they put on the play for their peers and tutors. Everyone watches quietly, refraining from giggling out loud even when one boy tries indiscreetly to do up his flies on stage or when another shakes with suppressed mirth behind his mask. Afterwards, while the actors are still on stage, Callan pronounces to the audience on what they have achieved.

He also asks the actors to tell everyone what they feel about the performance and about the audience response. Clearly, he sees the displays of music, drama and art as parts of a greater work of art which is being created every minute that the youngsters spend at Ingestre. He himself acts as a master of ceremonies, infusing even the mundane with drama and excitement: "I am an environment creator," he tells them, "as all good teachers should be."

Also on the last day there is an exhibition of the art group's "faces" designed with food. The 13 girls and one boy stand self-consciously in front of their portraits, some ingeniously decorated with polystyrene spring onions or shiny red paper grapes. They all admit they were stumped when they were first set the topic. "I was stuck for vegetables," says Sarah: "I needed something that would stick out. Then I thought of polystyrene."

Tony Biggin, the music tutor, has possibly the hardest job, teaching youngsters both to compose and to play music. For a while they are unable to do anything but play familiar tunes. Many are also playing on keyboards for the first time." Yet by the final performance they were pounding away on the keyboards and drums to their own compositions.

Carl, one of the musicians, said: "Before I came here I hadn't played that much music. I'd never touched a keyboard. It wasn't what I thought it would be like here. I couldn't sleep the first night. All the Hill Top pupils were affected by their time at Ingestre. Some remarked that it was particularly nice to be treated as adults.

Roz Mace, one of the two Hill Top techers who accompanied the youngsters, said: "They were struck dumb from the moment the coach came round the corner. It's quietened them down a bit and they've all learned something this week." Roz played a pastoral role. "If there were any problems, I know their backgrounds and could sort them out."

By the end of the week she reckoned: "A lot of them have gained in confidence. In the classroom at school, they're told to turn to page 15 . . . here they're encouraged to work on their own." So is the week at Ingestre a rarified, never-to-be-repeated experience? Is it a glimpse of an inaccessible world of grace and creativity, where adults treat teenagers with respect and courtesy?

Even as such it would be an experience to stay with successive generations of West Bromwich teenagers for the rest of their lives. Better still it could be followed up in their own schools. Roz, for one, plans to keep the spirit of Ingestre alive with her English set.

The vanguard of learning

SUSANNAH KIRKMAN

A play and learn van in Dorest helps alleviate the isolation of children in rural areas.

To a visitor, rural Dorset seems idyllic with its thatched cottages, stone farm buildings clustered on hilltops, and miles of empty countryside dotted with picturesque hamlets. But for the mothers and pre-school children who live there, the idyll can be tarnished by loneliness and isolation. The play and learn van run by DARSET the Dorchester Area Rural Schools Education Team, aims to alleviate some of the harsh effects of rural deprivation.

Education advisors in Dorset have been concerned about under-achievement by country children ever since a survey revealed that children starting at village primary schools were lagging behind pupils of the same age in the towns. The survey was carried out ten years ago, but the local education authority did not have the resources to help rural families until it received an education support grant from the Department of Education and Science in 1985 to improve provision in country areas.

The play and learn van has now been on the road for 18 months. Covered in a vivid rainbow mural painted by children at a village primary school, the van is visible for miles as it winds along country roads and muddy tracks to reach outlying farmsteads and remote hamlets. It is crammed full of games and toys designed to teach and stimulate under-fives.

Sue Harrison, the pre-school teacher who also drives the van, has made many of the games herself. She uses the DARSET office facilities but she is the only pre-school teacher and has no other helpers, as the DARSET project concentrates on curriculum in village schools. However, Sue is very appreciative of the support she has received from Dorset's primary advisor, Joan Hickmott. "I don't think I've ever felt so valued or encouraged in what I do," Sue said.

The first call of the day is on two year old Vicky and her mother, who live on a farm outside Dorchester. Sue shows Vicky how to do a jigsaw.

Vicky's mother values Sue's fortnightly visits very much. "We're fairly cut off. I don't have time to have other children up here and Vicky spends a lot of time on her own. She gets very excited if I say Sue is coming." Vicky's grasp of colours and numbers has improved and she is more talkative since Sue came.

Delayed language development is typical of rural children, according to Sue Harrison. "There's a lack of stimulus—no popping to the shops like town families," she says. Such children can also be shy and withdrawn. On a busy farm, they may be left to themselves and have very little contact with adults. Not all country families can afford their own transport, so some children may never be able to attend a playgroup.

Mothers may be lonely, too, and welcome the chance to discuss their children's progress. "In that situation, I'm a friend. They need someone to talk to and I can give them some support," Sue says. She includes parents as much as possible, explaining the learning concepts she is trying to develop and leaving games behind for mothers to play with their children. Sue plans an individual development programme for each of the 20 children she visits, which she carries out with the help of the parents.

Parents are given "link charts" where they can fill in the games and toys they've borrowed and add their comments. Sue passes the charts on to the reception teachers so they they get an idea of each child's development.

The education authority believes that parents who play an active part in their children's education before they start school are more likely to stay involved. Dorset primary schools encourage parents to help with school activities and to hear their children read. There's also a chance for parents to bring their under-fives into school for an afternoon's games or reading.

It's now mid-morning and time to park the van outside Charminster First School, so that mothers can return the toys they have borrowed. Two year old Roberta bounces on and starts doing up the zips and buttons on the gaudy cloth clown at the end of the van, which is designed to teach children how to cope with fastenings.

The mother of four year old Matthew wants a game with colours. "He's still not very good at recognising colours. I think he might be colour blind." The van is much more than a toy library; Sue tries to build up a relationship with mothers so that they can discuss problems and ask her for advice.

Over a cup of coffee in the school staff room, Sue hears of a little boy from a travelling family who is finding it difficult to adjust to school. She agrees to get in touch with the health visitor and see if there are any younger children in his family who might benefit from regular visits. The primary teachers feel that children who have received home visits from Sue are much better prepared to start school.

The play and learn van has improved links between village schools and the social and health services. DARSET ran an open day last year where Sue explained the work of the van to local GPs, health visitors, social workers and educational psychologists. Some of the families chosen for home visits have been referred by health visitors, although others refer themselves.

Country families have their share of problems, like unemployment, ill-health and homelessness. The play and learn van calls regularly at Greenfields, a bleak collection of old army nissen huts which now serves as accommodation for the homeless. The low-income, mostly single-parent families, are very cut off; there is little opportunity for the children to go to playgroups as their parents have no transport.

Before lunch, Sue parks the van outside the Milton Abbas playgroup, which is held in one room of the ancient almshouses. Milton Abbas is a model village, 18th century style, with rows of whitewashed thatched cottages either side of a wide village street and an air of competing for the best-kept village award. But there are only two buses a week and few facilities for young families.

Three year old Ben swaggers in on a red batman cloak. His mother says the van is teaching him that toys should be shared. Nicola, aged three, is already looking out for the van when Sue drives up to her home that afternoon. Nicola's father is disabled and before the family got a car, her mother, Frances, had to walk two miles to the nearest shop. There are no other children of Nicola's age in the tiny hamlet of Alton Pancras. "She enjoys somebody different coming in. She tells everyone about the play and learn lady—Sue's famous around here," says Frances.

Frances is proud of her daughter's achievements: Nicola can already count to ten and pick out colours and shapes. "Sue helps you to realise how much they can learn."

Some 350 families use the play and learn van and the demand is growing. The Dorset local education authority is now planning to expand the scheme, using outreach workers provided by a MSC community programme. Workers will make games and activities, help with record keeping and work with the young families themselves.

The Education Support Grant which funds the DARSET project has just been extended to five years, by which time the county hopes to pick up the cost. Dorset's education advisers are convinced that the play and learn van is the panacea for the isolation of rural families.

Singing for harmony

CAROLINE ST JOHN-BROOKS

A theatre project in Manchester involving schoolchildren broadens their horizons and gives them a new perspective.

Schoolchildren in Manchester have successfully written and performed their own musical.

I get weary
And sick of trying
I'm tired of living
But scared of dying
But Ol' Man River
He keeps on rolling
He just keeps rolling
Along.

The atmosphere in Ducie Lower School hall is hushed for a few minutes. The black schoolboy on the stage sways as he croons into a microphone that song of the resignation and dispossession of black America. The young black British dispossessed of the 1980s, in their anoraks and worn trainers, stop scuffling and elbowing each other, and listen. "You certainly had your audience in the palm of your hand," I say to the singer, David Rowe, afterwards. "Oh, I had them on their *knees*," he replies.

We're in Manchester, watching *Struggle for Freedom,* the fruits of a five-month project for the alienated children of the inner city. A hundred or so pupils from three secondary schools—two boys' schools with a large number of pupils of Asian and Afro-Caribbean origin, and a Catholic secondary school where 98 per cent of the pupils are second-generation Irish—have been brought together to research, write, design and act in a musical based on the life of a local black hero: Len Johnson.

Manchester is a city of racial tensions. At one of the schools involved, Burnage, an Asian teenager was stabbed to death in the playground last year, by a white schoolmate who was subsequently convicted of murder. And it is in Manchester that Viraj Mendis, a Tamil sympathiser, has taken refuge in a church in order to avoid deportation to Sri Lanka.

Len Johnson, born in Moss Side at the turn of the century, was regarded as the greatest middleweight boxer of his generation, but was never allowed a title fight because of his colour. He retired penniless, and spent the rest of his life fighting not in the ring but for the rights of the poor blacks and whites of

Manchester. He married an Irish girl, to the great disapproval of her family.

All this is very much alive to the 15 year olds involved in the play. A handful of young mothers are gathered at the back of the hall, black and white together. One has a toddler asleep in a pushchair. The school dinner ladies tap their feet to the reggae beat of another song, this time written by the cast.

Annie and Len were getting married
But the parents didn't agree
They only wanted to be together
And raise a family
He begged her mother
He begged her father
Let Annie marry me!
Her father said
Is this your lover?
It cannot be!
Chorus
They say no! no! no! no!
Her family wouldn't set her free
The people wouldn't let her be
Just let her be
Just let her be
Len Johnson was her man to be.

The musical has been put together, with the help of £3,000 from Manchester city council, by Frontline, a professional theatre group working in the field of culture and education in Manchester. Springing as it does from the life of working class Mancunians, it has been a big success, with more than a dozen performances all over the city.

The cast researched the history themselves with help from Frontline, interviewing local people and tracing the historical background. Then the young people acted out the 15 scenes in their own words. These were tape-recorded, and then members of Frontline developed a script using the recordings as a basis.

What difference has this cooperation made to relationships among the three schools? "Before the project," says one member of the cast after the performance. "Everyone just thought about fighting if we saw someone from another school. But now it's quietened down a lot." "When we joined together," says another, "we forgot we were from different schools after a bit. Because we had to rely on people, so we had to get on." "Though tempers did fray a bit sometimes," says a realist.

Over the last month, most of the participants have been working from nine in the morning until eight at night. And these, after all, are mostly unenthusiastic school pupils. Some are persistent truants. But they have responded to this "alternative curriculum," and their achievement will go down on their record and count towards any qualifications.

"It makes you feel different," says Lawrence Garry, the boy who plays Len Johnson. "The character you play comes into it; the character rubs off onto you. My election speech—it gives me the courage now to stand up and speak in front of people."

"You could say before that we never knew what any of these things were—communism, socialism. I'd never heard of that Spanish civil war," says one boy. "In a way we've been learning history, English, all sorts. Like, I never knew about Mosley and his blackshirts before."

It has also impressed them that the events they have been acting out really took place. "An old woman came up to me after one performance and said that she shook Paul Robeson's hand," says David Rowe, who played Robeson. The American singer visited Len Johnson in Manchester to support his campaign against the colour bar.

Another woman told the cast that her Jamaican father and Jewish mother had had to overcome a great deal of prejudice in order to get married, just like Johnson and his wife, Annie.

Part of the research process involved interviewing Wilf Charles and Sid Booth, Manchester men now in their eighties, who went to Spain with the international brigade. Then Charles and Booth came and watched a performance.

"It's very exciting for the kids," says Dan Baron Cohen, one of the Frontline workers who initiated the project. "All this oral history means that the people taking part in the project have really become aware of Manchester's past during this century. They've met trade unionists who've lived through the general strike, and they've been talking about the lives of the people they have met. What they've really been doing is struggling to construct their *own* freedom.

"Do you realise that after they'd written the script, they learned the whole thing in between twelve and 15 days? The meaning was all there already; the only work that needed to be done was memorising. I think that this five months has massively affected them—they tend to reason far more than they did."

Chris Glyn is a Manchester drama advisor, who has encouraged the project from the start. "What drama does," he says, "is to give youngsters a chance to succeed, which doesn't always happen in the traditional curriculum. What we wanted to do was offer them a worthwhile experience, which they would remember for ever. And I think they will. I don't think that this time last year any of them thought that they would ever be performing in front of an audience in Manchester Town Hall."

And what was the final verdict? "If you could get more things like this in school, it would be a lot better," says Lawrence Donnelly. "In a way, we're creating history. And we want it to happen again." And what effect has the play had on them? What do they think they would be like today if they hadn't taken part in it? "We'd be a bunch of yobboes," says one of them, laughing sheepishly.

It's never too late

CAROLINE ST JOHN-BROOKS

Burleigh College in Leicestershire aims to provide a community curriculum for all ages—from nought to 90.

Tricia Blossom never did much art when she was at school. "The education I had was absolutely useless," she says. "And when I first went to evening classes, I didn't know anything. I thought you could just flick a brush and get a picture. Huh!" She carefully lays another brushful of paint on the sky of her landscape.

Tricia is painting in a bright and busy school art-room, surrounded by teenage pupils. She is one of half a dozen adults in the class; the youngest is in her twenties, the eldest is retired. They're all part of a "comeback" scheme at Burleigh Community College, in Loughborough. Adults return to learn alongside sixth formers, at a cost of only £5 a year.

Tricia, just turned 40, is taking A level art. "I was a bit apprehensive about mixing with the kids at first," she says, "but it's worked out really well. You don't feel you're this old person sitting there." Marie Jessop, the art teacher, is sure that the school students (as they are always called at Burleigh) benefit too. "They're very used to having adults around, and it helps them to see that education doesn't stop when you leave school."

A living example of this philosophy is Alka Mandalia, who sits opposite Tricia, working on a picture. She was at school at Burleigh herself. "When I was here, I always knew I could come back again. I've got two little girls now, and I work in a chemist's shop, but really I want to go to art college. If I get a good enough A level, I want to apply to Leicester poly. When I was doing my exams before, I had problems at home, and then I got married. I was still coming to school after I was married. And then I went abroad, and then I got pregnant . . . But now, my mother looks after my children, and I get a day off from the shop on Thursdays, so I do this in the morning, and textiles in the afternoon."

Leicestershire has a strong tradition of community colleges: there are 35 in all. But since the new principal, Keith Foreman, came to Burleigh last September, there has been a basic rethink as to how a big college, with 1,500 pupils aged between 14 and 18, can give the local community what it wants and needs.

The idea of a community college is that it should be open to anyone, of any age, who wants to use it. "I like to think of it as a petrol station," says Trevor Riddiough, vice-principal, and in charge of the community education programme. "People can drive in and top up whenever they like."

Riddiough is working out a host of ways to attract people back into education. "How well known we are in the community is unclear," says Keith Foreman, "so we're surveying the local area, asking what people know about Burleigh, and what they need, and we've sent out 7,000 leaflets. If people don't know what to do and where to come, they won't come."

The "community" which Burleigh serves is mixed and divided, ranging from the very middle class university area to the rundown Ashby Road council estates. And one problem, as always, is to encourage people who have no family tradition of education, and negative feelings towards school, to use the college as a resource.

One method is "outreach." Burleigh has an outreach worker, paid by the local education authority, working on one of the Ashby estates, where there is a large number of young families. A father unemployed and mother depressed is an all too common picture. Burleigh's outreach worker is based in the "Hermitage Road hut" on the estate. Because young mothers are very reluctant actually to come into college, they do classes in the hut: keep fit, karate and women's health.

The hut has become a centre of activity. A community newspaper—written by people on the estate but using the college's equipment—is based there, and so is a parent and toddler group. The women have set up a community childwatch scheme. Volunteers keep an eye on the children as they play on the greens or in the streets, and in every street there is a "childwatch" house. Children know they can go to it if they are lost or upset, or approached by a stranger.

Trevor Riddiough aims to develop community education at Burleigh on four fronts at once: there is the outreach work on the estates; then there is the enormous programme of classes, from toddlers' swimming to psychology O-level to bricklaying and hairdressing, which 650 people attend every week; then there are the formal youth clubs and informal "drop-in" clubs for young people. The college is open from 8.00 in the morning until 10.00 at night, but the "twilight zone," from 4.00 to 6.00, is especially for teenagers. They can get advice or counselling, as well as go to classes designed for them, such as computing, or "be your own DJ."

Then there are the 102 local clubs and organisations who meet at the college and use its facilities. The number has more than doubled over the last year, as a result of the new initiatives. They include sports' clubs, tenants' associations, pensioners' groups, brownies, boys' brigade, hobbies such as stock car racing and religious groups such as the Shree Ram Krishna Centre.

This year, the college has a writer in residence. Rib Davis writes documentary dramas based on people's experience. He and a group of Burleigh students are interviewing local people about their lives. "Really, it's about life between the first world war and 1939," he says, "and it's important to get it onto tape now, because some of those people aren't going to be around much longer."

Take Mrs Bookes, for example. Her reminiscences take us into another world. "I was the thirteenth," she says. "There was two more after me, but they didn't all live. A bit crowded in the house, but it was three storeys. At school, the prize I got was for darning. We had to refoot stockings. We all had stockings, boys and girls as well, woollen ones. My mother used to refoot them when the darns got too much, I never knew how she did it. I watched her, and she cuts them out, cut the heel, then cut up a bit there, then come round that way. Then she'd get a sole part off another part of stocking and then that would be stitched on, so you'd got a respectable pair of stockings."

It will take Rib a month to write the script and the songs, then in the autumn a show will be put on in Loughborough's theatre, involving 70 or so people of all ages as actors, musicians, puppeteers and dancers.

Some of the teenagers who have been doing the interviews with Rib are using the project as part of their coursework for geography—an important aspect of community education which Trevor Riddiough wants to build up. "I want a real community curriculum for everyone from nought to 90," he says.

But what is a community curriculum? "The idea is that contact with the local community pervades the whole college and what people learn," he says. "It's not bolted on at the side in special projects, but it's more like a transparent sheet laid over the whole timetable." One example is of a CPVE (Certificate of Pre-vocational Education) course being taken by four sixth formers. Motorists and lorry drivers are using a road on a local estate as a short cut between the motorway and the centre of Loughborough. Three children have been badly hurt in traffic accidents, and one was killed. The four sixth formers have been asked by local parents to research the problem, and prepare a report for them to send to the borough surveyor.

"This will be part of their coursework," says Trevor Riddiough. "They'll get a reaction from the tenants, and a reaction from the borough surveyor too, and they're playing a real part in solving a real problem. That's what community education is all about."

Learning to share

ADRIANA CAUDREY

In a community education centre in Nottinghamshire, mentally handicapped people mix with secondary school pupils.

It's near the end of the school day. In the youth centre, behind closed curtains, dozens of mentally handicapped people, of ageless appearance, are clapping their hands and bending their knees, as the inane pop song tells them to. The Down's syndrome pairs are the most fluent dancers, but even the wheelchair-bound rotate slowly on the dance floor.

This is the lastest influx of "students" to the Dukeries Complex, in the mining village of Ollerton, Nottinghamshire—probably the most advanced community education college to have developed out of an ordinary secondary school. It is the only centre in the country where mentally handicapped people are catered for within school grounds, and can mix with pupils.

A blend of expediency and idealism lies behind the creation of the campus, which opened officially just over a year ago. The Dukeries comprehensive had been wasting £80,000 a year on classrooms that had been emptied because of falling pupil rolls. So Nottinghamshire County Council and Roy Sowden, the school principal, decided to recycle the space for other community purposes. Now, the "school" also houses a day centre for the elderly, a creche for under-fives, a youth centre, library, concert hall and theatre. It would have cost £1 million to build all this from scratch, whereas the conversion cost only £350,000.

At a recent debate on community education, held in the House of Lords, the Dukeries was held up as a model of the community education movement, whose aims are to break down the insularity of schools, foster lifelong learning and "raise the school leaving age to 90."

Like other community education centres, the Dukeries tries not to compartmentalise people, but to mix them—even to use them to help teach each other. But nowhere else had ventured to include the mentally handicapped in this human jigsaw, until just eight months ago, the Whitewater day unit—a huge bungalow which cost social services £650,000 to build and furnish—was opened on the campus. Eventually it will take 125 "students." For now, it looks after 80 men and women, aged between 16 and 55, most of whom live with their parents in and around Ollerton.

Although Whitewater is essentially autonomous, its students use the college facilities, including the theatre, swimming pool and mini-farm. Roy Sowden explained: "These people are no different from the children who come to us, the elderly people, or the other adults. They all have the same right of access to facilities, which should help them to reach greater confidence and independence." But when it was first proposed that Whitewater should be placed beside the school, it created quite a controversy. Sowden says that some officers within social services were worried about dispensing with the "discreet isolation" that normally surrounds such places.

Some parents of the mentally handicapped feared that their offspring might be taunted or teased, while parents of pupils at the school were worried for their children's safety. With help from Mencap, Sowden ran a short training course to prepare the schoolchildren for their mentally handicapped "neighbours." To begin with, children couldn't help staring at the handicapped students, but now they seem to accept them.

During lunch at Whitewater, a couple of schoolgirls walk quite unselfconsciously through the dining-room with one of the handicapped students, on their way to play dominoes or darts together. One of the spin-offs from allowing ordinary schoolchildren to mix with the mentally handicapped is that social barriers are nipped in the bud. Not only are the schoolchildren more relaxed with those whom society prefers to exclude, but the mentally handicapped themselves are given more of a chance to fit in with the rest of society.

The Dukeries runs on a network of symbiotic relationships. Although Nottinghamshire education, social services and leisure departments contribute to different parts of the campus, they all share facilities with each other. The managers, who run the individual units, regularly consult with each other and the students swap skills. Just as the schoolchildren have lunch duties at Whitewater, the mentally handicapped help out in the creche.

On a typical afternoon, a few children from the comprehensive are milling about in the noticeably disinfected entranceway of Whitewater. Many of them use the computer room and hairdressing facilities. All the training rooms are enormous, with long windows onto the fields. Coming from two of the rooms are the sounds of "All things bright and beautiful" and "These are a few of my favourite things," and the walls of these rooms are covered with primary school type collages and brass rubbings. Three middle aged "students" sit in one of the rooms planning their imminent holiday. "Are you going to have a bath before you go?" asks the instructor. "Yes," says one woman monosyllabically.

Nearby, other students are using the training flat, which has a bedroom, bathroom and two kitchens, where they can practice housekeeping skills. They're taught to budget for a meal, cook it and wash up afterwards. There's a Hoover for them to use and a bed to make. Often they're encouraged to simulate family life and just flop down in front of the television. The only thing they can't do is sleep in the bed. Today, one tiny, silent young woman is learning to rub butter and flour together to make scones. She doesn't change her expression as a motherly instructor encourages her with: "that's it, duck," but her fingers move more confidently.

In the adjacent kitchen two young men are making themselves a cup of tea. They are among the least handicapped students. Sarah Crookes, Whitewater's deputy manager, says: "We tend not to use the word 'independent' because the parents find it threatening. It means different things to different people. To one person it might mean being able to lift the fork to their mouth, to another it might mean being able to live alone." A few of the students, it is hoped, might eventually be able to live together in a threesome, or foursome, in sheltered housing, and as a team reach the self-sufficiency of one "normal" person.

But even for those who will never be able to live independently, Whatewater helps to integrate them into the community in many ways. For example, they are frequently taken out on shopping trips, so that the locals get to know them. A group of them are taking part in the Best Kept Village competition, organised by the parish council. And Whitewater has set up a scheme whereby local clubs and organisations can take on one or two students as members.

The students are also taught to handle their own finances. They frequently get a visit from a representative of the Trustee Savings Bank and one room is temporarily turned into a bank.

Many of them are even developing skills that their instructors don't have. For example, one of them has learned to milk a cow. Others have been learning to paddle a canoe in the calm waters of the campus swimming pool. One day, say the unit's instructors, maybe they will be able to paddle their canoes on the open sea.

Challenge to learn

ALISON WERTHEIMER

A network of teachers and pupils offers informal learning in people's homes.

Kay is a member of a group which meets at Julie's house, where Dave teaches them to meditate. As part of the same scheme Dave's wife, Eve, has been learning to play the piano. Meanwhile Kay has been teaching Dave how to cope with soil problems in his garden. Kay, Eve and Dave are all members of the Haringey-based Learning Network.

The project is one of a small but growing number of schemes in this country offering "deinstitutionalised" learning along the lines described by Ivan Illich in *Deschooling Society*. It is an approach which challenges many current educational practices; its advocates believe that learning can take place anywhere, not just in specially designated places like schools or colleges, and that almost everyone has got something they can teach other people; you don't have to leave it to people who are qualified teachers. As one member of the network puts it "It's about passing on to each other what you know . . ."

The Learning Network was set up in 1984 by Christopher Rourke who came to it via sociology, craft bookbinding and redundancy. Deciding, as he says, that it was "an idea whose time had come" he sold the scheme to the local adult education department who gave him the first base. This meant operating within the system it was challenging, offering a term-time only service from the base of an adult education centre.

But last year the scheme was re-launched in NHS premises and funded through the MSC Community Programme. The staff of five can offer a full all-round-the-year service now and the initial catchment area of Haringey has extended to Islington and Waltham Forest. Later this year they will be moving into Barnet and Camden too. Over 250 subjects are now on offer including Czech, carpet laying, reflexology and rock group management.

With this range of subjects it is usually possible to offer someone the names of one or more people willing to teach them—although it did take a year to find a teacher of Bulgarian.

Different teachers can also offer learning at different levels of ability. Scott, for example, has been learning to read music for his guitar with Wilhelm. Having learnt the rudiments of guitar-playing he's now ready to move on to a guitar-teacher as Wilhelm teaches people to read music but isn't really a guitar teacher.

About 750 people are currently members of the network, about two thirds of them as learners and the rest teaching. But many of the teachers are also learning, breaking down the barriers of "teacher" and "pupil." Wilhelm, for example, teaches reading music, piano and Portuguese but also manages to find time to learn modern Greek from another member.

Although no systematic study of the members has been carried out, the staff do know a bit about them. A high proportion are from ethnic minority groups, representing about 80 per cent of users although they only represent 40 per cent of Haringey's population. The fact that the scheme is free to its users also means that many members are unemployed or low wage earners.

Retirement motivates some to join the network, like the legal secretary who is about to retire and has offered to help people to draw up wills; or the former TV and film producer who wants to pass on his skills to others. For many, like Wilhelm, it's "because it's important to keep learning. I'll probably still be learning something new when I die!" he says.

The scheme can also offer work—albeit unpaid—to younger people still trying to enter the job market; like the music graduates keping up their skills in the network whilst looking for paid employment. Then there are others, like the man referred to the network by social services after he had left psychiatric hospital. They discovered he could speak Greek and teaching through the network has been an important factor in his recovery. It also provides a flexible and non-stressful sort of work as he can renegotiate sessions on days when he doesn't feel up to teaching.

Despite its apparent simplicity, the scheme may confront potential users with more of a challenge than adult education because, as Christopher Rourke says, "We don't spoonfeed them." Enquirers are given the names of other network members and then it's up to them to make the arrangements. Most people do—sometimes after quite a long time—but the project would like to be able to do more follow-up and find out why some don't follow through the initial enquiry.

Although Illich and others have suggested that learning can take place anywhere, from parks to churches, in practice members meet in each other's homes. Thinking this might be a problem, the project had obtained the use of community centres, premises but there hasn't been any take-up. People like Dave, who also teaches in more formal academic settings, have found "there's a lot to be said for informal teaching and learning in each other's homes." He has found the network provides a completely different experience in terms of the relationships involved: "It's more like a friendship . . . it's not a commercial relationship, and the question of authority simply doesn't occur," he says.

The one-to-one teaching seems to go down well, despite the fact that people may initially feel nervous. The scheme has also spawned some groups like Dave's meditation class or the local yoga teachers who got together to learn homeopathy.

Although the 250 subjects offered included many minority interest topics there are clear favourites too—photography, languages and computing being currently top of the list. Swimming and drumming have also proved popular, as well as dancing. Some people come to the network for subjects like dancing because they may not want to learn in more public settings like dance studios, although the network may give them confidence to move on.

That fact that people can use the network for free is a major bonus for people on low incomes although for some people it is, initially at least, a potential problem. Kay was one network member who found it difficult to accept. As she says: "I felt terrible about it and rang the office and asked if I could pay because I didn't feel I could teach anything in return." Now she realises that by helping Dave with his garden and by giving a lift to the meditation group to one of the other members she has been "contributing to the network without realising it."

The scheme challenges the more formal structures of adult education classes although Christopher Rourke is emphatic that they are there to supplement and complement traditional forms of learning, not to replace them. Sometimes people combine both, like one woman who goes to evening classes to learn Portuguese but who also learns with Wilhelm through the network.

The network can offer a much more flexible form of learning than adult education classes. Learning doesn't have to stop if the class gets too small. Indeed, people often come to the network because their usual class has been disbanded. People can also teach and learn at times that suit them. The flexibility suits people like Kay and Scott who both have jobs involving shifts which change every so often.

Sometimes people aren't even sure what they want to learn. Like the man who came to the network and went off with contacts for learning five subjects. He came back four weeks later asking for five more. Now he's happily and permanently installed learning the piano. As the network realised, he didn't initially know what he wanted to learn but he did know he wanted to learn something.

Not suprisingly the network's users are highly enthusiastic and perhaps the only question is why such an apparently simple idea hasn't caught on before.

Getting them started

MYRA BURGESS

One-day courses in Avon help parents get their children learning.

Getting parents to help in the education of their children is important. But how to do it? Little attention has been given to helping the parents. Many would like to be involved but don't know where to begin.

It is all a question of confidence, according to Geraldine Taylor, a matter of showing parents their own potential as teachers. She runs one-day courses designed to do just that: helping parents to help their children acquire the basic skills taught at primary school. "Provided you can get your child literate and numerate by the age of eleven, then if something happens at secondary school, or they have a rotten adolescence, they can still be rescued from the age of about 16," she says. "This is why primary education is so important; it's a kind of hedge against what can and often does happen to children during their teenage years."

The courses are attracting a growing following. Geraldine is a qualified teacher and counsellor but her interest in parental involvement grew out of personal experience. Eight years ago her five year old son was classified as backward by his teacher. Shocked, she devised her own set of exercises and games to encourage the child to learn. It was a success and other parents soon started borrowing her notes and ideas. Out of this came a book, *Be Your Child's Natural Teacher* (published by Penguin Books) and a series of courses in Avon, where she works as

Parent Involvement Tutor Organiser for Central Bristol Adult Education Centre.

She is now taking her course nationwide. Sixty people recently attended the first one held in north London, each paying £3 for the day. Nearly all were parents, and nearly all were women; only four men attended.

There is a fine line between involvement and exerting pressure. Parents can do untold damage by pressurising their child to conform to their own image of success. The child's only defence is to withdraw, thus becoming "stubborn" or "strange." Such cases are extreme, but serve as a salutary reminder. Geraldine Taylor has worked with cases where children are unable to develop academically because they are deprived of their parents' love and acceptance. She tells parents to make sure their children know that: "It's okay to be you. Love comes first; learning after." Once the child is secure in this parental acceptance, just ten minutes a day is enough to ensure that they grasp the basic skills they will need to carry them through secondary school and into the outside world. The course aims to show how to use those ten minutes to best effect.

A lot can be done even with pre-school age children. Glove puppets provide a good stimulus for storytelling. You can act as your child's personal scribe if you make up a story together, perhaps based on the events of a day out, and then write it down, using the child's words—"train-place" instead of "station," for instance—so that the story remains personal through its transition from spoken to written form.

Once children can read and write, a frequent exercise in junior school is to "write a story about . . ." This requires imaginative skills which parents have usually outgrown, but Geraldine Taylor showed us how our jaded, adult imaginations could recapture an eight year old's ingenuous capacity for the impossible—or at least improbable. "Imagine that your life depends on staying in this room; there's a monstrous danger outside. But there's an even greater danger inside. What can it be?"

Suggestions ranged from the sensible—gas leaks or fires—to the fantastic—triffids and space visitors. Any eight year old would have been proud of our attempts at storymaking. Our imaginations were running riot; we were divided into groups of four or five to write a children's story.

Some of these turned out to contain familiar themes, others were more original and obviously drawn from personal experience: the mother playing along with the child's game that it's raining in the kitchen, until she discovers that the bath is overflowing; the game of "ping-pong in the bucket" which comes to an abrupt end when the ball lands in Henry's open mouth and he begins to turn very red.

Although there was an occasional attemp to avoid sexist stereotypes—"Wendy's Daddy took Wendy and the baby shopping"—most stories reflected a stronger relationship between mother and child; hardly surprising, since most of the authors were women. Geraldine Taylor finds it natural, if not ideal, that more mothers than fathers attend her courses. An important element of her work is to give mothers, who frequently lack confidence in their own academic ability, the knowledge that they can help their children in this field. A number of women came back to say that they've managed to implement the things they learnt on her course and are feeling more confident of their ability to help their children. But what can they do for themselves? She is willing to help here, too. She sees the mother as still the central figure in the family; a strong and confident mother makes for a strong and happy family, she says.

Maths is one of the trickiest areas. But Geraldine is reassuring. "There's no such thing as New Maths—it's simply the same old thing put into a form which captures children's imagination." Maths belongs in the real world and this should be impressed on children right from the start. You can make up sets of things that go together: knife, fork and spoon; soap, towel and toothbrush. Use food to illustrate size; children are very astute when it comes to assessing which is the larger piece of a bar of chocolate, a half or a quarter.

It is the general knowledge which underlies maths that a parent can teach: telling the time, using money, knowing the days of the week and the months of the year. The language of mathematics is the basis for the language of instruction. If a child is not conversant with this language she will be lost when she goes to secondary school. There she will need to know which way to run round the gym when the teachers says "in an anticlockwise direction," which way a vertical line goes, which points are east and west. "Maths is all confidence," she says, and it is this confidence that parents can help their children discover.

Although her special area is working with parents, Geraldine has been approached to give similar courses for teachers. She is also involved in a project with a nursery school in a deprived area of Bristol, where the staff work with the parents as well as the children. This can be highly stressful and Geraldine has been called in to counsel the staff.

Inevitably, Geraldine's courses attract parents who are already to some extent involved in their children's education. At present it is only through her work with teachers and with the British nursery project that she can reach others. Her hope is that by taking the courses outside Avon, she will reach a wider public. She has also been asked by the Home and School Council to write a booklet about how she runs her courses as a guide for others. She would like to see other professionals encouraging parents to participate in their children's education. Parental involvement can take many forms; parent governors are one, but for those millions who cannot or do not wish to spend time at their child's school, Geraldine Taylor's course offers an alternative which is just as valuable, and probably twice as much fun.

Saturday school

JOY MELVILLE

Every weekend, a Cambridge primary school becomes a classroom for creativity.

Ten o'clock on a Saturday morning at Duxford primary school, Cambridgeshire, and you can't hear yourself speak: there's the sound of instruments tuning up; children of all sizes stampede down corridors, holding recorders and clarinets, plays and poetry books; adults, back to being pupils for a morning, sign the register, exchange greetings, and disappear into classrooms. "Where's Estelle?" shouts someone. "In the paint cupboard, teaching the oboe," someone else shouts back.

With 200 children and adults turning up, there's not a classroom, cupboard or corridor free. The Duxford Saturday Workshop is bulging at the seams: a startlingly effective form of community education in action. The idea behind it is to stamp out the elitism of "culture" and make it accessible, in all its forms, to everyone. It costs 10p a week for a child and 15p a week for an adult, plus £6 a year for instrument lessons.

Open any door at the school on a Saturday morning, and you could find a poetry recital, or adults and children playing chamber music; a flute lesson; a class of creative drama; a brass band. "What did you do on Saturday mornings before you came here?" I asked an eight year old, holding a recorder. "We just done shopping, sometimes watched telly," she said.

For her, and a great many adults and children in Duxford and surrounding villages, Saturdays now bring exhilaration rather than boredom. The enjoyment is evident in every room you go into, whatever is going on. "I think it's just more relaxed here than at school," said the drama tutor. "Everyone sees you about the village: you're not like a teacher, you're a friend. Right, then," she said, "round your cauldron." And the three witches in *Macbeth* gathered round a chair and gave an energetic rendering of "Double, double, toil and trouble." "If you'd offered them Shakespeare, they would have said 'ugh'," said the tutor, "but they like it because they chose it."

It was the same in the poetry class, where a twelve year old was reciting *The Owl and the Pussycat* with great feeling. "Most of them here don't possess poetry books," said the tutor, "they don't even have one in the house. I give them one set poem and let them choose another they like. They look in the local library, and what they come up with is lovely; and they write this beautiful poetry." She had a small stack of their poems by her side. "The TV rattles on like an old lady," begins one. Another starts, "How many times now have you looked out of the window?"

In the main hall, six small kids chugged by, pretending to be a train. "I'm getting bored," said one, "are we nearly there?" The deputy head was taking three to eleven year olds in non-scripted drama. "It gets them to control their bodies and their emotions. I try to give them situations whereby they are other characters and so get out of themselves and experience as many emotions as possible."

Other children were taking part in some Jamaican ring-games: "Lick an' Lock Up" (the whip and prison); and "Hurrah fuh Jin Jin" (Queen Victoria). There are no black children in the village, so this, said the headmaster, was a way of teaching the class about black history. the last song the pupils sang ("The girl couldn't cook/She couldn't read a book/So send she back to she mum,") also made a useful feminist point.

Next door, an adult, who learned to conduct at the school, was rehearsing an enthusiastic orchestra of all ages. "*That's it*: did you feel it?" he said. "You really hit it hard that time. Can we take it a little faster and a little brisker and *smile*." One teenage boy said he couldn't do that *and* play the recorder. "You can smile with your eyes," said the conductor. "The atmosphere is so friendly here," said one of the adult women members of the orchestra. "We're all in the same boat, learning, and I have learned to read music, which I never did before and I'm thrilled."

Boosting people's belief in themselves like this is another main aim of the workshop. "By utilising the skills in your local community," says Jill Steinberg, the founder of the workshop, "you give people confidence that they have a skill and can teach someone else—in all sorts of fields, not just music and drama and poetry. We had a woman here who was an absolute bag of nerves, and joining did a lot for her. She discovered she could do things for herself and did O levels and passed and now has a job.

The workshop directs people towards things they can be successful at because it generates an atmosphere where you are expected to succeed."

Jill Steinberg started the workshop 13 years ago, after stopping her drama class at the school, because of her young baby. The children kept asking when she was coming back, so she started Saturday morning classes in creative drama and dance, parking the baby in the classroom.

"And then someone said to me, 'Angela is marvellous with music,' and none of the children could play a note, they couldn't even tune any instrument. I phoned everyone I knew to borrow recorders, Angela started teaching it and slowly more and more children came. As well as the recorder group, we did drama and poetry, and took the children to concerts and pantomimes. Then all the kids wanted to learn the guitar, so I found someone in the village who could take a class and it went on from there. Parents brought their children, and stayed on themselves.'

With no money for tutors, the more experienced started to teach the beginners. And the workshop is now unique in that children and adults of all ages learn and teach together—as once a pupil reaches a level of competence, they themselves become tutors. One girl who came at the age of seven to join the first recorder group is now 16 and a tutor.

This allows a lot of individual tuition, but more important, it breaks down the elitism of music. "I think we're all equal when we are playing music," said one housewife. "We all have new music to learn and have to struggle through it, whether highly educated or, like me, not educated at all."

As you stand in the corridor, listening to strains of chamber music, rather than rock bands, you nevertheless wonder if it isn't all rather middle class. "You don't realise what rock bottom homes some of these children come from," says Jill Steinberg. "When we started it, it was 90 per cent working class children, and 10 per cent middle class; but the nature of the village has changed because of the growth of high-tech work round here, and now it's about 50-50. But we do a lot of work in recruiting the kids who really need to come. Some one-parent families can't manage the 10p charge, so we waive it. We also give interest free loans to any who can't afford an instrument."

What about the emphasis on classical music? "Rock groups don't like being taught: they create their own music. But the kids come here, learn how to read music, play the guitar, and go off to rock groups. We have had jazz, too: it comes and goes. You do what the kids want at the time: they change and we change."

Their Duxford workshop is a registered charity, raising money by donations. It has 30 unpaid tutors, and at the moment is run by three voluntary managers, who between them organise the instruments, run the register, records and finance; and organise the tutors and the classes. But now the numbers are 200 and growing, they are appealing for funds for a paid organiser. In time they would like to have holiday courses and a composer in residence.

A workshop like this can't be duplicated exactly: it needs to grow in response to grass roots demands. But with the collapse of funding for the arts and the cuts in education, there's an urgent need for more.

Housing

Designed for living

JOY MELVILLE

A scheme in Liverpool caters for the special housing needs of the elderly from ethnic minorities.

The 76 year old Somali, in a pale-coloured "longi," which he wears for sleeping or prayers, and small skull cap, sits eating curry and frowning over a Will Hay film on television. In between mouthfuls of curry, he starts to tell me, in broken English, how he first came to England in 1930 when he was a seaman, working in the galley. "I am still good cook," he says, pointing to his curry. Two other elderly Somali men, also residents of the house, sit alongside, on the comfortable brown sofa in the centrally heated room. It is all very different from the last place they lived in: a cold, damp and derelict house.

The neat terraced house they live in now is in the heart of the black community of Liverpool 8. Inside it looks essentially English, until you catch sight of the specially converted prayer room upstairs. The prayer room was carefully planned: Somalis have to pray five times a day, and although the house is near the mosque, the three elderly men may not always be well enough to get there.

This prayer room is all part of Liverpool's new approach to the special housing needs of elderly people from various ethnic minorities. The house for the three Somalis opened the year before last, one for elderly Afro-Caribbeans is expected to open this month and a further one for elderly Chinese is planned for this year.

The scheme for "group living with support" was initiated by the Liverpool Personal Service Society. The society, which had run a boarding-out scheme for elderly people since 1978, was offered a small terraced house by the owner, who said that if three people could be found to live there, she would be willing to act as "carer," by coming in every day. The idea was taken up and proved so successful that the society approached Merseyside Improved Houses—one of the largest housing associations in Liverpool—about developing it further.

"We recognised that there were not very many elderly blacks in our sheltered schemes," says Grantley Adams, an assistant manager of MIH, who has been involved with the scheme from its beginning. "And the Somali community, who in terms of housing need in Liverpool 8 were the worst off, had already come to us about the problems of some of their elderly. The three elderly Somali men they suggested for the scheme were living in appallingly overcrowded conditions."

Discussions took place between the Liverpool Personal Service Society and the DHSS over finance. The MIH was able to provide, renovate and furnish a house near the mosque, and the Somali Cultural Association advised on the interior design of the house and the way it was to be run. A Somali carer was found, Mrs Abdullah, who spoke the language, understood the men's cultural needs and was employed to come in daily, shop and, if needed, cook for them.

All ex-seamen, the men were already friends and shared the same political beliefs – important if they were to live together successfully. "As far as the carer was concerned," says Grantley Adams, "the men were initially a little bit worried about her being a woman because they see themselves as head of the household and the father figure and were reluctant to ask a woman for help."

Their wariness did not last long, however. Only one speaks English well and they now depend on Mrs Abdullah for both practical help and friendship. But they like to do as much as they can for themselves. Mrs Abdullah, a serene-faced Somali woman, wearing a blue kerchief, yellow blouse and long red skirt, smiles and says: "I am supposed to cook for them, but they usually say to me, 'I can cook myself.'

"But they are nice men. I talk to them when I arrive, to see if they need anything. I say, 'Don't be shy, just ask.' I will phone the doctor if anyone is sick. Then I clean the house, change the beds, go to the shops for them, or get them leaflets they want. They ask if my family is all right. I have a handicapped boy, after a road accident, and they always ask how he is going on. They know my husband – he was a seaman, too."

There are altogether about 20,000 Liverpool-born blacks in the city, and a further 2,000 Somalis and Arabs, 8,000 Chinese and 3,000 from the Caribbean live here. They form close communities. Don't they, traditionally, look after their own elderly? "That's a myth," says Grantley Adams. "It's just assumed that they are looked after by their extended family. But even the Chinese family network is breaking down and a lot of elderly Chinese are unable to be supported by the younger ones. In any case, they live in small houses: there's no room for the elderly."

He admits to having been criticised for segregating the elderly into their different ethnic groups. But, as he says, "There are religious differences and diet differences which would make a project like this very difficult to run with a mixture of elderly people from different minority groups." Some Somalis, for health reasons, chew raw garlic, for instance.

As far as Chinese are concerned, they cook a great deal so the house that is being planned for the elderly Chinese (who will be women, not men) will have low-level working surfaces and a large extractor fan in the kitchen. To cater for the Chinese enthusiasm for gardening, there will be specially raised flowerbeds in the garden.

Jeanette Abendstern, the social worker from the Liverpool Personal Service Society who coordinates the scheme, drops in regularly to the Somali house to see all is working well – thus giving the carer the reassurance that there is someone to back her up. "It's a very flexible arrangement," she says. "The beauty of it is that you can be very flexible and tailor the house to the needs of the elderly people living there, rather than expect people to fit into existing services. The present social services provision doesn't really cater for elderly people with different cultural needs from white people.

"The main aim of the scheme is really to hand over at a later stage the running of the house to the community that is involved. We are learning from the community what the needs of the elderly are and they are learning about the procedures of setting up the house, and the possible pitfalls. In answer to the demand of 'Why not give them the money and let them organise it?' we explain we are trying to give people the experience of working with a housing association and other departments."

Each man claims a hostel accommodation allowance of £87.50 a week, and all the bills – rent, rates, repairs, food and so on – come out of that. The scheme is working most successfully, so it's surprising to hear from Herbie Higgins who, on behalf of the Caribbean tenants for the new house opening this month, that he has been hitting difficulties. "The Afro-Caribbeans are too independent," he says. "They don't like to share houses: they like their own front door. I couldn't believe it, people in such bad conditions refusing to take up such a good offer. But they're proud. They think you are taking them to an old people's home, that they'll be treated badly. And unfortunately, past experience backs this up."

Jeanette Abendstern agrees that there have been some unexpected problems. "It's a big move for elderly people. It's a new idea and these people have had so little done for them, they are suspicious."

To begin with, the Somalis were just as suspicious of the offer of a house. But as Mrs Abdullah says, "Now they have seen this house, they look for another. They cry for one; but there are not enough."

Building a neighbourhood

DAVID WHITE

A community in Shropshire encourages a new style of cottage industry where modern technologies coexist with traditional crafts.

How do you set about growing your own neighbourhood? First, take a seven-acre field and divide it into 14 plots. Then encourage a variety of pioneering people, from bricklayers to teachers, to build homes and workshops. Sprinkle the enterprise occasionally with planning expertise, and watch the neighbourhood grow.

This, in a seed packet, is the story of Lightmoor, a new community launched by the Town and Country Planning Association three years ago. Lightmoor lies between Telford and Ironbridge. In its own small way, it could prove as significant a social and industrial development as either of these places.

Lightmoor is becoming a community which provides a pattern for postindustrial life. The aim is to encourage a new style of cottage industry, where modern technologies coexist with traditional crafts. Tony Gibson, Lightmoor's development officer, likes to think of it as a place where there is "computer in the kitchen and a pig in the backyard."

Telford Development Corporation have helped. They have sold 22½ acres of land on a long lease to the Lightmoor project at its agricultural value, but have granted planning permission for housing and light industry, which has given the project the security it needs for building society loans and the freedoom to develop home-based enterprises.

Lightmoor is also a community built by a community. Part of the project's purpose is to break down the barrier between the planners and the planned for. And so every effort has been made to involve the first phase of residents in decision-making. The 14 households have been encouraged to use moveable models to plan the neighbourhood and "soon-now-later" packs to order priorities.

One lesson that has emerged from the modelling sessions is that, at first, people will site their homes as far as possible from other people's. Later, as factors like the cost of roads sink in they bring them nearer.

"It's a neighbourhood that's being built, not just one's own house and then finish," Tony Gibson says. "People have to decide what they're going to do about pavements, and where the village green will be."

The growth of Lightmoor has been exponential, starting gradually and then, in the last six months, taking off. The first couple to put down roots were Dave and Brenda Cooksey. They moved in during the winter of 1984, when the site was a sea of mud. Everyone saw it as an act of faith in the Lightmoor project. Someone had to do something to get the new community really started.

Dave Cooksey is a bricklayer, with a down-to-earth view of Lightmoor. "Lots of people came here because they wanted a new way of life," he says. "We didn't. We just wanted to get more organised." They moved from a council house, with an allotment two miles away. Now they keep pigs and goats and grow vegetables in their back garden.

The Cookseys hope to finish building their home next March. "We did everything backwards," Dave says. "On a self-build scheme, you get a group of people wanting to build houses. They worry about the community afterwards. We started wanting to build a community, and then stood back and thought 'now, we've got to build a house'."

Paradoxically, hold-ups in the building of homes at Lightmoor have helped build a sense of neighbourhood. When the Severn-Trent Water Authority turned down their plans for individual septic tanks, the Lightmoor residents were faced with a costly bill for installing a sewage treatment plant. So they installed it themselves. It was back-breaking work, but everyone joined in, even the children.

For many of the early pioneers, the time spent on "infrastructure" was too long, and they left. Helen Brown would have left, had it not been for her husband Phil. "Phil has the strength," she says. "I almost dropped out."

Phil Brown is a former assistant director of town planning with Stockport borough council. "I had the opportunity of retiring early," he says. "We liked the idea of being part of a community. We wanted to do something with our lives. We needed to start again."

Helen now hopes to go into business as a cook and caterer. Phil is returning to his old profession of architecture. "Designing your own house and building it is every architect's dream," he says. "But it has taken two years to get this far. There have been times when we wondered if it would ever get started."

Everyone agrees that it was Gerwyn Lewis, the teacher, who got things going. Early this year, he built a shed to hold the tools to build a workshop. In the Easter vacation, he built his workshop and the footings of his house. And in the summer vacation, he began to build his house.

He had paid for outside labour. "It's a huge undertaking to build it on your own," he says. This is true of the whole Lightmoor project, he thinks. "The sheer size of it took us by surprise. We were hopelessly naive."

For Gerwyn and his wife June, an adult literacy teacher, the attraction of Lightmoor was the relaxed planning regulations. "I knew it was my best opportunity of being able to build what I wanted to build, and I wanted to build a workshop. This is my lifetime's ambition."

Gerwyn teaches woodwork at a local sixth form college. Even with his workshop going, he would keep the job. Self-sufficiency is not the aim. "Some people think of Lightmoor as a sixties commune. I'd never envisaged it being that. That is a greater degree of freedom. We do get a better say. But it's impossible to get away from the present-day bureaucracy. You still have to pay your rates. You still have to raise your money with the building society."

Miri and Ivor Hastilow, who moved in last July, had high hopes of Lightmoor. "For a long-time, we looked for more than living in a suburban neighbourhood," Miri says. But she was brought up in a kibbutz and is slightly disappointed that things in Lightmoor are not all that different from things outside. The men, for instance, do not seem to get involved in the community. "Everyone is so busy," she says. "We haven't had time for ideals."

Ivor Hastilow works for Sandwell council, but he is keen to develop some sort of enterprise of his own in his workshop. "I would like to do something, but I don't know what," he says. "I need someone else to develop a business. The hope is that there will be businesses on the site and the women will be involved too."

Rob Leverton has always dreamed of setting up on his own. "Twenty years ago I had the idea to farm a croft in Orkney," he says. "I never lost the idea." Rob is a former building site manager. He now operates the site's JCB. He and his wife Jackie will move in to one of the four low-cost homes for rent on the site eventually. The building hasn't started yet, but both of them know they have made the right choice. "I was reassured at the first meeting," Rob says. "They wanted what I wanted. How often do you buy a house where you like everybody living there? We know every single person in this community, we know their children."

Jackie, who is a teacher, agrees. "They are the sort of people who care about the environment, that's the thing."

Lightmoor, they say, is the sort of place where you cannot cut down a tree without holding a meeting to discuss the matter. And that is the way people want it.

Goodbye bed and breakfast

ANNE GROSSKURTH

Could short-term private lets solve one London housing problem?

As the problem of the London's homeless steadily worsens, local authorities have embarked on a frantic search for alternatives to squalid and costly bed and breakfast hotels. Their desperation has inspired some bizarre solutions: Barnet has set up caravan parks for homeless people; Camden is erecting temporary prefabs on vacant sites; Brent is converting derelict office blocks; the new Liberal administration at Tower Hamlets is even considering mooring a disused ocean liner in the Thames for homeless families.

But by far the biggest growth area is temporary accommodation today is "short-life" housing. Councils, short of the cash to bring their own dilapidated empties up to an acceptable standard for families, are trawling the more fertile pastures of the private sector.

The potential is enormous. The government may complain about the amount of vacant council housing goint to waste, but 70 per cent of London's empty housing (over 90,000 properties) is in private hands. The challenge has been how to persuade landlords to put it back into use for those who need it most – the homeless.

Paddington Churches Housing Association (PCHA), is partnership with the London borough of Brent, has led the way. Armed with a package of incentives, PCHA's emergency housing team has secured 120 dwellings from private landlords over the past year through its short-term leasing scheme.

Private leasing offers owners all the perks they claim have been denied to them by the Rent Acts. They are guaranteed not only vacant possession when desired, but comprehensive management services, grant aid with improvement works and, in many cases, rents well above the registered fair rents levels.

The strategy has been tried before, but never as ambitiously or successfully as by PCHA.

The immediate benefits for Brent council are impressive. The council is currently paying some £2.8 million a year to keep its 642 homeless families in hotels. The comparable outlay on private leasing is about £642,000. If every Brent family now in bed and breakfast were to be rehoused temporarily in privately leased property, total savings would amount to £2 million a year.

Private leasing enables councils to avoid two major obstacles to rehousing the homeless in their own stock: the long-standing government ban on buying private property, and the severe restrictions on capital spending which have brought council housebuilding to a virtual standstill.

As Mark Wilkinson of Brent Council's "Room at the Top" scheme – which aims to secure empty flats above shops – points out, private leasing is more than just a cost-cutting measure. "It's not just a question of pounds and pennies or a straight balance sheet exercise. The social benefits of taking families out of bed and breakfast are enormous."

A recent inspection of privately leased property by Shelter, the national campaign for the homeless, confirms that claim. In contrast to the typically cramped and unhealthy hotel rooms used for homeless families, the leased accommodation is spacious, and decorated to an exceptionally high standard. They are close to relatives, friends, social services and schools, because the association aims to get accommodation in Brent or as close as possible.

Stella Fisher, mother of two year old Jeffrey and expecting her second child, has just left one of Paddington's worst hotels for a privately leased flat. After an 18 month stint in dangerous and overcrowded accommodation, she couldn't believe her luck when she was moved to a spacious two-bedroom flat in Lincoln House, a new luxury block in leafy, middle class north Acton. Next door, Michael Phelan is settling in with his young family, from whom he has been separated in different hotels for over a year.

Both flats could fetch up to £65,000 on the open market. How did PCHA persuade the developers to pass up such a lucrative prospect for the sake of homeless families? David Fussell, a director of the small company which built the block, is frank about his motives. "We haven't got any ambition of housing the homeless of London," he admits. "But as long as we're getting a reasonable return on it, we're interested. Private leasing means we're assured of our rent, we don't have to get involved in management and we get the property back when it's needed. It makes the whole business of letting chore-free."

Fussell was also impressed by the eloquent approach of PCHA's Nick Sheil, who has developed the business of courting landlords into a fine art. In Sheil's experience, many councils and housing associations are failing to get private housing because they haven't learned how to talk to landlords. Too much time is being wasted, he says, sending brochures to owners of empties on the rates roll. A little wining and dining is far more effective.

Despite what now seem to be substantial savings, there are grave misgivings about the potential cost of private leasing. Many owners, aware of the high cost of hotels, are demanding exorbitant rents and huge improvement grants before passing their property over for temporary use by homeless families.

Many landlords and councils, too, have serious doubts about just how much temporary housing can be made available through private leasing. Despite a package of incentives guaranteed to lure even the most reluctant owners, surprisingly few are taking the bait. Out of a total letting portfolio of 13,000 dwellings, the Freshwater Group, for example, have committed just 60 to the scheme. Landlords have lost faith in the residential market, says Freshwater's David Hodges, and "it will take years of cooing by both political parties to entice them back."

More fundamental is the criticism that private leasing is simply substituting one temporary housing solution for another. Instead of lining hoteliers' pockets, councils are enriching private landlords. Families may get better accommodation through private leasing, but it is still only temporary. The scheme does not create any permanent homes, and fails to tackle the fundamental cause of rising homelessness in London.

PCHA is now extending the private leasing idea in answer to those criticisms. In the first scheme of its kind in the country, they are working with the Nationwide building society and other city institutions to use private mortgage finance to acquire empty property. A public-private trust, operating as a trading company, will buy houses on the open market using index-linked mortgages from building societies and pension funds. The properties will then be leased to Brent council for homeless families, along the same lines as the present short-term leasing scheme. Rent payments from the families and the council will pay off the mortgage. Within a few years, PCHA will buy the properties for permanent occupation by families nominated by Brent.

The aim is to get every Brent family now in bed and breakfast into a permanent home within two years. It's an ingenious way of dodging the government clampdown on capital spending by councils, and another example of the imaginative thinking going on at PCHA.

Building a future

STEVE PLATT

A group of young, unemployed people in St Paul's Bristol, are given the chance to build their own homes.

Four years ago, Chris Gordon, then 22, was sharing a rented flat with his sister in the rundown St Paul's area of Bristol, where the first of the recent wave of inner city riots occurred in 1980. A young black with no skills and few prospects, he had been out of work for a total of five years since leaving school.

Now he is a homeowner, half way through a City and Guilds plumbing course, with a share in a successful building company. His modern, well-furnished flat, where he lives with his girlfriend, Pat Caven, and their son Daniel, aged 20 months, is for sale at £23,000. Along with eleven other young people from St Paul's, most of whom were also unskilled and jobless, he has – quite literally – built himself a future.

What gave Chris Gordon the opportunities to which he could never before have hoped to aspire was the Zenzele Self-build Housing Association. Initiated by a "committee of advisers" set up by Bristol JP Stella Clarke in 1982, the association's objective was to enable a local group of unemployed young people to build and own their own homes.

"We wanted to demonstrate that a home of your own is a possibility for even the most disadvantaged members of society," said Stella Clarke. The skills and experience acquired in building that home, moreover, would also greatly increase the job prospects of the people participating in the scheme.

The Zenzele Housing Association was formally established in June 1983 following a series of meetings over six months. Chris Gordon was the first person to get involved and he became the association's treasurer. A friend's brother, Colin Simpson, joined soon afterwards and was elected chairman. Others came in twos and threes, until there was a settled group of twelve young people, aged between 18 and 30, nine of them black and three white.

"None of us really knew each other," said Colin Simpson, "and apart from a carpenter and an electrician none of us had much experience of building work. I wasn't remotely interested in building, and I was very sceptical at first, not just about whether we could do the work, but also I couldn't believe you didn't have to put any money up front."

The construction work was financed initially via bank loans guaranteed by the Housing Corporation under its self-build programme. But the cost was ultimately met by mortgages totalling £146,000 from the Bristol and West Building Society. Crucially, the society agreed to provide individual mortgages to all members of the association on completion of the building work – even if they were still unemployed at the time, in which case it was agreed to accept interest-only payments from the DHSS. The DHSS in turn, agreed in advance that it would meet the interest payments of jobless members.

The scheme was thus completely self-financing, and the unique financial arrangements made it possible for people without assets or income to take part, despite the absence of public subsidy. "All that was required," said Stella Clarke, "was commitment and motivation." And the prospect of owning one's home at the end of the project proved to be a very powerful motivator.

A suitable site, owned by Bristol City Council, was found in Coombe Road, Eastville; the association bought it for £15,000. Despite problems with uncharted cellars and old foundations, which increased costs by around £14,000, the twelve-flat development was finished within 14 months.

John Meehan, an experienced building tradesman, was employed as a site foreman to supervise the work. Otherwise the group had to rely on the limited skills its members possessed when the scheme started and those they learnt as work progressed. Chris Gordon, for instance, got a friend to show him how to do the plumbing on the upper floor, and then did it himself on the ground floor.

A straightforward design and the use of traditional building methods kept construction as simple as possible, so that the actual building work posed few problems. According to the architect, "The care taken over the construction of their own homes produced as good or better workmanship than is often experienced on the open market."

A bigger problem arose, however, when one association member did not "pull his weight" during the construction phase and had to be expelled from the group. But his explusion provided an unexpected bonus, in the end, when the group was able to take on a skilled plasterer as his replacement.

Other difficulties occurred because people found jobs and were unavailable during the day. Eventually it was agreed that jobless association members would work on the project during the day, while members with jobs would work in the evening and weekends. Even so, there was still some friction about whether everyone was doing an equal share of the work, and there were organisational problems in having different people working at different times.

"The building work was very, very difficult to fit in with a job," said Colin Simpson, who worked full-time for an electronics firm throughout the construction period. "I used to go to the site straight from work, grab a takeaway and start work again."

Occasionally they came close to giving up. "When you could see no obvious progress at the end of the week's work, and you had no chance to relax and recharge your batteries, the only thing that kept you going was the thought of having your own home at the end of it all," said Colin Simpson. Everyone in the scheme needed chivying along or their spirits lifting at some point, he said.

Yet work on the site never stopped – and for some people it continued long after the building itself was completed. Chris Gordon has built a pine-panelled partition wall between his bedroom and living room. Other residents have erected arches, built-in cupboards or breakfast bars. And everywhere there is evidence of never-ending DIY home improvements to these DIY homes.

In addition, three of the association's members, Joe Gordon, Clive Campbell and Chris Gordon, have used their experience on the self-build scheme to establish their own building and decorating firm – the Zenzele Building and Construction Company. "Doors have opened that were previously closed to us," said Chris Gordon. "The fact that we live in a place we built ourselves is the best advert we could ever have. It's given me a job as well as a home."

Everyone involved in the scheme had had a double return on their labour. Firstly, they have gained financially: the twelve flats are being bought on £12,000 mortgages, but they are worth at least £10,000 more than that. Secondly, and of equal importance though less readily quantifiable, the self-builders of Zenzele have learnt a lot – not just about building, but about themselves.

When you work with twelve very different personalities every day for 14 months, you find out a lot about yourself and other people," said Colin Simpson. "It gives you experience, knowledge, a sense of purpose and self-confidence." Above all, though, there was a sense of achievement affecting every other aspect of life: "It's a marvellous feeling to know that I could come back here in 50 years and this building will still be standing – a sort of monument that I can point to and say 'We built that. We did it ourselves and we didn't get anything from anyone else.' Not many people know how good that feels."

Happy in the high-rise

IAN SUTHERLAND

If the right steps are taken, hard-to-let tower block flats can become desirable residences.

Life in a high-rise block on one of Glasgow's deprived housing schemes is never going to be the model for an ideal late 20th century urban existence. But a Scottish Special Housing Association tenancy can at least make sure that such residency is not entirely nasty, brutish and short. Scotland's enterprising state-funded housing agency is experiencing the unusual pleasure in the public sector of actually having waiting lists for high-rise accommodation in Glasgow's Gorbals and Westercommon areas. Both neighbourhoods were bywords for decay, violence, crime, drug abuse and dampness less than a decade ago.

In the seventies, the SSHA multi-storey blocks were a target for vandalism. It left lifts useless, elderly tenants depressed and terrified, stairs and landings scarred with graffiti and strewn with litter and urine. In the Gorbals, until the introduction of both entryphones and an improved caretaker and security guard system, drug users, glue sniffers and dossers regularly slept in corridor cupboards. Such intruders are still a common and frightening feature of life in non-SSHA properties. At Westercommon – on the edge of the notorious Possilpark housing scheme, where GPS and other public services have refused to visit – ground-floor flats in the association's high-rise blocks consequently became unlettable.

Faced with the virtual break-down of life in their high-rise flats, the SSHA re-allocated its rent-collecting personnel as housing visitor-cum-assistants and began the process of consulting the remaining tenants – many of whom were hostile and ready to blame their state landlord for all its – on ways to improve life in the "village in the sky." The availability of commercial controlled-entry systems in the late 1970s seemed to provide a starting point for change. At public meetings, the demand by tenants for security against unwelcome guests and callers had come through loud and clear.

The association quickly found that controlled-entry systems alone were not the answer to the growing crisis in Glasgow tower blocks. Even where entryphones were not subject to vandalism, the sheer extent to which they were used often left newly-installed systems inoperable within days. Repairs and maintenance threatened to overwhelm resources. So the technologists began to study how locks, doors and entry systems could be adapted for constant heavy use, while housing workers and community development staff – in close contact and co-operation with tenants' committees and groups – began to address the different problems faced by tenants living in the grey concrete complexes.

In the Gorbals, the average age of tenants was increasing. Specialised housing provision for an older group would eventually become inevitable. If security could be guaranteed, the crisis-ridden tower blocks could be converted and upgraded to meet an already-identified demand to stay in the Gorbals area.

The SSHA began to convert some of their Gorbals flats into sheltered flats for the elderly, linked by inter-com to a warden scheme. Standard flats were modernised. Unnecessary entrances and exits at ground level were closed off.

At the same time, they took the opportunity to employ a new generation of caretaking staff, normally resident in the blocks, and chosen, in part, for their ability to relate to tenants. "The SSHA's tenants are its customers," says Gorbals housing assistant Sadie Hamilton, "and the staff attitude is that without them none of us would have a job." Smart uniform jackets have replaced the traditional dungarees, while caretaking staff are encouraged to use their initiative and to challenge anti-social behaviour.

At both Gorbals and Westercommon, extensive community facilities have accompanied the improved security and the general upgrading of blocks. At Westercommon, where the large number of children remains a problem, a tenants hall cum mini community centre funded by Urban Aid has been installed, providing modern youth club facilities near the flats. Fenced-off gardens have been built in front of ground-floor flats. Stark doorways have been softened with brick baffles. Plans are afoot to have the main doors recessed into the foyers, with the caretakers, as at Gorbals, gradually assuming the role of concierge or receptionist. Caretakers are encouraged to adopt a "quick response" approach to outbreaks of minor vandalism—they even hold stocks of chemicals on site in order to remove graffiti promptly. Closed circuit television cameras at Westercommon monitor at the main doors.

There are still problems. Tenants will accept advice, and even censure, from a permanent caretaker living in the same building. But where, as in Gorbals, on-site services are supplemented by outside security companies, there is a rapid turnover of private sector guards. Ideally, directly-employed guards would encourage the tenants to comply with, and even identify with, the new régime.

With a government paymaster dedicated to privatisation and

with spending cuts now intensifying north of the border, this is not likely to happen. Conceivably, if cuts and privatisation grow, the present caretaking initiatives could suffer. Against that day, SSHA staff have produced models of resident consultation and participation. Gorbals and Westercommon may no longer be in crisis, but they are still a long way from assured salvation.

What has in fact happened is that security has moved beyond technology. The technology will always have problems anyway. Even strong doors will be pulled open forcibly by those too lazy or confused to use a release system. Wind turbulence, which is a common problem with high buildings, can wreck a door in seconds. Television cameras and entryphones can and do break down.

Security, in the end, rests with people. And people will only defend that which they feel involves and defends them. True security is a *process*. Setting that process in motion demands high-quality professional staff, operating with confidence and autonomy, alongside at least a core group of involved consumers. It means that while the customer may not always be right, his or her views get priority when decisions are being made.

In one of the SSHA's rescued Glasgow blocks, the caretaker walks from top to bottom every Wednesday, checking that tenants have washed their stairs and landings. If they haven't and that's increasingly rare, he reports to management and the tenant is sharply reminded of his or her responsibility. In contrast, when council housing staff in Glasgow took action last year to enforce the payment of multi-million pound rent arrears, they were humiliatingly halted by angry councillors afraid of electoral reaction. The SSHA backs its staff and they, in turn, back the tenants.

The neds and the junkies, the slogan-sprayers and the housebreakers, are finding it increasingly difficult to get into Gorbals and Westercommon. They face security guards, entry-phones, alert caretakers, cameras, and single-entrance blocks. But they've also been beaten by rose bushes, community centres, weathered brick and smart new paint. Technology can't do it alone.

Home from home

AMANDA MITCHISON

A project in Liverpool lodges homeless 16 to 18 year olds with families.

Would you like to take into your family, and love as your own, an aimless, disgruntled adolescent who is perhaps on drugs, on probation or pregnant? There are many that would, and the Merseyside Accommodation Project, which lodges homeless 16 to 18 year olds with families, has been inundated with requests. The project, established by Merseyside Council for Voluntary Service, took off last year.

A teenager can help cover the mortgage, or break up the insularity of a nuclear family. In Maisie's case, she would feel lonely in her small semi-detached with only herself, her 16 year old daughter and her baby grandson.

Her house is what every working class teenager hates to love; streams of milky tea and scones from the kitchen, a telly in every room, and tiny bedrooms upstairs with floral wallpaper, Spanish dolls in glass cases, valences and candlewick bedspreads.

In the lodger's bedroom, the house rules (no borrowing without asking, no friends to stay without permission, meals for friends to be paid for) hang on the wall in a plastic folder. The room next door is locked and Maisie says, "They're not all light fingered but it's silly to put temptation their way." Maisie has experience—she began taking in young destitutes 20 years ago. "We had money then, but I've spent it all on the boys and girls. There's no comparison—the kids in those days were all crawling and matted."

Maisie is lodging Sharon (18) and Janet (16), who both left home after rows with their parents. Maisie says, "Teenage years are a major catastrophe—you can't get on with your parents. I've tried to put Sharon's mum at ease and I'll try and get them both to go back. Because they are not mine, I feel more responsible for them than their own parents do."

Maisie worries about the girls—especially about Janet who "goes drinking," wears hoolahoop earrings and braces, and frequently folds up in giggles. Girls, according to Maisie, are more difficult than boys because they don't communicate—they sulk and bottle things up instead. "And at least with boys you don't have to worry that they'll come home with a bump. I know, it happened to my own daughter."

Maisie believes that teenagers can't live alone. "I've seen too much of it . . . Before they go it's all a wild thing, they are on cloud nine. And then after a few weeks the bills come in and the basics runs out. Mandy (an ex-lodger), she's 19—she moved out into a council flat and now she's in debt for who knows how many hundred."

MAP's teenagers are constantly penniless or in debt to their householders, but most of them agree they would probably be worse off living alone. The "young persons" (or "YPs" in MAP terminology) receive £60 a week from the DHSS and are meant to give £50 to their householder for board and keep. The £10 pocket money "is enough to buy a pair of jeans every three months," says Jane Lichtenstein, project manager for MAP.

MAP will not arrange for the DHSS to pay board and lodging directly to householders. "The YP must learn to cope with money even if they learn by running off with it," says MAP, and the organisation will not cover debts to householders. Under a "rehabilitation" category, MAP is exempt from the four week rule on DHSS lodging payments and householders can have up to two £50-a-week lodgers without affecting their own benefit allowances.

MAP will not accept householders who "ask about money before we raise the issue," and families which lodge many people and keep a separate sitting room for lodgers are now being phased out. "Also, if householders are over-zealous it doesn't work. They try and mould and shape the kids," says Lichtenstein.

MAP is also suspicious of families "who say the kids can do what they want. Next you find they are not allowed in the fridge, or they have to be in before eleven, or they are not allowed to bring girlfriends or boyfriends home . . . We suggest householders make it clear from the beginning and have rules about music, where the kids can smoke and on staying out times—perhaps in by eleven or twelve on weekdays and 1 am on Saturdays." MAP finds that in households headed by a couple, one of the adults—not necessarily the woman—will invariably take on the mothering role for the YPs.

MAP also does some mothering—householders and YPs have separate extension workers who visit regularly. A full-time education officer tries to get those that have left school into further education and gives literacy classes—about half the YPs cannot read. At the MAP centre, day courses and counselling are given on careers, housing, family planning, working holidays, leisure, and personal problems, such as bereavement and alcoholism.

There are also occasional MAP parties, holidays and outings, which are sometimes quite rowdy. MAP is staffed by 4 full-time staff (funded by MSC, Laura Ashley and Crisis at Christmas), and by 12 MSC community programme workers who themselves receive part time training in social work and counselling.

"There is an absolutely massive number of people whose life starts going wrong at around 14. They drift into crime, or stop going to school," says Lichtenstein, who claims the project fills a gap in provisions by social services. At present MAP has 66 teenagers in residence; about a quarter of them have come out of residential care and a few are victims of violence or sexual abuse.

But the majority have simply left home or been thrown out because of family quarrels. A MAP employee says, "You'd be surprised how many parents kick their children out. One lad, when we asked him why he'd come to us, said, "my mum always kicks us out when we turn 16." Lichtenstein notes, "What we often find is that families expand—for example, the older sister has a baby, a step-father arrives. And at that time it is the horrible 16 year old that gets ejected."

The YPs coming out of care are the most uncommunicative, but also "the easiest to deal with on a day to day basis"—a couple of crewcut orphanage and foster boys wouldn't answer any questions with more than monosyllables and sniggers. According to Lichtenstein "something really awful" has to happen before middle class teenagers become homeless and they tend to be some of the "most bolshy and difficult" YPs.

A few of the teenagers have returned home—for example, pregnant girls often return home after their parents recover from an initial period of rejection—others are thrown out by householders, disappear or drift into vagrancy. Most, however, manage to settle down and MAP tries at the end of two years to place them in permanent accommodation. But perhaps for one MAP charge the future has more in store than merely a housing association flat. A rich childless householder says he will bequeath his fortune to the perfect YP, if he ever finds one.

Crime and Community

Peace and goodwill

JOY MELVILLE

Warring neighbours in Kent are reconciled by volunteers, rather than taking each other to court.

How do you reinstate the Christmas spirit after one respectable elderly lady in her seventies living next door to another respectable lady in her seventies shouts, "You old cow," over the hedge?

This sudden rush of blood to the head was because the fast-growing box hedge belonging to one was now blocking the other one's light. Going on the attack, the neighbour in the shadow went out one day, deliberately cut down all the bits of hedge within reach, and flung them up and over into the other woman's garden. In turn, this woman rushed out and threw it all back again. At that point the three-letter word ripped through the air.

Fortunately, it happened in Bromley, one of the few towns that deals with neighbours' rows through a Mediation and Dispute Centre, run on a voluntary basis as an extension of the Citizens Advice Bureau. The centre has now been operating for some three months with a dozen conciliators—CAB workers who went on a training course earlier this year—who listen to both sides of the story, don't place blame, and suggest solutions.

The conciliators try to get the warring protaganists in to the centre, to tell their side of the story. If they come through the door looking daggers at each other, they are put in different waiting rooms. "Where is *she*?" said the hedge-owning lady when she came in. But at one point, when describing how she threw the hedge clippings back, she laughed. "It was the first little breakthrough," says Joyce Sutton, the organiser of the bureau and one of the conciliators. "Then when the other woman came in, she laughed too and said, 'It does sound silly.' We had a fairly heated time with them, but in the end we helped them come to an agreement about cutting the hedge and keeping it trimmed. When I phoned them a month later, they were both happy."

The issues neighbours fight over sound trivial enough: bad

parking in shared driveways; having bonfires which ruin the washing; making a lot of noise; leaving lights on and disturbing people. Yet if such a problem isn't solved, and goes on for months, even years, it can lead to obsessive bitterness and sometimes mental breakdown. There have even been cases of neighbours killing each other. "It seems to penetrate right through the whole of the family," says Joyce Sutton "It starts with the parents and then the kids pick it up."

Once obsession sets in, it's only too easy to decide that someone is acting maliciously. In one case the Bromley Centre had to deal with, a couple had a fishpond with very expensive carp and the lady next door had a cat. The couple thought she was deliberately letting the cat out to eat the carp. "We managed to convince them that she couldn't control her cat and the only way was to cover their pond," says Joyce Sutton.

Most people telephone in, rather than have any kind of confrontation with the neighbour themselves. About 100 calls have been received in the first three months. Once a call is received the person is asked if they would talk to a coordinator', who listens to the problem and then writes to the neighbour. "Pratically every time they have answered," says Joyce Sutton, "though sometimes they get indignant and say, 'What's all this about?' Often when the conciliator has talked to both sides he or she will suggest to the person who made the call that they go and talk to the neighbour, have a cup of tea with them.

That's not always an easy step. One woman rang up, for instance, and said that the neighbours kept on having a barbecue outside, right next to their living-room. She and her husband told them to remove it and both sides got angry and started abusing each other. Finally the husband jumped over the fence and grabbed a steak off the barbecue and threw it slap in the neighbour's face. "We hoped to sort it out," says Joyce Sutton, "but though the person who complained was willing to come in, the other wouldn't: they wanted an apology. And the complainants said, 'No way.' We will have to wait till barbecue time next summer to see what happens.

"What I have found is that people seem to get all het up when they try to speak to the other party and instead of saying something friendly, blurt something out that sounds rude and the other side reacts, and from then on no progress is made at all. People have got to be able to feel that they can come in and face the other person and this is always a major difficulty. I wonder sometimes whether it's an English trait, being too polite to tell your neighbour that they are infuriating you. So often when people know why their behaviour is upsetting, they stop it."

One youngish couple, for instance, both working, had two

dogs and a dog flap and the dogs got out and barked day and night. The woman next door got immensely upset because her two children were taking their O and A levels and were being woken up in the middle of the night. She would bang on the neighbours' wall and once yelled at their window from the street.

A conciliator arranged a meeting and found the people with the dogs just did not understand the effect the barking was having. After both sides listened to each other, the dog owners agreed not to let their dogs out at night and the family next door offered to look after the dogs when the owners went away. They shook hands and the agreement held.

Another time a young family had a climbing frame in the garden. Next door there was an old widower living alone. The mother phoned to say he was getting very angry about the children being able to see into his garden and we talked to both sides and it turned out he was extremely lonely and resented the family next door being young and happy. And once the mother realised why he was making such a fuss, she bent over backwards to help him.

"Often it's a lonely person who will cause the problem," says another conciliator. "If you're feeling a bit down, it's quite easy to get upset. And once it starts, all reason goes out of the window. You get the revenge element, with both parties trying to cause more annoyance and there's just no end to it. But if they go to the solicitor the cost can be £300 or £400, out of all proportion to the complaint. The solicitors often advise the complainant not to proceed, but they're in a lather to get their own back."

It it's a question of a dispute over driveways or a property matter, conciliators go back to the deeds. Otherwise their job is to talk—and keep talking. It's hard to keep figures of their success: often, after negotiating with neighbours, they hear nothing—which hopefully means both sides are now back on good terms. As the word gets round about this free service, the number of neighbours asking for help is growing, along with the need for more voluntary conciliators.

"It would be very nice to get to the point where people, when they feel that they are getting themselves into a state, come along and say, 'Can you help?'" says Joyce Sutton. "What we want is to sort it out at the beginning before it goes too far. But it's a new concept for them—like the Citizens Advice Bureaux when they first started." And, for the un-neighbourly British, obviously just as necessary.

Safe and sound

STEVE PLATT

A community programme scheme provides crime prevention counselling for the vulnerable elderly.

"I haven't got anything of any real value, you know," the old man said. "Just a few old coins that aren't worth very much." He didn't see the point of talking to crime prevention counsellor Bill Cooles about protecting himself from con-men, muggers or thieves, but he was a little lonely and welcomed the chance of a friendly chat over a cup of tea.

The "few old coins," however, turned out to be gold sovereigns, over a century old and in mint condition, with a minimum value of £2,000 or so. The old man kept them in a battered wooden box, oblivious of their real worth and vulnerable to the first confidence trickster or thief that chanced upon them.

It was, according to Bill Cooles, "fairly typical" of his experiences during ten weeks of crime prevention counselling: "The elderly people I've seen always say they haven't got anything of value. They don't understand that what might be an old table or a pretty vase to them is a valuable antique to someone else. And they don't really believe that there are lots of people around who would have no scruples about conning them out of it or stealing it from them."

Bill Cooles is one of five members of a crime prevention counselling scheme run by Arrowhead Community Enterprises in Chertsey, Surrey. Set up in January 1985 under the Manpower Services Commission community programme, the scheme offers a unique service reassuring elderly people who are worried about crime and showing them how to protect their property.

Members of the counselling team make contact with elderly people at local clubs and day centres, where they organise special talks and video shows on crime prevention, usually in cooperation with Age Concern and the Surrey police. The emphasis is on non-alarmist discussion about the risks of crime—and bogus callers, burglars, street thieves and so on—and how to take precautions against it. Simple advice is offered on the use of door chains, locks, security marking devices and identity checks on unknown callers.

Most importantly, though, the elderly are also offered the opportunity of making an appointment for a personal visit to their homes by members of the counselling team. Usually about a third of them take up the offer, enticed perhaps by the free ultra-violet security marking service the team provides, or by the prospect of some company and social contact.

"The social side is as important as the actual counselling," says John Dean, who set up and organised the scheme. "Our counsellors are trained to sit down and chat, to take their time and, if necessary, to go by a roundabout route to get a solution to an old person's crime prevention needs. We're not there to tell them what to do; our aim is to help people to solve their own problems."

Jane Bennett, another member of the counselling team, agrees: "A lot of old people are very set in their ways. They don't want anyone to come in and order them about. They'll say they've always left their back door unlocked, for example, so why should they start locking it now?"

Simple precautions, which cost nothing, are considered most important—remembering to lock doors and windows when going out, finding out who is at the door before opening it (and accepting that it is not bad manners to do so), knowing what to do when going away and so on. "It's amazing how many old people still leave notes for the milkman saying they won't be back until such and such a day," says Jane Bennett, "or how many leave the front door wide open while they pop out to the shops."

The counselling team also provides impartial advice on different locks or other security devices, although it can't install them itself. "It's frustrating not being able to finish the job by fitting locks where they're needed," says Bill Cooles, "especially when you know that a professional locksmith might charge £60 or £70 for an hour's work. But we can sometimes help people who couldn't afford it otherwise by referring them to groups like Age Concern, the Lions or the Rotary Club who will do it for them."

The main practical service offered by the team is ultra-violet security marking of valued items with the elderly person's postcode and house number, so that if they are stolen and subsequently recovered, the police can return them to their owner. The counsellors mark any item, on request, regardless of their own assessment of its value.

"What matters is whether an old person considers something to be valuable," says John Dean. "That means we get asked to mark all sorts of peculiar things—from fur coats and toy dolls to every individual item in a canteen of cutlery." The only thing he has ever refused to mark was a television: it turned out to be rented.

The counselling team is taught to respect the judgement of the elderly, not to impose their own ideas. John Dean points out that sometimes what may appear to be foolish or needlessly risky behaviour can actually be quite rational: "A lot of old people are very cost-conscious and astute. They might weigh up the price of new locks against the risk of burglary and decide that it's not worth installing them. Or they might keep large sums of cash at home because they would be ineligible for social security if they put it in a bank. We might suggest ways of reducing the risk of theft, but in the end the decision has to be theirs."

"We are able to do what the police and social services can't," says John Dean. "We have a very different relationship with people. They can confide in us and we can spend the time with them that other organisations don't have." Follow-up visits are made as a matter of course: "You can tell what effect you had on your first visit by whether or not they look or call out to see who you are before opening the door."

Almost 1,000 old people have been counselled since the scheme started two years ago, and John Dean would like to see it expanded to cover the whole of Surrey. The only obstacle is the current standstill on further growth in the community programme, which is fixed at 255,000 places nationwide.

"When the Prime Minister held her crime prevention seminars at 10 Downing Street last year, she announced the provision of 5,000 community programme places as part of her anti-crime initiative," says John Dean. "What she didn't say was that these were not *extra* places, and that they couldn't be taken up until existing projects came to an end. Because of this we haven't been able to even think about expanding the schemes."

Dean and his colleagues are understandably aggrieved at this. He argues that the crime prevention counselling team is of benefit not only to the elderly, but also to those it employs. The nature of the work means that potential applicants have to undergo a rigorous vetting procedure—"We are not afraid of rejecting people," says Dean—but once they are accepted their future job prospects are greatly enhanced.

Virtually all of the ten people who have been counsellors with the team now have jobs, one of them as the head of a large group of security personnel. Jane Bennett, a single parent who was out of work for four years before joining the team last November, says she gets as much out of the scheme as the old people she visits. And for Bill Cooles, a former engineer who was unemployed for twelve months, it is "a way of retraining myself for some kind of social work."

Above all, the team provides an invaluable means of educating old people into the ways of a world that has become immeasurably more criminal than when they were young. One of the cautionary tales told by the crime prevention panel in Chertsey is of a local con-man who uses a five year old boy to trick his way into the homes of the elderly. Teaching old people to be less trusting, even of children, might not be everyone's idea of the most satisfying of tasks, but it is one that has become increasingly necessary—even in the leafy suburbs of Surrey.

Playtime in prison

JENNY CUFFE

Provison of a crêche at Winchester Local Prison eases the tensions and frustrations of visiting times.

In the visiting room at Winchester Local Prison, it's the children who are behind bars. While their parents sit at rows of tables in the centre of the smoke-filled room, and officers stand guard, a group of six or seven children crouch on the floor of a huge playpen in one corner. They're as intent on their jigsaws and building bricks as the adults are in their conversation. Occasionally one of them will run out of the playpen gate to join mum and dad. A little boy wants his father to help make a fire engine out of Lego. When an officer stops the prisoner from leaving his table and getting inside the bars, the child begins to cry.

Winchester Prison crêche is a modest affair. Any more than ten children in this corner and they'd be standing on top of each other. Sometimes the volunteer play leader has a cluster of small children fighting to climb on her knee. In one afternoon, with three batches of visitors over a two-hour period, she may cope single-handed with up to 30 children. The noise level is excruciating. But the group of women who have set up the crêche know how important it has become.

Until two months ago, Winchester was like almost every other prison in Britain in providing no facilities for visitors' children. Seeing them sit restlessly at bare tables in the locked room, you might have wondered if they were being punished for the sins of their fathers. In a way, the crêche was born out of curiosity. Fiona Clarke, whose home is between the railway station and the prison, noticed groups of women passing at the same time each day, pulling or pushing often reluctant children. A mother herself, she wondered what was in store for those children at the prison. When she found there was nothing for them, she decided to set up a playgroup of some sort.

A woman welfare officer at the prison was prepared to champion her cause, but a request to the Home office remained unanswered for twelve months. Then Fiona got a telephone call asking her to set up a crêche within a week. Thanks to a local network of willing mothers, she set up a rota whereby 13 volunteers take turns to be in charge. But not everyone is suitable. "I had to sort out those who wouldn't mind dirty nappies and snotty noses," Fiona says. "I didn't want anyone going in as Lady Muck. They had to get down on their hands and knees and attend to the children."

The prison provided money for toys and there was a donation from a group for prisoners' families in Portsmouth. Then space was allocated in the visiting room, but this caused dissension among some prison staff. At first they complained that they were losing two visitors' tables, which meant more frequent trips to and from cells and the prison gates, escorting prisoners and their families. Some argued that the crêche should be in a separate building, but Fiona maintains that it's essential the children are in sight of their parents during the visit. Other critics claim that children shouldn't be exposed to life inside, yet only the most punitive would stand up and deny a prisoner the right to see his children, or their right to see him.

Most of the critics have now been won over. And those in charge of the prison are so pleased with the effects of the crêche that they're considering another addition for visitors—a room for nursing mothers. The deputy governor, John Lawrence, feels there have been benefits all round. The children, he says, are receiving care and attention they may not get elsewhere, because their mothers are too harassed trying to cope on their own. And the prisoner and his wife or girlfriend are able to have an uninterrupted conversation. Visiting times are short—a quarter of an hour daily for men on remand; half an hour twice a month for convicted prisoners—and there are often important subjects to discuss, things which can't be put in a letter. "The crêche," says John Lawrence, "means that the visits go better and the inmate returns to his cell feeling he's had a useful time with his family, rather than going back frustrated because he's been unable to talk."

As with any useful service, the crêche has quickly become taken for granted, though prisoners' wives with experience of the other places of detention admit that it's reduced the tension of visiting time. Pointing to the three year old clinging to her skirts, Lorraine remarks on how difficult it is to have any conversation with the likes of him climbing all over the table, asking to play. Another mother agrees that you can't speak openly in front of the children, yet there is no one who can look after them at home and, besides, it's good for them to see their dad.

Considering the obvious benefits of the crêche, it is remarkable that the Home Office has remained so indifferent to its existence. A spokesman tells me that, as far as he knows, there are no such facilities at any other prison in England and Wales. But then he didn't know about the Winchester initiative. Certainly, the Home Office has no plans to provide similar crêches at other prisons, and it will need persistent volunteers like Fiona Clarke and her Winchester group to get any such scheme off the ground. "Any idea or suggestion to improve facilities would be welcomed by the governors of individual prisons," says the Home Office. "However, with the pressures on funding, it obviously depends on circumstances and resources."

Meanwhile, back in the visiting room, the play leader suggests to four year old Katie that she paint a picture for daddy. "Don't want to," comes the reply. But another day she'll do half a dozen paintings to show him, and he can watch her happily occupied until it's time to say goodbye.

Bridging the gap

TOM ASTON

An organisation critical of the penal system befriends those in prison and provides advice for ex-offenders.

Except for his visits from New Bridge volunteers, Paul, a remand prisoner at Brixton Prison, is completely cut off from the outside world. Since he lost touch with his sisters and his parents died, he has had no one else to support him. He even had difficulty contacting his solicitor until New Bridge did so for him. He is just one of over 500 prisoners around the country who are visited by the volunteers.

It is usually up to the prisoners to make contact with New Bridge, an organisation which befriends the inmates of prisons (including those on remand), youth custody centres and special hospitals and provides an advisory service for ex-offenders. Some hear about it through the grapevine. Paul wrote to them during his first spell in prison three years ago.

However, New Bridge does regularly hold introductory meetings with inmates of youth custody centres: "We heard about a number of youths who had committed suicide in custody and we weren't getting referrals so we took the initiative," said deputy director, Jerry Westall.

Two years after the first meeting with "trainees" (as the inmates are called) at Rochester youth custody centre, 50 volunteers now visit and write to more than 100 trainees in 13 custody centres. The scheme is growing rapidly: at the beginning of last year New Bridge associates visited only 40 trainees.

Set up by a group of intellectuals, including Stephen Spender, Victor Gollancz, Lord Longford (who has just retired as president) and Lord Montagu (who himself was imprisoned for homosexuality), New Bridge will be celebrating its thirtieth anniversary later this year. Jerry Westall admits that in the past the organisation was somewhat paternalistic: "After the clamour for radical reform of the penal system in the sixties we took a downturn in the seventies. The real crunch came in 1980 when the money ran out and a group of members broke away to form SOVA, the Society of Voluntary Associates. They thought we were stuffy and a bit detached from the world. It was then that we became much more down to earth."

The youth custody scheme is a good example of this new outlook. When it started the voluntary associates were simply too old to communicate with the trainees. But the scheme is now organised by a 21 year old psychology graduate, Alessandra Lemma, and the VAs are all in their early twenties or younger, and 20 of them come from ethnic minorities. "The boys often say to us: 'I expected someone who was going to preach to me.' We help break down the image of the white middle-class prison visitor," said Alessandra.

"At first the staff were suspicious, but we got them to trust us. Now they welcome us, if only because we alleviate the tension inside the centre." After the introductory meeting, which is an official part of the "introduction week" at two centres, trainees can write to New Bridge if they want a visitor. The one-to-one meetings are unsupervised and confidential.

"Often the youths want to talk about the drugs coming into the centre, many still know very little about AIDS and want more information about how it can be transmitted. Some of them are fathers even at 16 or 17, sometimes having children with more than one girl, and they want to talk about it. Some of them just want a girl to talk to," said Alessandra. "One boy who has AIDS is confined to the centre's hospital and has asked for a VA to visit him as his mother lives in Grimsby and cannot see him regularly."

The success of New Bridge was illustrated recently when the governor of Dover youth custody centre phoned New Bridge and asked representatives to visit his centre, all expenses paid. The scheme is also getting started in a woman's youth custody centre, Bullwood Hall, although as yet trainees can only meet VAs just before they are released. "One girl coming out this week is a bit scared of taking the train back to London and wants someone to go with her. Some girls want to talk about their babies, who are either left with parents or taken into care—they feel they've failed as mothers," said Alessandra.

VAs often visit inmates of youth custody centres and adult prisons where the conditions can be much harsher. Even remand prisoners, like Paul, may have to cope with days in strip or semi-strip cells (empty cells with only a blanket, or cardboard furniture and few possessions) and up to 23 hours' incarceration a day.

During an earlier spell in prison, Paul's VA, Eric, provided him with a steady supply of letters and regular visits, occasional tobacco and food. And when he moved around the country from prison to prison, Eric stuck with him. Local prison-visiting groups would have lost touch with him as he eventually passed through five prisons, some of them twice during his two-year sentence.

Another member of the organisation is John Ferris, a former convict and now chairman of New Bridge's Alton branch. A year after he was released from Wandsworth prison, John married Liz, his VA. "The first-timer is likely to feel bewildered, frightened, very depressed and alone," he said. "For the guy who has no friends or family to write to him or visit him there becomes a desperate need to communicate regularly with an understanding, caring person outside."

When helping to train new VAs John says they must be "a friend and comforter, an advisory service, a vehicle for the guy's anger and frustration. Often you're expected to be a marriage guidance expert, or just a liaison between him and his wife or family." One prisoner described his volunteer as "an emotional lightning conductor."

Half of the prisoners who ask for VAs to visit them are serving more than seven years, many of them are lifers convicted for murder, or sexual offenders who can be isolated and beaten up by other prisoners. "Some people have, quite literally, been kept alive," said Jerry.

John Ferris, who also works on the Bridge's management committee, emphasises the important role of a VA after a prisoner is released: "For anyone who wants to go straight, the prospects are very grim if you don't know the right people. During this settling-down period the temptation to commit more crime can be very great and they need the strength of a friend to draw on."

Over 100 ex-offenders are still seeing their volunteer visitors. New Bridge also runs three employment offices covering the London area which can help with curriculum vitae, interview techniques and building up an ex-offender's confidence.

On an annual budget of about £125,000, New Bridge manages to provide three employment officers and four staff in its Notting Hill office, pay the travel expenses for 150 VAs and run its newly opened Manchester branch. About a quarter of the funding is from the Home Office and London councils; the rest comes from a range of trusts, companies and individuals.

The Bridge is openly critical of the penal system. The chairman, Lady Ewart-Biggs, has made some powerful speeches in the House of Lords calling for reform of the prison system. Jerry Westall, who is a former member of Radical Alternatives to Prison (RAP) says: "Prison is irrelevant to crime. If people would realise that it would be a great shaker. It doesn't solve problems it creates them."

Council goes local

STEVE PLATT

Decentralisation by a Labour Council brings in a new kind of democracy.

When the last of its 24 neighbourhood offices opens in July, Islington—one of the smallest boroughs in the country—will have completed the first phase of the biggest decentralisation programme yet attempted by a British local authority. No resident will be more than a ten-minute walk from their nearest council office; services which were once spread among half a dozen different departments in as many different buildings will all be available under one roof; and neighbourhood forums to determine how services are provided and how money is spent in each area will usher in a new style of local democracy.

Islington's ambitious plans for devolved local government have taken four years to get off the 1982 election manifesto drawing-board. The council has had to overcome professional rivalries, staff resistance, tenants' doubts, unanticipated legal and financial problems, and a series of trade union disputes.

"It's been damned hard work," says Maurice Barnes, who chairs the decentralisation sub-committee. "People have wanted to change everything but themselves."

Yet change there has been. The council has rewritten half its workers' job descriptions to create a completely new structure of local government. Each neighbourhood office now provides all the basic council services, including most housing functions (repairs, improvements, lettings, rent collection, advice and benefits), environmental health duties, social work field services, welfare rights assistance and community work. Eventually, home helps, caretakers and street cleaners will also be locally based (though they are currently engaged in a campaign of "disruption and direct action" in protest at the way the "go local" plans affect their jobs).

When decentralisation is complete, each office will resemble a tiny town hall, employing between 30 and 50 white-collar staff and 40 to 90 manual workers. In addition to the street cleaning and area repair teams, which will remain largely autonomous, four mini departments under their own neighbourhood officers will deal with housing, environmental health, social services and office organisation.

Instead of an overall office "boss," there is a heavy emphasis on cooperation and teamwork, something which one neighbourhood officer described as "a far more revolutionary concept for most of our workers than that of decentralisation." His own office had been racked by personal conflicts and professional competitiveness since opening last year. Technical officers had "retreated behind a veil of expertise"; social workers had erected filing cabinet partitions in the open-plan office "to symbolise their separation and secrecy." Elsewhere, though, departmentalism has been successfully challenged. Common files have been created, and social work case conferences have begun to involve staff from outside the usual social services network. In some offices, rent arrears cases are now being dealt with as part of a package involving a range of workers. Housing benefit hold-ups are attended to, advice is given on other welfare entitlements, and outstanding repair or transfer requests—which may have contributed to the accrual of arrears—are sorted out as part of a single plan of action.

Local people are also being involved—often for the first time. The Archway neighbourhood office, for example, has halved the number of empty properties in its area by bringing tenants, lettings officers and the building works departments together in a coordinated effort. Tenant cooperation and vigilance has also substantially reduced the squatting of newly repaired property.

The reduction in empty properties (though the council still

owns well over 2,000) is a reflection of decentralisation's most dramatic success story. Two years ago, a centralised direct-labour organisation had a repairs backlog of three to four months. Now the new area repair teams have reduced it to under three weeks, and some have backlogs of a fortnight or less. What is more, the turn-around has been achieved in the face of a massive growth in demand. Repair requests have increased from 1,400 a week in 1984 to 3,000 a week—"The better we do, the more we get asked to do," as one building works foreman grouchily remarked.

The same surge in demand has hit other services too. The social services department reports a "greatly increased" case-load. Section 1 emergency payments have risen to over £500,000 this year. Housing benefit take-up has also increased, partly because new welfare rights workers have been employed at every office. Some offices are now dealing with up to 700 callers a week (a fifth of the area's adult population in one case), and additional staff are being employed to cope with the unexpected demand.

Maurice Barnes believes that use of the offices will fall after an initial surge, and this has already begun to happen in the first four to open. But he also says that improved service take-up "was a major reason for decentralisation in the first place."

Barnes is also encouraged by the degree of involvement in the neighbourhood forums which have been set up in each area. Potentially the most radical aspect of the entire "go local" scheme, the forums are seen as a means of devolving power as well as services. At present they control £1 million of local spending and have a powerful advisory function which has so far focused on issues such as planning, traffic, crime, street lighting, repairs, empty property and the use of community facilities.

Any formal extension of the forums' powers would require legislation (which the council may promote) as well as some changes of attitude. The local tenants' federation, for example, had been unwilling to relinquish its right of direct access to the housing committee, or to permit non-tenants to vote on tenant issues. Some tenants' associations are also reluctant to become involved in decision making which might mean that they have to give priority to different improvement schemes. "They want the power," says Maurice Barnes, "but not the responsibility."

There would also need to be a more uniform method of selecting representatives to the forums. Although the council insists upon the involvement of "people who have previously been under-represented in local democracy," such as ethnic minorities, the young, elderly and disabled, the precise selection method is left to each area. Some, such as Archway, have opted for direct elections. Others, such as Quadrant, which attracts 70 or so people to its meetings, allow any local organisation to nominate members.

None of the neighbourhoods has more than 12,000 residents; the average is 6,900. This is clearly a decisive factor in encouraging community identity and involvement. So, too, is the accessibility and friendliness of the neighbourhood offices, which were specifically designed to create a welcoming environment. As well as comfortable waiting areas with children's toys and playspace, vending machines and public telephones, the offices also provide typewriters, photocopies and duplicators for community use.

The improvement has, inevitably, been expensive. Building work alone has cost £10 million, and at least 220 extra workers have been employed. The council says that many of them were taken on to provide new or additional services. It also argues that, while public participation may be costly at first, "it can result in a more cost-effective and efficient service in the long run."

Another view was expressed at the official opening of one office recently, when a *Daily Mail* reporter asked an old age pensioner what she though about the costs involved in decentralisation. "Marvellous, isn't it?" she replied. "It saves me 60p in bus fares every time I come here."

Snappy workers

STEVE PLATT

A partnership in Stoke Newington taps the resources of a heterogenous community.

Stoke Newington, in the north-east corner of Britain's poorest borough, Hackney, is often portrayed as "the place where gentrification meets urban blight and yuppies bolt their pine shutters against the video marauders . . . house prices have risen by 25-35 per cent in the last year, but most streets contain derelict houses that the council can't afford to repair and the post delivers giros to one house in five."

The words are those of Mark Lushington, a "community links" worker with the Inner London Education Authority, who is based at Stoke Newington secondary school. But Lushington also says that "the conventional picture fails to give a good likeness."

Not that he denies the coexistence of poverty, dereliction and decay alongside the more prosperous communities of middle class incomers now taking over the Victorian terraces of this north London suburb. Rather, he prefers to emphasise the variety of classes, races and cultures which combine to create a rich blend of skills and resources.

It was to utilise those untapped resources and provide an outlet for those underemployed abilities that Lushington and others initiated the Stoke Newington Area Partnership. Based at Stoke Newington School, and assisted by small grants of several hundred pounds each from ILEA and Hackney council, SNAP aims "to bring together people of all ages, cultures and interests who live or work in the area so that we can share ideas and resources."

Its objectives are deliberately open-ended, even vague. "We are trying hard not to define our relationship with the community too tightly," says Lushington. "We are essentially a communication network. We don't want to impose ourselves on existing community organisations, or to take them over. But we do feel that there is a need for some sort of umbrella organisation linking the school with the community groups, and the community groups with each other."

Thus, SNAP concentrates on acting as a sort of clearing house "to help guide people through the maze of services and organisations that exist," and to provide a common forum through which people from different groups and cultures can communicate and cooperate with each other. There is an emphasis on small-scale, practical assistance: arranging the loan of the school minibus to a homeless families group, for instance, or opening up the school premises for special language classes, meetings or other community activities, or putting one tenants' group in touch with another which recently got a grant to buy certain equipment that it needed.

The inspiration for SNAP, according to Mark Lushington, was in the 1984-85 miners' strike, when a wide range of groups in Hackney came together to organise a massive Christmas party in support of the strikers. Up to 5,000 people took part altogether, thousands of presents were collected for miners' children; local businessmen donated toys and food; local performers put on free entertainment; and Turkish and Asian groups in the borough organised the catering. "The different communities in Hackney came together in a way that we hadn't seen before," says Lushington, "and some of us wanted to preserve the magic of that moment, and build on it for the future."

The teachers' industrial action during the next two years, and the painstaking work involved in bringing together what were often very different – and sometimes conflicting – organisations, meant that SNAP developed slowly. The idea of closer links between the school and the community was tested first on a very small scale – four pupils working with a local over-60s project, informal discussions with the Turkish Education Group about the school curriculum and language resources, and so on.

But there was a demand for something more. "What we want is a partnership with the school," said Aydin Ali Ahmet of the Turkish Education Group. The same idea was reiterated again and again by people from other community groups, and by teachers, parents and pupils.

A steering group was set up, therefore, to develop such a partnership. Its members – who include an actor, a journalist, three teachers, a black parent-governor, the vice-chair of the Bengali Homeless Project and the chair of a local residents' group – tend towards the yuppie end of the Stoke Newington community, but other active supporters include school students, as well as the local Labour councillors and Stoke Newington School's headteacher, Robin Chambers.

In April, Chambers enthusiastically supported SNAP's first major public event – a community fair at Stoke Newington School, with food, entertainment and stalls provided by a variety of local groups. Posters and leaflets publicising the fair, which went to about 10,000 people in the area, were paid for by adverts from local businesses, including shops, pubs, cafes, a gymnasium (which also put on a keep fit display) and art gallery. Pupils from the school helped organise the fair and clear up afterwards, and despite heavy rain all day it was a huge success, attracting around 1,000 visitors.

The fair also marked a deliberate break with traditional forms of organisation and structure. "The biggest parents' meeting we've ever held at our school was attended by about 35 people," says Mark Lushington. "Most people simply won't turn out for meetings, and those who will are usually overcommitted already. So we decided to centre the organisation around an event or activity, rather than a meeting."

After all, he adds, that is the way in which most people lead their lives – arranging things informally with friends, "rather than going through endless committee meetings and discussing every little detail." Even the steering group is organised informally. It does have elected officers, and a fully fledged management committee is to be set up in the autumn, but this is mainly to satisfy outside bodies that the organisation is properly constituted. Lushington insists that an informal chat over a cup of tea will remain the principal organisational method.

SNAP's latest project involves the production of a regular broadsheet for the area, probably financed by advertising and money raised from events such as the fair. Lushington sees this as a logical extension of the "informational network" already established around the school.

"The school is a sort of informal Citizens Advice Bureau," he says. Half of its 1,000 pupils are from ethnic minorities; 10 per cent are of Turkish origin, and perhaps 15 per cent come from Bangladeshi families in nearby bed and breakfast hotels for the homeless. Often the children are the only people in the family who speak good English, and their only way of finding out what services are available, or what organisations may be able to help with their problems, is through the school.

SNAP, however, is in danger of folding before it has even properly got off the ground. The temporary hut which had been earmarked as a base for the project has been discovered to contain asbestos and can't be used. And Mark Lushington is one of the ILEA staff currently facing compulsory redeployment as a result of falling school rolls. He is angry about this threat to SNAP's future.

"It would be two years' work down the drain," he says, "and the stupid thing about it is that by 1991 our school will have an extra 400 pupils, so they'll have to start taking on staff again. SNAP would still survive in some form if I went, but without a community links worker it would almost certainly lose its connection with the school, which would be a disaster."

Lushington quotes the former ILEA leader, Frances Morrell, with bitterness: "She used to say: 'this is the age of initiative, not resources.' She didn't say that the ILEA would be smothering initiative by taking resources away."

Families and Young People

Friends in need

STEVE PLATT

Linkworkers in Hertfordshire befriend high risk children to keep them out of care and custody.

John Steen was woken by the knocking on his front door, but by the time he got downstairs there was no one there. Up on the balcony above, however, outside his bedroom window, was a teenage boy, Billy. "What are you doing up there?" asked John irritably. "Front doors are boring," Billy replied.

John Steen is a "linkworker" with the St Albans Diocesan Link Scheme in Hertfordshire; Billy is an "at risk" youngster with whom he has been "linked." The idea of the scheme, as outlined by one of its coordinators, Ian Carty, is "to get ordinary people from the local community to deal with some of the problems of that community by linking them with youngsters who are in danger of going into – or just coming out of – care or custody." The adult linkworkers "befriend" the youngsters, typically meeting them for six to eight hours a week over six to twelve months, and helping them through crises.

"Sometimes you just sit and have a cup of tea together," says John Steen. "The young person might simply want someone they can talk to or pursue an interest with. You might see each other for a short while, and then that's it. With others, it's a longer term commitment. Sometimes you need to be available to them 24 hours a day, seven days a week. I saw one lad 87 times in 92 days."

"If you can form a friendship with the youngsters you're linked with, they'll listen to you in a way that they won't listen to their social worker or probation officer, or even their own family," says Sue Carty, who has been a linkworker since the scheme started three years ago. "You can also get a lot of warmth and satisfaction in return, if you're prepared to put the effort in to make the relationship work."

In the case of Kim, a young girl with whom Sue is still linked, that effort included having to help her deal with being thrown out of college and getting evicted from her lodgings. Kim says she can't talk to her mother about her problems—"we always end up having rows"—but she feels able to discuss things with Sue. She's now been accepted back into college, has found new accommodation and has got a Saturday job, all with Sue's help. "Of course it could all fall apart again tomorrow," says Sue, "but if we've done nothing else, we've given her time to grow up a little and shown her that someone cares."

The linkworkers, who are paid sessional fees for their work, are selected according to enthusiasm and commitment, not professional qualifications. "We recruit people warts and all," says Dave Kellett, the project leader, who is seconded to the scheme by Hertfordshire county council (the council has taken over responsibility for funding the scheme from the DHSS, which financed it for the first two and a half years). "The linkworkers include factory workers, firemen, housewives, unemployed people, market stallholders—even social workers!"

One of the linkworkers is a former heroin trafficker, who served four years in prison. Kellett's view is that "when you're dealing with children at risk you have to be prepared to take risks. Someone who's been in trouble is more likely to be able to help these kids than someone who's well-meaning, but doesn't really understand their problems."

Each worker is vetted, of course, and has to go through an intensive ten-week induction training. After that, they spend a month getting to know each child assigned to them before a planning meeting is arranged between the child, linkworker, project coordinators, social workers, probation officers and anyone else concerned. A contract is drawn up stating how often the child will meet with his or her linkworker and specifying concrete objectives.

Regular review meetings are then held to assess progress, and there are also meetings at which the linkworkers can get together for mutual support and discussion. "In the end though, it's up to the individuals concerned," says Dave Kellett. "And it can be bloody hard, exhausting work."

In all, 166 young people have been referred to linkworkers since the scheme began. Because the organisers are concerned to avoid "unnecessary net-widening," they only accept referrals of youngsters in "high risk" categories. Even so, they have succeeded in keeping most of those referred to them out of custody or care. And they have done so at an average cost, in sessional fees and expenses, of only £80–117 per placement.

The project has an equally successful "homelink" scheme, whereby children facing a crisis are accepted into a family's own home, usually for a maximum of six days. The intention is to provide an immediate alternative to custody or care, and to give a young person "breathing space" in which to deal with their problems.

"The time limit concentrates minds wonderfully," says Dave Kellett. "We usually find that the people involved come up with solutions within the six-day period." Most often, the young people will go back to their parents' home, the time apart having enabled both sides to sort out the problems which led to the crisis in the first place. The average cost of each placement, for which the families are paid a fee of £15 per 24-hour period, is just £80. And of 117 youngsters accepted by the homelink scheme all but 27 have avoided care—a 77 per cent success rate.

Jake, a 17 year old youth from Stevenage, was kept out of custody by the link scheme. One of five children being brought up by his mother on her own, he admits—with only a hint of irony—to have "an explosive nature" (a year or so ago he blew up a Portacabin on a building site). John Steen took him on as a frustrated, cocky adolescent following his appearance in court on an arson charge. They went together to see Chelsea play; John taught Jake windsurfing, Jake taught John ten pin bowling.

Now Jake says he's changed completely: "John and I hit it off straight away. He helped me to calm down and sort things out at home. He was someone to talk to apart from my mum." Jake's feelings for John run deep: when he visited him one night, and couldn't get a response, even though the lights and the television were on, he says he started to panic: "I thought he was ill. I was about to try to break in or something, when he suddenly appeared, walking up the road. I could have killed him for worrying me like that."

Robin, another 17 year old on the link scheme, has deeper problems. A lifetime spent in children's homes has left him bitter and isolated. He was sleeping rough before coming into the scheme, and though he now has lodgings in Stevenage, he feels he has little else to keep him there. "The loneliness is the worst thing," he says. "Sometimes all I do is sniff glue all day." He describes his linkworker, Martin Fogarty, as "a gift from God. He's always there when I need him, even when I know he'd rather be doing something else."

"There were 30 different workers at the children's home I was in," Robin continues. "So we were brought up in 30 different ways. I'd never had a one-to-one relationship before I met Martin. Having someone like him gives you that extra bit of support that you don't have when you come out of care." Robin looks across at me as though I could never begin to understand the depth of his loneliness: "It means you're not *totally* on your own."

Stepping into families

SUSANNAH KIRKMAN

An organisation, which provides counselling for stepparents, is setting up local groups throughout Britain.

Forming a stepfamily is like taking the first five people you meet on the street and saying, "We're going to live together," according to Clive Goodwin, who has been a stepfather for five years.

"You're suddenly presented with a grotty little 13 year old you loathe but have to live with. It's not a normal relationship," Goodwin explains. He and his wife set up the Winchester branch of Stepfamily three years ago, using their own experiences to try to help others going through the mill of stepfamily life. It's a self-help group offering support and a chance for stepfamilies to get together and air their difficulties. Families gather in each other's homes to share a buffet Sunday lunch, and parents can also meet on their own to discuss particular problems.

The Winchester branch is one of about 50 local groups affiliated to the national Stepfamily, which was started in Cambridge four years ago by Elizabeth Hodder, who has five stepchildren as well as two of her own. Hodder believes that stepmothers often have the worse deal. Hodder says "You feel like a skivvy in your own house; you're not in control of the situation, but your stepchildren are. A natural mother can set parameters; a stepmother often has no say over rules and standards."

Yet in Hodder's experience, the onus is often on the women to work things out. "Men are liable to say, 'You sort it out'," she explains.

It's not surprising that many stepmothers lose their self-esteem and start to blame themselves for everything that goes wrong. One of the most important things Stepfamily can do is to reassure anxious stepparents that it's not their fault. When they start to get in touch with others in a similar situation, they soon realise that they're not alone.

"It was marvellous to read other people's experiences in the Stepfamily newsletter," says Judith, whose teenage stepson nearly wrecked her marriage. "I was battling with two different lifestyles under one roof, but when I criticised my stepson's behaviour, my husband became defensive. He felt I was attacking him through his son."

Contact with other stepparents helped Judith to feel less guilty about her relationship with her stepson. "I started to understand that you may not always love your stepchildren, but you can care about them in a special way."

Judith herself contributed some of her own experiences to the Stepfamily newsletter, in answer to a letter from a woman who felt bitter towards her husband's first wife.

Telephone counselling is another way of linking and helping stepparents. Stepfamily runs a telephone help-line staffed by stepparents round the country. "We would never give advice. We let them talk, suggest alternatives in different situations and get them to solve their own problems," says Goodwin. "People often want to bounce ideas off a third party because they find it difficult to talk to their partners." Couples whose first marriages have failed are often afraid to discuss their problems together because they do not want to admit that their second attempt at matrimony is threatened.

Stepfamily's pool of experience has helped to produce guidelines which can be helpful to stepparents. One solution to the resentment and jealousy of a stepchild, for instance, may be for the natural parent to set aside special time for that child. It is common for parents to be over-lenient towards children who are grieving for the loss of a natural parent. But Goodwin suggests that rules on bedtimes, pocket-money and punishment should be sorted out early on, as they are all potential areas of conflict.

Very often, stepparents just want someone to listen to them. "The process of hearing grievances and identifying with them personally is the important thing," says Maggie Belshaw, who is one of 16 professional counsellors and therapists involved in Stepfamily's new telephone counselling service. Callers so far have ranged from "people in dire distress—if you wrote fiction you wouldn't get near it,"—to stepparants who simply felt isolated and wanted to get in touch with other people.

The counsellors, all volunteers, can link callers up with local support groups or they can send Stepfamily leaflets offering suggestions on particular topics, like teenage stepchildren or stepparents who decide to have their own children.

Typically, most of the callers during the first six weeks of the new service were women. Men seem far more reluctant to seek help, according to Stepfamily counsellors. One worried stepfather called from a call box.

"At first, he said he just wanted information, but it turned out that he was ready to quit," said Donna Smith, who helped to start the professional counselling service. At the end of the call, he did agree to talk to his wife about his feelings.

Women often fail to understand the stepfather's side of the problem, says Elizabeth Hodder. "He has to father someone else's children while the children he really loves may be many miles away. A woman can also be unaware that she and her children appear a close-knit unit, sometimes excluding the stepfather."

Television documentaries and even *The Archers* have given the problems of stepfamilies a high profile recently, but Hodder is dismayed at the negative view portrayed. "It's made people think that stepparents are a bunch of complete inadequates. I'd like to see a more positive public image. Fergie's wedding helped because everyone could see she had a nice stepmother."

If they manage to work through their problems, stepfamilies may be stronger families, says Hodder. "They're more open with each other and understand each other better." Her own experience has confirmed this—she now has an enormous extended family and finds her grown-up stepchildren "delightful."

To keep up with the surge in interest and the increasing demands for help, Stepfamily is rapidly expanding its activities. The BBC has consulted the group about a soap opera based on stepfamilies and Stepfamily is also discussing a course about stepparenting with the Open University. A training course for prospective stepparents, "Learning to Step Together," is being piloted. Special counselling for those involved in incestuous relationships and for stepchildren is also being considered.

Despite its energetic and highly professional approach, Stepfamily runs on a shoestring. During its first three years, it helped 10,000 families on a £4,000 annual grant from the DHSS and smaller grants from charities like the Gulbenkian Foundation. Members pay a £10 subscription. Publicity is limited to leaflets and posters in libraries and doctors' surgeries. Some stepfamilies are referred by social workers, GPS, marriage guidance counsellors or child and family guidance.

Goodwin thinks Stepfamily deserves a higher priority. "Half of marriages involving stepchildren end in divorce, with an awful lot of trauma. At very little cost, we can prevent families breaking up."

Family focus

SUSANNAH KIRKMAN

A family centre in Avon provides an oasis of friendliness and help in the bleakness of a notorious housing estate.

"The doctor told me it was either Valium or the family centre," Angie recalls with a laugh. Three years later, it's hard to imagine that vivacious, energetic Angie ever suffered from depression; she's now an active member of the parents' council which helps to run the Fulford Family Centre for parents and under-fives on the bleak Hartcliffe estate, five miles from the centre of Bristol.

"The centre has given me the confidence to take control of my own life," Angie says. "I've made friends here and we've been able to help each other," she adds, smiling at Katy, another parents' council member.

Project workers at the Fulford centre believe in giving parents the support to work out their own destinies, including the chance to plan activities at the centre. Before the centre opened three years ago, project staff interviewed 100 families in the area to find out what services they thought young families needed. In response to the question: "What are the best things about living in the area?" the highest response (41 per cent) was, "Nothing." "We firmly believe social work should be done with, not to, families," says Owen Gill, deputy project leader. "Too much social work is based on professionals imposing their views on young families. We want to bring parents in similar situations together so that they can gain confidence and work out their own solutions."

The approach at Fulford is also unusual because community work goes hand in hand with therapy for families with problems. "There's a huge polarisation between community and individual therapeutic work in this country. But we think the difficulties in Hartcliffe stem from the community as well as within the families themselves," explains project leader Christine Stones.

Before Barnardo's set up the Fulford Family Centre, partly with short-term funding from the DHSS Under-fives Initiative, more children were being taken into care in Hartcliffe than in any other social services area in Avon. Through partnership with parents, the project aims: "to provide opportunities for growth and development for parents and under-fives and, where appropriate, to prevent the needless reception of children into care."

Like many of the young parents on the estate, Angie is single and knew no one when she first arrived. Hartcliffe has few amenities; although many young families live in blocks of flats, there are no proper play areas. Patches of scrubby grass between the flats are covered with empty glue bags and dog muck. There is no launderette and the tatty shops offer little choice. The community centre has a long waiting list for membership and the spartan pubs don't have children's rooms. Most homes have been burgled at least once. Hartcliffe has such a bad reputation that only those who are desperate for a roof over their heads, usually one-parent families, will accept accommodation there.

To many parents, the cosy, bright Fulford Family Centre, now partially funded by the local authority, is a haven from the chilly world outside. Converted from three hard-to-let flats, the layout of the centre is still familiar enough to make parents feel at home.

At the twice-weekly "drop-ins" for parents and their under-fives, the immaculate Princess of Wales, Barnardo's patron, gazes serenely down from a photograph onto the hubbub below. Musical tortoises, jack-in-the-boxes and dolls' prams are strewn over the floor, but most of the children are involved in a painting session next door, giving their parents a chance to chat. "It gives you half an hour's peace," says Maria, who comes to the centre with three year old Claire and Alex, aged two. "If you've got a problem, you can talk confidentially to someone," she adds. Maria's marriage broke up shortly after she moved to Hartcliffe last year.

It is up to parents to decide what they need from the centre. Pauline, who has three children aged from eight to four, asked for individual counselling when her marriage was going through a shaky patch. "When my husband lost his job, he used to sit around all day not doing anything. I felt he should give me a hand," Pauline explains. Living with relatives put extra strain on their relationship. But therapy helped Pauline and John to communicate with each other. "There were things I couldn't tell John which I can now. Before, if I was in a mood, he'd just snap at me. Now he asks me what my day's been like."

There is also a once-weekly fathers' "drop-in" to encourage the men to become involved. Chris, who's been unemployed for four years, is keen for more men to attend. He says he is already looking forward to using the new woodwork room in the centre when it's finished. Chris's family had a holiday together last year in one of the caravans that the centre owns at Burnham on Sea. It was the first time he had been away since he left school.

The scope of services and activities offered at the centre is vast. There are self-help groups for women who have men in prison, for parents with hyperactive children—both initiated by parents—and for parents of handicapped children. Activities have ranged from painting the Pied Piper mural which brightens the stairwell at the centre, to photography, reading, writing and cookery. "We got sick of cooking chips for lunch and thought we'd learn how to do quiche," explains Katy.

The focus of therapeutic work at the centre is the family group day with families whose children may be taken into care because of neglect or abuse. Here parents learn to play with their children. A movement session encourages loving physical contact between parents and children. Afterwards, parents have the chance to watch their own behaviour on video. They also fill in an evaluation sheet to assess how much they and the staff have achieved during the day. There is no stigma attached to attending the centre for a family group day because it is used for so many community activities as well.

Advice on welfare rights, including social security benefits and fuel bills, is given on Thursday afternoons. Even here, parents are not spoon-fed. "We're aiming to equip parents on the committee with the basic skills to check someone's entitlement," says Phil Holford, the worker in charge. "They make you get on the phone yourself and sort it out," says Angie. "Phil is very good at problems; he gets angry for you and pushes you into doing something yourself." Members of the welfare rights committee, one of the five parents' committees which help to run the centre and make up the parents' council, now want to help at advice sessions.

Tenants' groups at the centre have already succeeded in changing council policy in two ways. One group's survey of burglaries on the estate showed that most people were afraid to go out in the evening in case their homes were broken into while they were away. Most burglars entered flats from the balconies, the survey revealed. After the council had seen the survey, it bricked in the balconies and improved the lighting; burglaries dropped by 80 per cent over the next three months.

Another centre survey showed that, contrary to official council policy, many flats in three high-rise blocks in the Hartcliffe area were occupied by families with children under five. These families were so desperate for housing that they had not only accepted high-rise accommodation as a last resort, but had agreed to waive their rights to extra housing points as high-rise tenants with young children. They therefore stood little chance of being rehoused. After the survey was published, the council improved the facilities for the young families and agreed that they should not have to waive their rights to extra points.

"The centre is something to be proud of," says Katy. "And we're proud of the project workers for sticking with us. Not one of them has left since the centre opened." From the frequent visits of interested doctors and health visitors from outside the area, parents realise that the Fulford centre is a model of good practice. They now plan to encourage more families to attend the centre regularly by visiting parents in their own homes.

Strength in weakness

KATIE OWEN

In Leicester, parents volunteer to help young mothers cope.

Anne sits nursing her coughing baby on the floor of her new council house. He was born while she was in hospital recovering from the battering his father had given her. She fled back to Leicester where her family is based after a failed attempt to "start a new life" in Nottingham. She had previously been badly beaten by the father of her two other children, the elder of whom, Linda, has been in care all of her three years. Anne says she will not feel complete until Linda is back, but already has two small children to cope with. Today her two brothers, both unemployed, have come to call but Anne has little contact with former friends in Leicester. "I often get on better with strangers." A stranger, Christine Tracey, has come to see her today.

Christine is one of the two senior organisers of Leicester's Home-Start Scheme. She has come to see if Anne wants a volunteer from the scheme to come and see her. She does.

Christine explained that Anne's situation is typical of the problems that arise when council estates like this are set up. They tend to group together single mothers who are told it is temporary accommodation—so they make little effort to put down roots or make friends.

The Leicester scheme is a model of cooperation between statutory authorities and voluntary workers. It has been followed not only in other parts of Leicestershire (where there are now six such schemes) but all over the country.

Albert Clarke, legal and administrative adviser to the Leicester consultancy which was founded in 1981 to give advice on setting up new Home-Start schemes, suggests that the "ideal blend" in Leicestershire has to do with the mixed nature of the community, its relative prosperity and the Labour colour of its council. The many initiatives of the Leicester Council for Voluntary Services, of which he is chairman, have been welcomed by statutory bodies. The six Home-Start schemes now in action are directly funded by Social Services as part of their overall childcare strategy. They are receiving a total grant of £30,000 over the next three years, £10,500 of it coming from the government's "Under Fives' Initiative" scheme. Eleven of the 80 Home-Starts spread through the country come under the umbrella of this programme.

The idea for Home-Start came, 14 years ago, to Margaret Harrison. Herself a mother of young children, she was doing evening classes in social studies and began visiting children in care in Leicester. She found herself wishing that she could have got to know the children while they were still in their homes, before official care became necessary. She was also doing voluntary work at a local family service unit, keeping an eye on children in the kitchen while the mothers were receiving counsel next door. She was struck by how often mothers passing through would appeal to her for advice: "They wanted me as another parent, as a friend. They were craving my individual attention."

She conceived a scheme that would offer help to any family with a child under five with any sort of problem. The only qualification for becoming a volunteer would be to be a parent yourself.

Her first step was to persuade representatives from established voluntary groups and statutory bodies to join together on a "steering committee." A committee of this kind, she says, is the vital pre-requisite for a Home-Start scheme. Social workers and health visitors are involved from the start so, instead of rivalry and suspicion, there is shared experience and guidance.

Official bodies, she says, have to realise that while they have the funds, voluntary workers are not necessarily "naive do-gooders." They have larger resources of freedom and, above all, time to initiate preventative schemes like Home-Start, which can ease the burden of the hard-pressed social workers. For the cost of one new scheme—£200 a week for the expenses of 35 volunteers, each spending six hours a week working face to face with one or two families at the most—local authorities would have to pay the salaries of eleven official workers.

"Our strength in Home-Start," says Margaret, "is our weakness." Because the volunteers have no official status, they pose no threat to families. They concentrate first on the harassed mother as a person by just listening, and then give any practical help as the need arises. The aim is to act as "an enabler," to help the mother relax, gain her trust and boost her confidence.

Margaret cites Joan as one of her first successes. When Margaret met her she was terrified that her children, just back from care would be taken away again. They were not eating properly and the health visitor was insisting they should be taken to the clinic and weighed. Margaret's role was to take the pressure off. She would do the cooking with Joan. They would go to the shops and buy the ingredients together. The children were encouraged to help with the cooking.

Margaret at first went to Joan three times a week, and each time "they had the front door open and were waiting on the doorstep." She persuaded the family's social worker to let Joan join in the case conferences being carried out so she could give her own views. "The statutory workers were bowled over by how well she presented herself." After three years of help, Joan herself became a Home-Start volunteer.

"Home-Start is a two-way process, a scheme of reflections," says Margaret. Volunteers always have their own difficulties and the central consultancy set up in 1981 is for their advice and direct support. Margaret travels all over the country to give the benefit of her personal experience to anyone wanting to set up a new scheme. She treats every potential group of organisers as "a new family." She organises short but vital training schemes for volunteers where they learn the rudiments of child development and "become well informed, not just well intentioned."

The emphasis on reciprocity means that the real triumphs are where families who have benefited from help—like Joan—come to feel that they have learnt enough to want to do the volunteer training course themselves.

Margaret says one of the things she's learnt is that "there's no right way of doing things. No one should dictate." She quotes a book on mothers and children to illustrate the principle of Home-Start and its pattern of functioning. "There are three stages in a child's development: enclosure, extension and separation. But it isn't just children who go through these stages. Home-Start comes in when the *mother* is at the stage of 'enclosure'." By spending time with her and encouraging her to articulate her worries and problems, the volunteer brings the mother to the second stage, where she has the self-confidence to trust the statutory authorities, and play a part in the community herself. "This is where we begin and end."

Carli cares

PHYLLIS WILLMOTT

A pioneering project keeps teenage girls at risk from being put into care.

Basildon is one of the earlier new towns begun in the postwar years. Lying between the A127 and the Thames estuary, it is centred on one of the flatter windswept parts of Essex. Thirty five years later, the rows of neat semis with their gardens and green verges look quietly pretty. With a population of around 130,000, some of the young parents who left London in the early fifties in search of their dream home may now be the grand-parents of the teenage girls who are the focus of the CARLI project (Care, Alternatives, Resources, Liaison and Information).

At least £20 million a year is "wasted" on placing less than 1,000 young women in residential care, according to the Rainer Foundation, a voluntary organisation working with young people at risk. The CARLI project is one of the first community-based alternatives to residential care that the foundation is pioneering. Launched in October 1984, and funded for five years by Essex social services, the aim of the project is to develop ways of helping 13 to 17 year old girls heading for trouble—like the 13 from the Basildon area who went into care for the first time the year before CARLI began. In its first year 35 girls were taken on by CARLI, most of them coming from Basildon's social workers and the rest from child guidance, the Church, the police and so on. So far only three of the 35 have gone into care.

Although CARLI does not claim all the credit, Jane Duffield, the project leader, says: "Just by having another resource means that somebody else doesn't have to do all the worrying. Whether that's the parents or social workers, we can share the misery of it, and that takes a lot of the burden off."

There are three full-time project staff (there are in addition sessional staff and some volunteers), all in their late twenties or early thirties. Duffield is a blonde Australian, a former teacher who has had eight years' experience of intermediate treatment work in the inner city. Sue's background includes experience in the youth service and a Brooke Advisory Centre. A trained social worker, she has also worked in residential care where, she says, she "learnt about what institutionalisation really is." She is particularly interested in women's issues and how these link up with the kinds of problem girls get into. Mike is the member of the team who works on the family side. He is a graduate in psychology, as well as a social worker, and he too has experience of working in institutions, which has led him to believe it is better not to land up in them.

The project is based in a pleasant two-storey detached house that was formerly a family-type children's home. It is charmingly furnished (wall-to-wall carpeting, Habitat-type furniture and plenty of hard bright colours) with an atmosphere designed to dispel the feelings of failure and worthlessness that parents and girls arrive with. Upstairs there is a music room (with key board, electric guitars and a drum set much used to express aggressive moods), a room for crafts, others for photography and computer work and another for thumping about and sobbing in. Downstairs, as well as the comfortable roomy lounge, there is the kitchen dining-room, furnished with solid pine table and chairs; also an office and a small, quiet room for individual counselling.

How or why do some girls, who have been brought up in a relatively favourable environment, such as Basildon, come to problems that threaten to put them into care? As Mike points out, it is only girls, as a rule, who are seen as being "in moral danger"—one reason for receiving them into care. Sue confirms that problems unique to girls arise from anxiety over behaviour that would not be noticed in boys. "Girls," she says, "get punished for behaving in an outrageous fashion because it's seen as unfeminine, not because there's a law against it. And they end up in an institution because they're rebelling." One result, Jane goes on, is that this can mean an indeterminate sentence—"And it can seem to the girls a punishment because they and their families didn't get on." CARLI also work with a few girls already in care, and from this they have learnt that it is then much harder to improve things.

The first time a girl comes to CARLI it is usually with her social worker and her parents (although subsequently fathers are more difficult to keep involved.). This first meeting is generally at a time of crisis and it can last for two or three hours. Mike tries to use this time to relieve some of the pressure and at the same time to put over to the parents that the project is there to help them, but not to take over from them. "We challenge the idea early on of parents' helplessness, the feeling they can't cope with this young person; that this young person is bad. We have to get across the idea that they might be able to work things out. If we got into the notion of us sorting out their kids, I think that can make parents feel even more helpless."

Most of the work with the girls is done after school or after work hours. It includes individual counselling, group work, activities and a residential weekend—programmed to fit the needs of each girl. At the moment, of 22 girls 14 were using one or more of the groups, six were getting individual counselling and nine were having regular meetings with Mike and their parents. One night a week any of the girls who want to can come to the "activity group." They choose what they want to do within a framework designed to develop both initiatives and interests. Some activities are run as courses—there is one on computing, O-level English, car maintenance, photography and many more. Some girls take on jobs about the house, or they use the evening to get to know each other and share problems. The project staff also help girls to take up outside activities like squash and horse-riding.

In another group, limited to a maximum of six girls, the aim is personal development. Through discussion together confidence is built up, and feelings and situations that young people like themselves find difficult are worked at. It is all very informal—nothing in the project is compulsory—and the girls can lounge on the sofa or stretch out on the carpet or rush off to bang on the drums or the punch bag, or make a cup of coffee or tea. "It's really good," says 15 year old Mary, "because if I've got the hump or got problems or I'm pissed off or anything, there's always somebody here that I can talk to—and they'll listen to me." Tessa, a 16 year old who has arrived tearful and disturbed because of serious problems with both her natural parents and her stepfather, says much the same thing. Cheered up, she later sparks off a discussion on prick teasing (which she is strongly against). Sue joins in to point out that its not always easy to draw a clear line between leading a boy on and a girl saying "no" because she does not feel ready to go any further.

One indication of the project's success is the number of enquiries it has received—over 50 so far, from social workers and agencies—about how it works. Another is cost. CARLI's budget last year was £54,000. Today, it costs at least £10,000 a year to keep one girl in care in an ordinary residential home, and in a community home for education a staggering £50,000—£52,000. Set against this, CARLI must be a bargain.

Youngsters in trouble

JEREMY LAURANCE

A CSV scheme finds places for difficult children where both they and the local community can benefit.

Tom and Bill are incorrigible flirts. Well, wouldn't you be if you lived with 33 old men and had the company of a beautiful 16 year old girl? "She comes in the morning and we gets a whoopee," says Tom, winking at me. "I'm brilliant, ain't I Tom." says Sarah, lowering her huge, almond-shaped eyes. She sits demurely staring at her slender fingers twined together in her lap—grinning broadly.

"Tom checks the time I come in," says Sarah. "I've told her she's got to report to me," says Tom, aged 76, winking at me again. "So you miss her?" I ask. "Oh yeah." "I've got to come back tonight," says Sarah. "I know what you're coming for. To dance with me," says Bill, 78, sucking a sweet. "I can't dance," laughs Sarah. "She's got a big mouth," adds Tom. "Can she use it?" I ask. "No, she's very polite." "Shut up," says Sarah. "All she says is shut up," grins Bill.

The transformation in Sarah is dramatic. A few minutes earlier, she had sat mute and stiff, as Arthur Polfrey, who runs the Cardiff old people's home where she works, discussed her qualities in his office. "Sarah, if you don't talk to people they won't know what you're like or what you can do," he reprimanded her. "I don't speak to people I don't know," she replied, biting her lip. In his gruff, warm way Arthur clearly admires her. But his parental concern is overbearing. Sarah displays the signs of someone who has never been granted the freedom to discover what she *is* like.

She is a little ray of sunshine in the lives of Tom, Bill and the others in Deane House, a council home for elderly men. But what do they do for her? That may sound an odd question to ask of someone working voluntarily, as Sarah is. But she is no ordinary volunteer.

At 14, Sarah was taken into care after her stepfather began to ill-treat her. Over the next two years she moved through four children's homes. She became anorexic. She bunked-off school. She was judged unmanageable and was in danger of coming before the courts and being sent to youth custody.

She was placed at Deane House by the South Glamorgan Local Partnership scheme run by Community Service Volunteers. She is a far cry from the sixties image of the CSV volunteer: ex-public school filling in a year before going to university. But voluntary work can help the giver, too. Sarah's placement is an expression of CSV's conviction that it can improve a person's image of themself, and the wider community's image of them.

The scheme has been run with the local social services department since 1984. Its specific aim was to reduce the crime rate among some of the most difficult children in the care of the local authority. In the first 20 months it placed 72 young people, most of whom had previous convictions. Many had not attended school regularly for years. But only eight made court appearances during their time on their projects, though twice this number started to reoffend after they left the scheme. The projects lasted four to five months, on average.

It is too early to tell what the long-term impact will be. But the scheme is already popular with the young people and their social workers and is over-subscribed. Similar projects have been started in many other parts of the country by CSV. Sally Fowler, the human dynamo who runs the Cardiff one with considerable verve, says their success proves that a policy of looking at the positive qualities of young people and giving them responsibility "really works."

There is a striking contrast with the community service orders handed out by High Court judges to offenders like these: the work may be exactly the same but the element of compulsion removes the sense of responsibility and commitment that are inherent in the CSV schemes. Their principal aim is to give the young people a sense of their own worth. They tap a fundamental, even radical, idea: that those in need of care are also able to give it.

Sarah is one of the success stories. She has been on the project a year—and she loves it. She wants to train to be a care attendant but she will have to wait until she's 18. In the meantime she's going to evening classes. She gets her dole money plus £1 a day pocket money. Not long ago she was told she would have to go on a YTS scheme—and was threatened with the loss of her benefit if she refused. She was so upset she cried and begged Sally to help. Sally phoned a few officials—and Sarah won a reprieve. "The key thing is that she's met new people," says Sally. "She's starting out on the right lines."

David, 17, is another keen recruit. He has been in care for 18 months since his mother gave up trying to cope with him. He lived in a hostel. "We were kicked out each morning. We had to go looking for work. There was nothing to do. We were just on the streets like." Thin, wiry with curly ginger hair and an Adidas jacket, he has the easy nonchalance of the streetwise truant. He got into trouble with the law more than once for "borrowing" cars. His social worker suggested CSV.

"I didn't like the idea at first. I came for a look around and tried it for a couple of weeks. It was really good." He is designing posters for local community groups and doing photography on a media project. "It's interesting. I look forward to coming here." They are strange words to hear from someone earlier described as "very anti-social" and "impossible to work with." His mother is pleased, too. He has patched things up with her and is moving back into the family home.

But selling the scheme to the young people is only half the task. Those who run the projects have also to be convinced that youngsters in trouble can be effective, reliable volunteers. This depends on Sally Fowler's capacity to sell the idea and support her volunteers through the bad times that inevitably follow. She has been remarkably successful establishing places on projects for the elderly, the handicapped, in conservation, with the RSPCA and so on. "We go from what the kid wants," she says.

A key element in the scheme's success, according to Sally, is that she is *not* a social worker. There is no control element. She is not part of the system nor is she seen to be part of it. "It is easier for young people to come to our office than to the social services department. It's informal, we have a one-to-one relationship, we are more flexible." But this informality has its drawbacks. "The most important thing I've learned in three years is that you have to set up boundaries. You have to tell the young people how far you can help them—otherwise you'll be overrun."

In fact, the question of who should run the scheme has been the topic of a fierce debate between CSV and the local social services department. CSV management insists that its role should be to innovate. Once a project is established, it should be taken over by the statutory sector, as has happened with similar CSV schemes in other parts of the country—with mixed results.

South Glamorgan social services, which funds the project, is unconvinced. It argues that keeping the project at arm's length is essential to its continued success. But this year it has cut its grant because the department does not see why it should pay for youngsters who would be just as well served by an MSC scheme. The result is that some of south Wales's neediest young people will be denied a chance to help—and be helped.

Making space for kids

MADELEINE FULLERTON

Police in Staffordshire provide facilities and activities in an attempt to reduce juvenile crime.

A young policeman, arms crossed, helmet pulled over his eyes, gazes across Hanley Park near Stoke on Trent. A scruffy teenage girl darts out from a crowd of youngsters and wrestles him to the ground. He retrieves his helmet and, arm in arm, they drift back into the crowd.

It is "International Day," organised by Staffordshire Police Activities Community Enterprise (SPACE). There are Chinese dragon dancers, Asian groups, a steel band and members of a black theatre group teaching children to breakdance. SPACE is a unique police operation designed to reduce juvenile crime during the summer holidays by keeping the county's ten to 16 year olds occupied with a range of activities from football and rope climbing to tile printing and theatre workshops. And it seems to be working; burglaries in August dropped by 17 per cent between 1981 and 1985 despite an overall rise in crime. The incidence of criminal damage also dropped considerably during the same period.

But the aims of the project go further than cutting the crime rate. One of the special objectives for this year's SPACE programme has been to involve disabled children and their families. Forty disabled children, all needing one-to-one supervision by police officers and volunteers, attended a day of swimming, games, a barbecue and a disco. A special effort has also been made to involve more older girls this year. Traditional girls' activities such as make-up and hair-dressing classes were planned, but the police found to their surprise that, once the girls gained the confidence to attend, they soon joined in the more outgoing pursuits such as rock climbing and football.

Police visit schools, mosques, Gurdwaras and community centres to show videos about the scheme. One Hanley police officer arranged for all information leaflets and registration forms to be translated into Urdu and Punjabi this year, and more youngsters from ethnic minority backgrounds joined the scheme this year than ever before.

"We aim to give all kids a chance to see what they can achieve with a bit of patience and hard work," says Chief Inspector Ken Ainge, head of crime prevention, community relations and coordinator of all 31 projects in the county this year. A major aim of SPACE therefore is to improve police relations with young people and help them discover and develop new interests.

Children pay £1 for their SPACE registration card—the fee is waived if they can't afford it. The card entitles them to join in all activities free of charge throughout the six week holiday. Twenty six thousand registered at schools or police stations last year and numbers promise to be well up this year.

"It's an extraordinary sight," says one police officer, "to see crowds of youngsters clamouring to get inside a police station—you register them, then they demand to be shown around."

Children gather daily at their local "SPACE base"—usually their school lent by the local education authority. They then disperse into activity groups or go on outings—1,000 children went to Alton Towers last week. If nothing interests them they can simply hang around the school which operates as a drop-in centre supervised by police officers from ten till four each day.

Up to 200 police officers can be involved in running activities on any one day, and many of them give up a great deal of their spare time. Some enjoy working with kids so much that they go on to apply for youth training certificates. The fire service, the RAF, the army, St John's Ambulance and many school teachers also offer specialist skills and the 1,000 volunteers required as general supervisors are recruited from unemployed parents and young people.

Police in each subdivision organise a major day event to which thousands of children arrive in coaches paid for by SPACE. International Day is Chief Inspector Perrin's idea: "The kids need to be shown that culture didn't start with the Beatles and fish and chips," he says. Meanwhile police officers are swapping headgear with the Chinese dragon dancers and sampling free food provided by two local Gurdwaras and the Caribbean restaurant. A Sikh stirring a massive cauldron of chick pea curry explains that they are supporting this day because Chief Inspector Perrin frequently visits the Gurdwaras and helps sort out any problems that may arise in the Sikh community.

Most of the children, however, prefer to queue for free SPACE beefburgers. "SPACE is ace," says a 13 year old girl, sporting pink lipstick and a SPACE baseball hat. This is her third year on the scheme: "My mum's at work all day and she worries sick if she thinks I'm wandering about with nothing to do."

So what do she and her friends like best about International Day? "Canoeing," they all shout enthusiastically. And what do they think of the police? "Really kind," says one girl, "we play basket ball every night with loads of them at the poly."

Three boys waiting for the steel band explain that the day is about "people from all over the world." They spent the morning trying out security locks with a police officer and collecting dozens of leaflets telling children to beware of strangers. Their favourite activity is football. So what would they be doing if they weren't on SPACE? "Sitting at home dead bored," says one. "Watching telly," says another. "The police are much kinder than you think," volunteers one 15 year old. "And much less strict," adds a younger lad. "In fact, they're not strict at all," shouts another. But the others think this is going too far and remind him of the time a boy was sent off the coach for throwing tomatoes at the driver.

All the children I spoke to could reel off a long list of police officers' first names and many now know the police who cover their area well. "It's an eye opener for the officers too," says Ken Ainge. "They get to see the good side of kids and soon realise they aren't just a load of trouble."

Six camps are run on the edge of moorlands for children who would not otherwise get holidays. These children are referred by probation officers, social services and community police. On the camps, officers volunteer as cooks and supervisors: "For some kids, the camps are the first time anyone's bothered to get to know them," says Ken Ainge.

SPACE involves tremendous organisation. Police officers and Manpower Services Commission workers start raising money and planning for the following year as early as September. In 1985, SPACE cost about £160,000. Financing comes from a wide range of sources. Chief Inspector Perrin wrote to a number of tourist boards telling them about SPACE and the international day he was organising and Caribbean Airways promptly gave two tickets to Bermuda to be raffled. "There was such a rush for the raffle tickets," he says, "that the money raised paid for the whole of the day."

Grants are made by Urban Aid, the council and various trust funds. Local firms also give generously and the rest of the money is raised through jumble sales throughout the year. Any money left over goes to the NSPCC, or to local child health clinics.

But is it not risky to divert so much police time away from normal duties? Ken Ainge, still breathless from running round taking photos of youngsters learning to breakdance, says: "Some forces might disagree, but we in Staffordshire are convinced that preventing crime by helping kids grow into valuable citizens is an essential part of our job."

Employment

Taking the plunge

CHRIS TIGHE

A scheme in East Middlesbrough is teaching people how to create their own jobs.

Decaying tenements, barefoot children and men lounging in flat caps on street corners are the images of poverty in the 1930s. Today's deprivation is harder to summon up. Take, for instance, the Thorntree, Brambles Farm and Netherfields estates in East Middlesbrough. Some of the houses on the estate look dingy and ill-kempt, but many more have neat curtains and gardens. There is even a scattering of neo-Georgian front doors, a sure sign of the ex-council tenant turned home owner. The shops, some with To Let signs, have a generally bleak air, and there is graffiti on some street signs; but there is nothing to make anyone look twice.

How deceptive appearances are! Unemployment on these estates is almost 40 per cent. Nearly half the male population, left stranded by the contraction of the steel, chemical and construction industries, of shipbuilding and engineering, is without work. Add all the households of pensioners, of single parents and the disabled, and you have a majority of homes totally dependent—officially at least—on state benefits. Some residents have to turn their ovens on, to try to keep warm. Teenagers loaf around. There are few resources.

When Martin Murphy arrived on the Thorntree estate three years ago, he decided "the only thing I could do was see what the people had to offer." He came as an employment development officer, recruited by Cleveland County council to try to help the estate dwellers create their own work. The unemployed are traditionally apathetic and Murphy does not deny it exists, but he sees the dangers of harping on the fact. "If you accept apathy, you accept that what can be achieved is very little, so it's not worth doing in the first place."

The problem on these estates is not that residents have become demoralised into inactivity, but that they have few prospects, they have adjusted their lifestyle and expectations accordingly in a way which isolates them still further.

Resignation, says Bob Flory, secretary of the Thorntree Residents Association, is the biggest problem with high unemployment. "People have become so used to accepting it, it becomes very hard for them to get out of that way of life."

Murphy believes that many people in such an area, having lost confidence in their own capabilities and potential, don't really know what their problem is. "There's an awful lot of people who don't know what the system is about, and how flexible it is to work within," he explains. "There are few limits in this country to what you can do."

In his three years, Murphy, working from his community centre office, has nursed between 40 and 50 people from the estates into self-employment. His influence has also spread more widely in Cleveland, which has the highest county unemployment rate in Britain. He has recently been appointed Senior Community Employment Development and Training Officer, heading up a team of four other workers posted in comparable housing estates.

"Martin has filled me with confidence to do things," says 23 year old Kevin Doody, who last November started his own mobile sewing machine service and repair business. "Being on the dole you think you can't do things. Everybody talks negative. He was positive and he filled me with good ideas."

At his office, Murphy operates an open-door policy, welcoming local people who come, however diffidently, to discuss their employment problems. There are plenty of skills on these estates, but they are locked into the contracting heavy industrial base. The possessors of these skills want to use them, to modify them so they are relevant but they are bewildered as to how to begin.

When they first approach Murphy with the notion of creating their own job, they are full of uncertainty. "They're uncertain about whether they've got an idea, about how even I am going to respond to it," he says.

Murphy offers them, free of charge, his wide experience, his sharp mind and above all his time. It took 23 hours of it to get Doody launched. Often the initial proposal is shown under analysis to be unrealistic. But once the idea of self-employment is planted, Murphy perseveres with his clients, encouraging them to examine every conceivable possibility. Four fifths of those coming to him with an idea end up doing something else, says Murphy. He talks them through the pros and the cons of entrepreneurship; he is not above counselling a return to the dole if a self-employed person is floundering and becoming ill with worry.

He steers them towards sources of grants, like the Prince's

Trust and schemes like the £40 a week for a year enterprise allowance. And he advises them to keep their plans to themselves: family and friends, on the lookout for their own main chance, are the worst enemy, he says. Some, even with his support, can't bring themselves to take the plunge. Those who do, return to him as often as they want for advice. Many, he says, begin by undercharging. "They are absolutely staggered that people want to pay them for what they are doing." The first bridge of confidence has been crossed when they put up their charges. Doody has just raised his.

Businesses launched so far include a fish shop, catering and clothes making firms and a flower arranging service. Now, an increasing number of projects are manufacturing orientated. "People are beginning to see how much is being brought in from abroad," says Murphy.

The big challenge, however, lies ahead. Murphy's work on the estates has produced a Residents' Initiatives Group. These local people, fired with a new sense of purpose, want not only to create their own jobs, but to help train and motivate other residents.

They have their eyes on the soon-to-be-vacated local infants school, where they want to establish their own employment centre. The group's members, with help from Murphy, have developed their own self-employment project. One wants to manufacture play equipment, another to repair sports equipment; one has even designed a prototype hovercraft.

But the group are keen to develop work for the community as well as for themselves. With the help of a £2,000 feasibility study grant from the county council, they are formulating plans for community businesses including a small printing firm. Despite reservations about MSC projects, they are also considering ways in which a Community Programme scheme, managed by the employment centre, could help develop local skills and test out ideas.

The group are anxious to offer more than just workspace; training facilities are a top priority. Their aim is to create a focus of hope and activity, relevant to the community's needs and skills. And most significant of all, whilst they want Murphy available to advise them, they want to run it themselves.

Despite the estimated £28,000 start up finance required the residents are optimistic. "The world's your oyster," says Flory. Murphy, knowing all the financial hassles and frustrations which lie ahead, is more circumspect. Although delighted at the confidence he has imparted he wonders if the residents' enthusiasm could rebound. "It worries me that this confidence and competence will give them a cockiness which might kick them in the teeth."

Clubbing together

STEVE PLATT

Self-help jobclubs offer free jobhunting facilities, support and friendship for the long-term unemployed.

The government's Restart programme offering individual help and advice to the long-term unemployed went nationwide at the beginning of July. The aim is, between now and March 1987, to offer everyone who has been out of work for over a year one of eight options from a "menu" which includes training, self-employment, voluntary work and places on community programme schemes.

One of the more popular options is likely to be provided by the network of self-help jobclubs currently being set up at job centres around the country. Over 200 are due to open by the end of the year, with a further 250 to follow.

The jobclubs combine counselling and the provision of expert advice on jobhunting techniques with free facilities such as telephones, typewriters, photocopying equipment, stamps and stationery. After attending a short introductory course, club "members" can use the facilities until they find work.

The Northampton jobclub is one of 26 set up in advance of the Restart programme. The brainchild of centre manager Mike Richards, who came across the idea on a management training course in Sheffield, it opened in August 1985 and now takes on a new batch of recruits every fortnight.

Four young people were finishing their two weeks' introductory training when I visited the centre. "Come back in a month," one of them said. "If we're all still here then you can write how useless jobclubs are. But if we've gone – well, they must work, mustn't they?"

The initial training consists primarily of advice on jobhunting techniques – writing letters, completing application forms, producing CVs and dealing with interviews – but it is also designed to build confidence and generate enthusiasm.

"People come to jobclubs when they're at rock bottom," said Mike Richards. "They've tried everything else and failed. The jobclub gives them the opportunity to reassess and re-evaluate their own worth." Both the self-help element (users do most of their job-searching on their own), and the mutual support of being with others in the same position, are important in that process.

"You get so discouraged when you're turned down for one job after another," said Caroline Pick, who lost her last job, as a shop assistant, 18 months ago. "You think it must be *you*, that it's your fault you're out of work. And because you're paid so little on the dole, you start to think that's all you're worth."

The jobclub, and the support it offered, rebuilt her faith in herself, she said. Equally important, it helped her identify where she was going wrong and how to improve her chances of getting a job.

Melvyn Millar, who has been unemployed for over five years, agreed: "I used to go to the unemployed centre a lot. But most of the people have given up. They keep telling each other they'll never get another job. The group here is very different. It's much more positive."

The jobclub fulfils a similar role to the unemployed centre, however, in breaking down the isolation of the jobless. Friendships made through it outlast people's involvement in it; Melvyn Millar, for instance, has just moved into a spare room in Caroline Pick's house.

"The hardest thing is getting people interested in the first place," said Frances Currie, acting leader of the Northampton jobclub. "When you get them in, they start to talk and help one another, they show each other job adverts or help each other with typing and so on." The unemployed might mistrust the job centre, the staff or the system, she added, but they don't mistrust each other. The camaraderie of the group is almost as important as the actual services provided.

Not everyone sees it that way. Mike Richards says that some women have dropped out because there weren't enough other women involved. A 38 year old man quit because there was no one else of his age. And one woman left because she couldn't cope with talking about herself in front of other people (the group meetings during the first fortnight can be a bit like therapy sessions).

Others use the jobclub largely for the free facilities. Koltar Singh, for example, a 51 year old architect who first joined the club six months ago, has never mixed much with other club users. Yet he calls in regularly to use the telephone, write letters, follow up job applications or seek advice.

Jobclub users are encouraged to make speculative approaches to employers, and some do so on a grand scale: one made 45 telephone calls and wrote 115 letters, another made 116 speculative telephone calls and 95 personal visits. Since the job centre foots the bill for such efforts (including any travelling expenses), unemployed people are able to make far more approaches for jobs than they would otherwise be able to afford.

It does, of course, require considerable self-motivation. "We ask for a lot of commitment," said Richards, whose own motivation and commitment is boundless. His glass-windowed office door is always open to both jobclub users and his staff.

"Out there you're outside the system, a bit of an outcast," said Caroline Pick. "But in here you feel part of it again." Like other jobclub users she was full of praise for the friendly and accessible atmosphere created by Richards and his staff. Locked doors and partitioned interview booths are banished from the Northampton job centre – though not with the total approval of all its workers. One grumbled noisily to me about "claimants being allowed to wander wherever they like."

But the system does seem to work. Of 146 people who joined the Northampton jobclub this year, 54 have found jobs and 29 have accepted community programme places. The job centre folklore is now full of the 59 year old woman, out of work for two years, who got a job as a clerk-typist after a few weeks with the jobclub; of the ex-office manager, aged 62, who found his first job in four years; and of Clive Uter who, after three years' unemployment, finally found work – with the job centre.

Yet the jobclub has so far reached only a small fraction of Northampton's 4,000 long-term unemployed. And John Paviour, the local Restart team leader, admits: "There is a danger of jobclubs becoming a middle class domain." He hopes the Restart programme will make jobclubs available to a wider range of unemployed people, including the less able, articulate or self-confident.

The aim of the Northampton jobclub, untidily scrawled on a scrap of paper on the office wall, next to charts showing how many job applications or inquiries each club member has made, is "To find the best possible job in the shortest possible time."

In Northampton, at least, this is not just bogus optimism. Unemployment, at 10 per cent, is well below the national – or even county – average; and a flourishing warehousing and distribution industry has enabled the town to withstand job losses in its declining engineering and leatherwork sectors.

Elsewhere, jobclubs may have more problems; they can't create jobs where they don't exist. But even if the users don't find work the clubs can still help them to cope with unemployment and not give up.

Koltar Singh, who had just been turned down for another job when I spoke to him, is now the Northampton jobclub's longest-standing member. The jobclub has kept him going through a long series of disappointments and let-downs. If and when he finally finds employment there will probably be a small party to celebrate his departure. The jobclub is one of the few places on earth where people show genuine friendship by telling each other: "I hope I don't see you next week."

Lisa's story

BOB HOLMAN

What happened when a job was created for a teenager who was otherwise unemployable.

In times of high unemployment, any teenager finds it hard. But Lisa's predicament was even more grim. Sacked from her first job for bad timekeeping and from her second, accused of fraud, her prospects seemed negligible. Her friends were worried about what the effects of these rejections combined with long-term unemployment would do to her. What could they do to help?

The Roundhill Project (formerly the Southdown Project) had been operating in two Bath council estates since it was started by the Church of England Children's Society in 1976. It started in my house, and I came into contact with Lisa – then eleven – because she lived nearby. The project workers – Dave Wiles, Jane Sellars and myself – got to know her well as the years went by. She often dropped in, and came with the youth club on its annual holiday. Then schooling became a problem. She says she hated school. The teachers were not too pleased with her cheekiness and her pranks like setting off the fire alarm; once, she was suspended.

During her final school year, Lisa and a friend would sometime call at our house and convince us that they were on study leave. Of course, they should have been at school. The outcome was an irate headmistress, who accused me of condoning the truancy. Feeling conned by Lisa, the project workers expressed their anger against her. It was fortunate that our long-standng friendship proved strong enough to endure the row.

Many teenagers go through such unsettled and uncooperative phases. Lisa's adolescence was more complicated, because it coincided with the breakup of her parents' marriage. Even now, she still feels upset and wished they were all back together. At the time, Jane Sellars helped Lisa's father through the initial shock and helped with the baby and household chores.

In doing so, she also drew closer to Lisa who was shaken not only by the splitting of her siblings between the two households, but by the arrival of new step-parents. For a while, Lisa moved out altogether.

When she left school, Lisa started work. Her job involved shifts, weekend rotas and a long walk to work. All the same, with encouragement from Jane, she stuck it for 18 months until her bad timekeeping resulted in the sack. Within a few weeks Lisa, now 17, was taken on as a cashier at a petrol station.

All went well until she was abruptly dismissed. When Jane Sellars tried to claim the wages owing to Lisa, she was told to get lost. Soon after, Lisa was arrested and charged with fraud. Under intensive questioning at the police station – with no solicitor present – she confessed. Once home, she vehemently denied the charge and wanted to retract her statement. The project staff believed she was innocent and appeared for her in court. Her mother and father also supported her in every way possible throughout a number of appearances which dragged on for months. Finally, a jury found her guilty.

Lisa was shattered by the arduous proceedings, the cross examination in the dock, the reports in the local press, and the verdict. She seemed to withdraw into herself. We at the Roundhill project feared that a long period of unemployment would see her drift into apathy and defeatism. So the team decided that she should be given a job with the project itself, which had recently moved into its own centre and been strengthened by an extra worker. Morever, they resolved she be awarded a decent wage as an indication that value really was placed on the contribution she could make. An application was hastily put together and, fortunately, a trust agreed to finance the post for two years.

After some hesitation, Lisa accepted the job. At first she helped in the office and went to the local tech to learn shorthand and typing. Our early working partnership was not always one of harmony; sometimes her forgetfulness and scatty ways evoked a sneaking sympathy for her former employers. But Lisa persevered and mastered typing, reception work and office routine.

She found she could master other tasks as well. She helped in the creche and the junior youth club. As the months went by she gathered confidence, would have a go at anything, and began to take on leadership roles. She took her turn at opening the centre at 8.30 am for the Before School Club. She learnt to deal calmly and sensibly when provoked by some of the older teenagers. And she also opted to spend a fortnight with the sailing ship *Arethusa*. Lisa's upbringing meant she rarely went out of the city, and she was reluctant to try new experiences. That she was now prepared to mix with new colleagues and sail around Europe in tough conditions was an indication of her developing character.

By the summer of 1985, Jane Sellars was about to leave to have a baby, I was working part-time, and Dave Wiles had become project leader. Lisa's full involvement was appreciated all the more because the remaining two full-timers were almost at breaking point. For the first time in the project's history, it might have closed down. But Lisa was against shutting the doors in the summer, when children made heavy demands on the project. So she, the part-timers and volunteers kept it going on their own. There were some complaints from neighbours about the noise of the record player and motorbikes. But she coped with them: no mean feat for a 19 year old.

As the end of her funding approached, Lisa began to look for another job. Eventually, she found one in an hotel. By this time, she was wanting to go. She had grown in confidence, and was now equipped to move out.

When I recently asked Lisa what she gained from working with the project, she replied, "I've learnt to cope with myself and other people." She explained how she had watched the project staff respond to pressure, observed that they did not over-react and tried to behave in the same way.

The ploy of creating a special job for a teenager has obvious limitations. In an era of mass unemployment, one post does not make much difference. Yet the impact on this particular individual was considerable.

What are the factors that led to this successful outcome? First: location. The project is set in a neighbourhood. Lisa formed her initial contacts with the project team because she lived near them. So when the crisis came, she knew where to find help.

Secondly: time. The project workers have a long-term commitment to the area. Lisa is the kind of person who takes a long time to form a close relationship. Such a friendship eventually came with Jane Sellars, whom she describes as "one of the closest people I've ever been to."

Thirdly: method. The team's approach was not to treat Lisa as a client but as a colleague, albeit a junior colleague. She went on courses, attended meetings and took responsbilities like the rest of us.

Fourthly: the trusting trust. The charity we approached responded quickly and with a grant of sufficient size to ensure that Lisa received a decent wage rather than pocket money peanuts.

So, one small project maintained a job for at least one teenager – and brought her through the period of trauma and vulnerability.

Art for all

DELWYN SWINGEWOOD

An Exeter-based organisation brings art to special-need groups.

"In a sense we're stimulating people. We go in and set things up and get them rolling," says Sue Way, a dance and movement artist working for Artshare, an organisation based in Exeter trying to bring the arts to people with special needs – from Bristol to Penzance.

The 1985 Attenborough Report, *Arts and Disabled People*, went some way to encapsulate the organisation's philosophy when it said: "The arts should never be regarded as open to a privileged elite. The arts are for everyone. To some degree it is within everyone's capacity to reinterpret their own experience and to share the experience of others, by involvement in the world of art. Over the ages, the arts have been the field for and have prompted some of the finest achievements of the human spirit." Artshare and its team of 100 freelance artists sees itself as trying to gatecrash those cultural institutitons and theories that have made art something for a cultural elite.

Sue Way's music and movement class at a hospital for the mentally handicapped is typical of the organisation's work in institutions. Star Cross – a picturesque village on the River Exe famous for its appearances on British Rail commercials – is the present home of The Royal Western Counties Hospital. The institution is gradually closing, but in the meantime Sue takes eight adults for a weekly dance lesson.

Most, like Joe, now in his fifties, have been there since childhood and are completely institutionalised. However, Sue believes her class has given them a sense of fulfilment. "Through movement they can improve their language – such as it is – and improve their coordination and general sense of well-being. Although it's only a simple form of art it isn't separated from life at all, it's become a way of living for them, and that's how it should be."

People from the Nichols Adult Training Centre gain obvious pleasure from their improvised music sessions with Deasy Bamford at Exeter city's art centre, in another Artshare venture. The supervisor, Michael Phipps, feels the prized outing is of tremendous importance to them all. It benefits people like Timmy, who is mentally handicapped as well as being partially deaf and suffers from a speech impediment. "It's helped him with his speech therapy. Even his therapists are saying how much of an effort he's making. But I think this sort of work is more important on another level. It shows the whole process is really about drawing feelings out of them, rather than feeding stuff in and trying to press the right buttons in the hope that you'll get some sort of socially acceptable response."

A creative writing project at Channings Wood Prison enabled some of the inmates to find outlets for their innermost thoughts, feelings and beliefs, and the result, *HMP Writes*, contains some wistful, funny and readable poems. Other Artshare artists have started work with the housebound at Wadebridge and St Austell, and a young leukaemia sufferer in Exmouth is being helped to develop his interest in photography.

Artshare coordinator Philippa Warin says the organisation – one of 14 throughout Britain – exists to "respond to practically anyone who has a special need for their help or advice about arts activities. In a rural area like the south west, the demands placed on Artshare can vary tremendously and have prompted it to experiment with non-institutional projects, such as working with the housebound. The team stress that they are not looking for a finished painting or object; indeed, they feel that to encourage such values could be counterproductive.

Bill Sleeman, a former long-distance lorry driver, is 62 and partially paralysed after a series of strokes and heart attacks; he relies on a walking frame to get around his neat bungalow in the Cornish village of Tregadille. He says he was prone to depression after his incapacitating attacks; "At times I just felt like giving up and dying." A chance meeting with the Launceston artist Breyan Gillead persuaded Bill that he wanted to take up painting. Breyan in turn persuaded Artshare that Bill should be taught at home: "I couldn't draw up a rigid curriculum designed to take him through areas in paintings, that would have been too much of a strain, too frustrating. What Bill needed, and what he gets, is satisfaction from his painting. We tend to iron out problems, such as coping with perspective, when we get to them."

Bill says of the past twelve months that he has been painting: "It's brought me to life, it's brought somethng out of me I never knew I had."

Philippa says the work Artshare is doing with Bill is beginning to blur the edges and challenge the assumptions of what are acceptable forms and practices of art. In some ways Artshare sees itself as being fundamentally political; by working with special need groups it not only wants to support their needs and demands, but also sweep away a system it sees as continually oppressing and marginalising the disabled, the elderly and people in trouble.

Such an outlook prompted the organisation to launch an ambitious experimental community arts project on an Exeter council estate. Women and children from the estate were invited to arts and craft sessions to which disabled people were introduced from all parts of the city. Philippa describes the experiment as only partially successful and somewhat problematical. Physically taking people to the centre proved a major headache. However, the main problem was overcoming local prejudice against the company of disabled people. She feels the eventual integration of disabled children into ordinary state schools will one day help break down such barriers. Meanwhile, one of the most powerful educators – television – could be a potent force in removing any prejudice to the disabled.

Artshare can also benefit the artist. "While it is emphatically not an employment agency for artists," says Philippa, "It realises that there is an enormous wasted resource among artists who're often taught to think of themselves as having skills that are not particularly practical. In fact they're ideally suited to work with people in the community because they often have a kind of energy that's developed from them being proficient at dance, music, painting, drama and so on."

This practical view of life is carried through to Artshare's financing of itself. It manages to match its grant from South West Arts by fund raising and sponsorship. It is also hoping to sell a package to the Cornwall social services department or the Devon Health Authority. "We could offer a contract to provide an activity for this many people for so many pounds over a set period," says Philippa. "The selling point would be that many of these authorities have a policy to serve their local community. Some, like Exeter, are actually deinstitutionalising their services. We can offer our services and expertise to help them meet their obligations to the community."

Down memory lane

JOY MELVILLE

A theatre company dramatises memories of the elderly, to the delight of old and young alike.

Scene: a sheltered housing unit in south London, where the musical show *The Time of Our Lives*, is about to start. The elderly audience comes in slowly, some pushed in wheelchairs. The show is based on leisure time in the 1920s and 1930s, reminding them of day trips, rambling, cycling, courting, dancing. One 78 year old man sees the old piano on stage and stops in the doorway, remembering out loud how "We used to have the beer barrel right by the side of the piano when we had a party."

The cast of four young professional actors, dressed in authentic thirties' clothes, starts singing *Ain't Misbehavin'*, and the audience join in, word perfect. The show begins and the actor playing Bert starts questioning his sister Elsie about her boyfriend: "What do you want to see him again for?" he says. "He's only nine pence in the shilling!" The audience laughs. This is their sort of language.

And in a unique way, it is their show. For *The Time of Our Lives* is a dramatisation of the memories of pensioners in south east London and is just one of a number of shows put on by the Age Exchange Theatre Company, a theatre and publishing company that works with older people. The entertainment is therapeutic. Encouraging old people to reminisce is an effective antidote to depression and has been shown to help them cope better, personally and socially, than those who never recall their past lives.

The company started in 1983 when Pam Schweitzer, a community worker with the elderly, tried to find ways of bringing the young and old together by getting the younger ones to help the old with the decorating and gardening, and so on. But they weren't interested, so she reversed the coin by making the old people the experts and getting the young ones to ask them about life in the twenties and thirties.

"It worked very well," she says, "and one particularly successful aspect was when we dramatised the elderly people's experiences on tape and played it back to a group of them. So we extended it to the idea of setting up a theatre company which would employ professional actors who would tour all over London with plays and entertainments based on the memories and experiences of the elderly in different districts of London."

Funded by the GLC, the company got under way, with a small

administrative staff headed by Pam Schweitzer as artistic director and five professional actors. Since April 1983, it has produced eight shows, playing to approximately 20,000 people a year. They go to community centres, sheltered housing units, arts centres, schools and colleges, pensioners' clubs and conferences.

The actors may contract for travelling with one show only, but the company encourages them to stay longer, as this is no ordinary acting job. Once the subject of a show is decided upon, they are regarded as part of the team, helping to interview the elderly and record their memories, working with a script writer or perhaps improvising themselves.

Pensioners are consulted at rehearsals, where they can quickly spot if clothes and words are accurate – the real audience being quick to notice a mistake. The other day, a character on stage announced that he was going off to get the No. 46 tram from Greenwich to Blackheath, and a pensioner in the audience immediately called out: "You mean the No. 36."

"When the company goes to schools and colleges, we invite the local pensioners in," says Pam Schweitzer. "That way, after the show, they can talk about those time to the younger ones in the audience." This bringing together is one of the aims of the project; the pensioners are usually pleased at finding how much detail they remember, and delighted at being listened to with interest. The intention is to give a value to their experiences and boost their self-respect.

A further aim is to stimulate them into talking to each other and so make new friendships. Wardens and supervisors are particularly enthusiastic over this. "They tell us that the elderly have gone on talking about the show and the past some while after the event," says Pam Schweitzer.

Certainly, *The Time of Our Lives* successfully involved the audience. "Bert has asked me to the dance on Saturday at Greenwich Baths," says Peggy, another character on stage – causing an 86 year old woman in the audience to turn to her neighbour and say: "That's where my Jim used to take me," and fish out a photograph of Jim from her bag. "Shall I walk you home?" Bert asks Peggy, and her reply of "I don't mind," is greeted with "Ooohs." That was the accepted start of a courtship in those less permissive days. "When we were first married, we lived in the Guinness Buildings," whispered one 80 year old to the woman next to her. "Oh, I remember those," she said. "Look at that old iron, I had one just like it," said the pensioner next to me.

At the end, the actors came down from the stage and chatted, stimulating the audience again into a barrage of memories: "You could leave your street door open then, we had one key for the whole street and hung it up at the end"; "We used to shove the piano out in the street bank holiday Mondays, and I used to hang a skipping rope from one pavement to the other, tied to the lamp-posts and we'd all skip to "One potato, two potatoes, three potatoes, four"; "Remember the buskers who used to come round with their street organs and how we'd dance?"

The Time of Our Lives is a light-hearted show, based as it is on the way people once enjoyed themselves. Other shows have caused rather more emotional discussion afterwards, like *Can We Afford the Doctor?* and *Fifty Years Ago,* which is memories of the 1930s and tackles not just hop-picking and Edward VIII, but subjects like living on assistance and the Blackshirts. Two new shows planned are to be based on the memories of Jewish people in the East End and of Irish women who came over to England in the 1930s to work as maids.

The company also publishes its own books, full of photographs, based on the reminiscences recorded for each entertainment, on sale at the show or from the company. It hires out special exhibitions as well, based on the shows, and runs reminiscence workshops. But all this costs money. Greenwich and Lewisham councils have replaced the GLC in funding, and a number of other organisations are helping. "But we are so short-staffed and we desperately need money to cope with new projects," says Pam Schweitzer.

"Our latest one is for two or three reminiscence workers to go into long-stay hospitals and old people's homes and have weekly sessions talking to the very frail elderly. One of the therapists where we were yesterday was very thrilled at the sight of an 88 year old lady who, like so many living in institutions, was withdrawn and uncommunicative, sitting with us with a broad grin on her face."

There were the same broad grins during *The Time of Our Lives*. An act of remembering made the past seem more valued.

Further Information

The name of the contact person is indicated in italic at the end of each entry.

WOMEN

Bilston Community College, Room 66, Green Lane, Wellington, Road, Bilston. Telephone 0902-475 333 ext 146. *Mary Higgins.*

Northumbria Police Headquarters, Community Services, Ponteland, Newcastle upon Tyne NE20 0BL. Telephone 0661-72555 ext 4244. *Gavin Aarvold.*

Merseyside Women and Girls Sport and Recreation Project, The Royal Institution, Colquitt Street, Liverpool L1 4DE. Telephone 051-709 6818. *Sue Aldridge.*

Islington Young Women's Project, 8 Manor Gardens, London N7 6LA. Telephone 01-263 6270. *Aqueela Alam.*

Strathclyde Police HQ, 173 Pitt Street, Glasgow G2. Telephone 041-204 2626. *Angus Kennedy.*

ETHNIC MINORITIES

Leeds Council for Racial Equality, Centenary House, North Street, Leeds. *Yvonne Lewis.*

Oxford Council for Community Relations Urdu Project, 44b Princes Street, Oxford. *Alison Shaw.*

Ashram Community Service Project, 23-25 Grantham Road, Sparkbrook, Birmingham. Telephone 021-773 7061. *Ute Jaeckel.*

The San Jai Chinese Project, 60 Hill Street, Glasgow G3 6RH. Telephone 041-332 3978.

Institute of Linguists, 2 Maners Way, Cambridge CB1 4SL. *Ann Corsellis.*

Asian Community Centre, 108 St Thomas' Road, Derby. *Hardial Singh Bains* or *Jarnail Singh Birring.*

Ethnic Minority Business Development Unit, City of London Polytechnic, Room 125, 100 The Minories, London EC3. Telephone 01-283 1030 ext. 456. *Cosmos Charles.*

HANDICAP

The London Innovation Network, Unit 8, Hornsey Street, London N7. Telephone 01-607 9740.

The Belfast Voluntary Welfare Society, Bryson House, Bedford Street, Belfast. Telephone 0232 225835.

CSV Independent Living Scheme, 237 Pentonville, London N1 9NJ. Telephone 01-278 6601. *Fiona Dawe.*

The Disfigurement Trust/Disfigurement Guidance Centre, 52 Crossgate, Cupar, Fife KY15 5HS. Telephone 0334 281.

Charnwood Nursery, St Paul's Road, Heaton Moor, Stockport SK4 4RY. Telephone 061-442 7767. *Brenda Kyle.*

Community Service Volunteers, Islington Social Services Department, Highbury Crescent, London N1.
Telephone 01-226 1234 ext. 4031. *Deborah Livingston.*

Friday Club, 3 Evesham Avenue, Whitley Bay, Tyneside. Telephone 091-252 4338. *Jim* or *Peggy Williams.*

KIDS Parent Support Link Project, 13 Pond Street, London NW3. Telephone 01-431 0596.
Naomi Dale or *Caroline Woollett.*

Hackney Disability Unit, The Town Hall, Mare Street, London E8. Telephone 01-986 3123.

Advocacy Alliance, 2 St Paul's Road, London N1 2QR. Telephone 01-359 8289. *Sally Carr.*

HEALTH

Dr James Anderson, 23 Shelley Road, Worthing.

Mersey Aids Prevention Unit, 10 Maryland Street, Liverpool L1 9BX. Telephone 051-709 3511. *Alan Parry.*

The Beth Johnson Foundation, Parkfield House, 64 Prince's Road, Hartshill, Stoke-on-Trent ST4 7JL. Telephone 0782-44036. *J. A. Flynn.*

Save a Life Campaign, Royal Society of Medicine, 1 Wimpole Street, London W1M 8AE. Telephone 01-491 0982. *Penny Webb.*

Druglink, Trefoil, Red Lion Lane, Hemel Hempstead, Herts. *Sue Bamford.*

Occupational Health Unit, The Robens Institute, Surrey Research Park, 30 Occam Road, Guildford, Surrey GU2 5YW. Telephone 0483-68637/68673. *Dr Hawkins.*

The Psychogeriatric Travelling Day Hospital, Department of Services for the Elderly, St James's Hospital, Milton, Portsmouth PO4 8LD.

Wallasey Council for Voluntary Services, Carers Care Centre, 245 Liscard Road, Wallasey, Merseyside. Telephone 051-630 2598. *Val Higginson.*

EDUCATION

St Leonard's Storybook Project, St Leonard's County Middle School, Black Lane, Blandford Forum, Dorset DT11 8SW. Telephone 0258-54928. *Simon Adorian.*

Ingestre Hall Arts Centre, Ingestre, near Stafford, Staffs. *Kevin Callan.*

Dorchester Area Rural Schools Education Team, Puddletown First School, High Street, Puddletown, Dorchester, Dorset DT2 8RY.

Frontline Culture and Education, 121 Princess Street, Manchester M1 7AG. *Dan Baron Cohen.*

Burleigh College, Loughborough, Leicestershire. *Trevor Riddiough.*

The Learning Network, Prince of Wales's Hospital, Tottenham, N15 4AW. Telephone 01-808 1081 ext. 222. *Alan Cleveland.*

Central Bristol Adult Education Centre, 189 Newfoundland Road, St Paul's, Bristol BS2 9NY. Telephone 0272-556415. *Geraldine Taylor.*

Duxford Community Primary School, Duxford, Cambridgeshire. Telephone 0223-833229.

HOUSING

Liverpool Personal Service Society, 34 Stanley Street, Liverpool L1 6AN. Telephone 051-236 5255. *Jeanette Abendstern.*

Town and Country Planning Association, 10 Hilton Terrace, St Georges, Telford TF2 9AG.

Paddington Churches Housing Association, Canterbury House, Canterbury Road, London NW6 5SU. Telephone 01-372 5671.

The Zenzele Self-build Housing Association, Gatcombe Court, Flax Bourton, Bristol BS19 1PX. *Stella Clarke.*

Bristol Self-build Development Agency, NFHA, Company House, Jacob Street, Tows Hill, Bristol BS2 0QE. *Chris Gordon.*

Scottish Special Housing Association, 75 Bothwell Street, Glasgow. Telephone 041-204 2588.

Merseyside Accommodation Project, Mount Vernon Green, Hall Lane, Liverpool L7 8TF. Telephone 051-709 0990. *Paul McCoy.*

CRIME AND COMMUNITY

Bromley Mediation and Dispute Centre, 83 Tweedy Road, Bromley, Kent. Telephone 01-464 6023.

Arrowhead Community Enterprises, 22 Guildford Street, Chertsey, Surrey KT1 9BQ. Telephone 09328 62227.

Fiona Clarke, 3 Clifton Road, Winchester.

New Bridge, Room A, 1 Thorpe Close, Ladbroke Grove, London W10 5XL. Telephone 01-969 9133. *Jerry Westall.*

Decentralisation Unit, c/o Islington Town Hall, Upper Street, London N1. Telephone 01-226 1234.

Stoke Newington Area Partnership, Stoke Newington School, Clissold Road, London N16. Telephone 01-254 0548. *Mark Lushington.*

FAMILIES AND YOUNG PEOPLE

Stepfamily, 162 Tenison Road, Cambridge CB1 2DP. Telephone 0223-460136/460312.

The Fulford Family Centre, 1 Fulford Road, Hartcliffe, Bristol BS13 9PD. Telephone 0272-782441.

Home-Start Consultancy, 140 New Walk, Leicester LE1 7JL. Telephone 0533-554988. *Margaret Harrison.*

Rainer Foundation, 89a Blackheath Hill, London SE10. Telephone 01-691 3124.

South Glamorgan Local Partnership Scheme, 23 St Mary Street, Cardiff. Telephone 0222-388224.

Staffordshire Police Activities Community Enterprise, Chief Constable's Office, Cannock Road, Stafford ST17 0QG. *Ken Ainge.*

EMPLOYMENT

Northampton Jobclub, Northampton Job Centre, 47 Prince's Walk, Grosvenor Centre, Northampton NN1 2EE. Telephone 0604-21222.

Roundhill Project, Mount Road, Southdown, Bath, Avon. Telephone 0225-331109.

ARTS

Artshare, Exeter & Devon Arts Centre, Bradninch Place, Gandy Street, Exeter EX4 3LS.
Telephone 0392 218923/219741 ext 24.

Age Exchange Theatre Company, 15 Camden Row, London SE3. Telephone 01-318 9105. *Pam Schweitzer.*